Scotland, class and nation

Scotland, class and nation

Edited by Chris Bambery

BOOKMARKS

London, Chicago and Sydney

Scotland, Class and Nation – Edited by Chris Bambery
First published 1999
Bookmarks Publications Ltd, c/o 1 Bloomsbury Street, London WC1B 3QE, England
Bookmarks, PO Box 16085, Chicago, Illinois 60616, USA
Bookmarks, PO Box A338, Sydney South, NSW 2000, Australia
Copyright © Bookmarks Publications Ltd

ISBN 1 898876 51 7 (Hardback)
ISBN 1 898876 52 5 (Paperback)

Printed by Larkham Printing and Publishing
Cover by Sherborne Design

Bookmarks Publications Ltd is linked to an international grouping of socialist organisations:
- **Australia:** International Socialist Organisation, PO Box A338, Sydney South
- **Britain:** Socialist Workers Party, PO Box 82, London E3 3LH
- **Canada:** International Socialists, PO Box 339, Station E, Toronto, Ontario M6H 4E3
- **Cyprus:** Ergatiki Demokratia, PO Box 7280, Nicosia
- **Denmark:** Internationale Socialister, PO Box 5113, 8100 Aarhus C
- **Germany:** Linksruck, Postfach 304 183, 20359 Hamburg
- **Greece:** Socialistiko Ergatiko Komma, c/o Workers Solidarity, PO Box 8161, Athens 100 10
- **Holland:** Internationale Socialisten, PO Box 92025, 1090AA Amsterdam
- **Ireland:** Socialist Workers Party, PO Box 1648, Dublin 8
- **New Zealand:** Socialist Workers Organisation, PO Box 8851, Auckland
- **Norway:** Internasjonale Socialisterr, Postboks 9226 Grønland, 0134 Oslo
- **Poland:** Solidarność Socjalistyczna, PO Box 12, 01-900 Warszawa 118
- **Spain:** Socialismo Internacional, Apartado 563, 08080 Barcelona
- **United States:** International Socialist Organization, PO Box 16085, Chicago, Illinois 60616
- **Zimbabwe:** International Socialist Organisation, PO Box 6758, Harare

Contents

Alex Callinicos is Professor of Politics at the University of York and the author of many books including *Is There a Future for Marxism?*, *Marxism and Philosophy*, *Against Postmodernism*, *Making History*, *Theories and Narratives*, *The Revenge of History* and *Social Theory*. He is a leading member of the Socialist Workers Party.

Neil Davidson is a civil servant in the Scottish Office and a Tutor/Counsellor in the Social Sciences faculty of the Open University in Scotland. He is the author of an article on Tom Nairn's theory of nationalism and of a forthcoming book on the origins of national consciousness in Scotland.

Angus Calder was formerly Reader in Cultural Studies and Staff Tutor in Arts with the Open University in Scotland and is now a freelance writer. He is the author of *Revolutionary Empire*, *The People's War* and *The Myth of the Blitz*, and has co-edited *Time to Kill: The Soldier's Experience of War in the West 1939-1945*.

Jock Morris is an English teacher and the EIS representative at a comprehensive school in Glasgow. He is a member of the Socialist Workers Party.

Jimmy Ross is a teacher of learning support in Glasgow and a member of the Socialist Workers Party. He has been a member of a number of folk bands and has written folk and political songs.

Chris Bambery is a national organiser for the Socialist Workers Party. He is the author of *Ireland's Permanent Revolution* and a number of articles including an analysis of fascism in Europe. He is currently writing a major history of Ireland.

Introduction

Chris Bambery

Scotland enters the new millennium with a new parliament, with the stranglehold the Labour Party has held on Scottish politics for at least three decades weakening in the face of rising support for the Scottish National Party, and with over 100,000 people casting their votes in the May 1999 Scottish parliamentary elections for socialist candidates.

Yet on the left what is striking is the lack of any debate and discussion from a socialist perspective about Scottish history and culture in general or of Scottish working class history. There is for instance no biography of John Maclean in print, with the exception of an excellent pamphlet by Dave Sherry. The debate on Red Clydeside which flared up in the 1980s has long since gone off the boil. It is now nearly two decades since there was any attempt to provide a socialist history of Scotland. Nor has there been anything to match the cultural writing of David Craig in the 1960s and 1970s.

Scotland, Class and Nation is an attempt to revive this discussion and debate. With the exception of my own essay, the other pieces are based on talks given at the **Socialism in Scotland** conference held in Glasgow in November 1998. This weekend of 34 separate meetings, forums and debates organised by the Socialist Workers Party and attended by over 500 people covered a wide range of topics going well beyond Scottish history and contemporary politics. One of the aims of **Socialism in Scotland** was to kick start a discussion among socialists in Scotland on a wide range of topics. Its success means it is now set to become an annual forum of debate and discussion.

My essay contrasts the making of a bourgeois Scotland in the late 18th and in the 19th century with the explosion of working class struggle and organisation which formed Red Clydeside during the years of the First World War. Alex Callinicos's examination of the debate on the national question among Marxists is a vital starting point for any discussion of Scotland's own national question.

While England's bourgeois revolution in the 17th century has produced a wealth of study and debate, with Marxist historians like Christopher Hill and Brian Manning in the forefront, Scotland's own transformation from feudalism to capitalism has received far less attention. Neil Davidson's keynote essay at last provides a readily accessible history of Scotland's own extended bourgeois revolution.

Modern Scotland can only be understood in connection with the British Empire. Angus Calder provides an examination of just how central Scotland was in creating and running the empire.

Lastly Jock Morris and Jimmy Ross look at Scotland's two greatest poets—Robert Burns and Hugh MacDiarmid. Burns needs rescuing from his reduction to an image on a shortbread tin. MacDiarmid will forever escape that fate but his whole life and work centres on the relationship between nationalism and socialism, the latter albeit of a Stalinist sort.

Gone are the days when British imperialism and Scottish nationalism could exist side by side. Scotland remains a virulently class divided society from which we await liberation.

Whatever you take from this book, let us hope that it plays a part in reinvigorating a debate among Scottish socialists on our past, our history of struggle and on the way forward.

Chapter 1

Two souls of Scotland

Chris Bambery

The history of Scotland I learned from an early age was that the Scottish nation stretched back to the dawn of time. In this version Scotland was one of the oldest nations in Europe. But this was false. Far from there being a seamless evolution of the Scottish nation, modern Scotland was created by a series of convulsions stretching back just a little over two and a half centuries. These convulsions centred on class struggle. The Hanoverian victory over the Jacobites at Culloden in 1746 marked the victory of the new capitalist order over the old feudal one. The beginning of this century, the years of Red Clydeside, saw the Scottish working class burst onto centre stage.

Certainly before then there was, within the Lowlands, at least a common identification that people belonged to a Scottish nation. This Scotland was defined in opposition to the Catholic states of Europe, the Irish and—within the territory of the Scottish state itself—the Highlanders. But it was also defined in opposition to the English, who were allies in the fight against the Catholic absolutist states but were also a potential threat to the independence of the kirk. This continued hostility to England was unsurprising, given Scotland's recent past.

Feudal Scotland had gone through a series of wars with its southern neighbour, preventing its incorporation into the English state as had happened to Wales. At sporting occasions today the words of 'Flower of Scotland' bellow forth about sending proud Edward and his army 'homewards to think again'. The victory to which it refers, Bannockburn in 1314, became a nationalist reference point. More recently the film *Braveheart*, with its hero Sir William Wallace, portrays a nation

1

united against a common oppressor, England.

Yet the Wars of Independence of the late 13th century and the 14th century were not simply wars between Scotland and England. Robert the Bruce, like most Scottish feudal magnates, had considerable lands south of the border. Opposing him were the Balliols and the Comyns, who drew significant support among Scottish nobles. Highlanders were at Bannockburn to fight Edward II, but their motives were to secure the hegemony of Clan Donald rather than to secure an independent Scottish state. As elsewhere in Europe, the nobility conferred in French, the administration was carried out largely by clerics in Latin, and among the peoples of Scotland there was not only a divide between those who spoke Gaelic and the Scots dialect but also a wealth of accents which could differ significantly within a few miles.

Feudalism came late to Scotland but it took root fiercely, with the great nobles becoming petty kings within the areas they controlled.

The much heralded Declaration of Arbroath in 1320, far from being a statement of nationalism as it is now quoted, was a warning to Bruce that he was king only so long as the nobles were prepared to accept him and reserving their right to rebel.

The feudal state created by Robert the Bruce after Bannockburn passed into the hands of the House of Stuart in 1371 and survived up until the Union of the English and Scottish Crowns in 1603. These were years marked by civil wars, rebellions, feuding and English invasion. In order to survive, the Stuart monarchy had to search out an alliance with France. Unlike Spain, France or England no absolutist monarchy emerged able to use the wealth of the emerging bourgeoisie to create a state which could tame the feudal grandees. Scotland was too poor for that. Rather, for most of this time, power was fought over by rival feudal magnates.

Even the division between the Highlands and the Lowlands was not so clear until the onset of the great European wide crisis of feudalism in the mid-14th century. The onset of plague was the first indication of that and, in common with large parts of Europe, Scotland suffered a dramatic loss of population.[1] In the Highlands the chieftains still held the land by feudal charter despite later claims that there was no such thing as clan lands owned by clan members. Because of the poorer quality of the land north of the Highland line these chieftains took to raiding their neighbours and the Lowlands for cattle.

Increasingly a contrast would develop between a largely cattle rearing, Gaelic speaking area—with a culture largely imported from Ireland

and with its own laws—and the arable economy of the Scots speaking Lowlands. Lowlanders commonly described the Highlanders as being 'Irish'.

The distance between the two states on the island of Britain was apparent at Flodden Field in Northumberland in 1514, when a Scottish feudal army led by King James IV invaded England at the behest of the French. Though vastly superior in numbers, the Scots force was chopped down by a more technologically advanced English army.

Scotland's long bourgeois revolution reflected the strength of feudalism and a lack of the elements which provided the backbone of Cromwell's New Model Army, manifested in the weakness of the towns and the absence of a gentry and yeomanry increasingly tied to the capitalist market.

Cromwell pointed one way forward—the complete integration of Scotland into an all-British state. But the restoration of the Stuarts returned Scotland to a pre civil war status firmly ruled by the nobility. Attempts to enforce Anglican stule organisation on the kirk led to opposition, including rebellion by the Covenanters in the south west.

But there was a gaping contrast between Scotland and England. In the former, famine was a reality in the 1690s. In England it was a thing of the past. The attempt to create an independent Scottish colony in Panama, the Darien Scheme, was a disaster, virtually bankrupting the country. The forces for full union between the two countries were growing.

The survival of the Scottish nation rested largely on the fact that the 1707 Treaty of Union incorporating the Scottish Parliament into Westminster created a situation described by Christopher Harvie as 'semi-independence'.[2] Scotland would be run for the next century by magnates like the Duke of Argyll and the Dundas dynasty. More importantly the kirk (after an initial hiccup), together with the legal and educational system, remained separate. In this Scotland contrasted with Wales and, more starkly, with Ireland under English and then British rule.

Why was this? In part the Scottish ruling class was able to gain a high price for its approval of the Hanoverian succession—the priority for the post-revolutionary settlement English ruling class. In part too it flows from England's own bourgeois revolution. It is hard to see Scotland achieving the position it did within the new United Kingdom in Jacobin France, with its rigid centralisation and its desire to create a 'one and indivisible' French nation, nor under Cromwell's republic, when Scotland was incorporated into and ruled by the British state. The 1688 'Glorious Revolution' rested on a series of compromises which were designed to ensure there was no repeat of the popular unrest of the 1640s. One of those compromises meant allowing Scotland to continue to be ruled by a feudal nobility.

Yet within a decade it was clear Scotland was on the verge of bankruptcy. Famine stalked the land. Parliamentary union in 1707 met with widespread popular opposition including the urban poor and the merchant class. Memories of the colossal failure of the Darien Scheme were still fresh. But in all the debates on the Union, there was no real alternative put forward as to how Scotland could develop. The famine and mass deaths in the 1690s were too vivid a reality:

> And the economic spurs working Scotland towards union were decisively important. [The Earl of] Roxburghe pointed to them in a letter of 1705 in which he predicted that the Edinburgh Parliament would swallow union, 'The motives will be trade with most, Hanover with some, ease and security with others, together with a general aversion at civil discords, intolerable poverty, and the constant aversion and oppression of a bad ministry, from generation to generation.'
>
> The Scots were poor and getting poorer. The English upper and middle classes waxed fatter every day. The disparity in wealth between the two countries, marked in 1603, was still greater now. This partly explains how the English could be generous.[3]

Prosperity would not come until after the final triumph over the old feudal order at Culloden in 1746 but it was followed by a spectacular reversal of fortunes for Scotland. The strength of Neil Davidson's article in this volume is to destroy the notion that what was at stake in the '45 rising was some ancient Anglo-Scots struggle. The reality was that a majority of Scots were opposed to the Jacobites and viewed Highland society as something alien and fearful:

> More Scots had fought for Cumberland than for Charles Edward; more Scots than English soldiers thereafter wasted the glens; it was Scots landlords and factors, not Englishmen, who forced the Highlanders on to the emigrant ships.[4]

The destruction of Highland society was under way before Culloden. Many of the chiefs who rallied to Charles Edward Stuart did so because of economic desperation. Clan chiefs had already begun evictions and the forced emigration of their followers to the New World. But the forced clearances of the Highlands which gathered pace after 1815 were of a qualitatively different order, both in terms of their scale and their brutality.

Scotland and Ireland

Scotland's position within the new United Kingdom is worth contrasting with that of Ireland. There was a fundamental difference between Scotland and Ireland after 1690. The Irish Parliament was very much more limited in its powers, while the new rulers in London could depend on the Protestant Ascendancy which controlled it and the land to rally against any Jacobite bid to reverse that settlement. To that must be added the quiescence of Ireland following the final defeat of the Jacobite forces at Limerick in 1691.

The Scottish Parliament, in contrast, exercised much greater power. Most importantly it could choose not to recognise the Hanoverian succession. The pro-Jacobite nobility of the north east and those clans who supported the Stuart cause could provide an armed force. This meant that Scotland could gain union on favourable terms. Its ruling class became an integral part of the new British ruling class (and remains so today).

The contrast between Scotland (outside of the Highlands) and Ireland became even greater in the final decades of the 18th century. The new British state did not overly interfere in Scotland, which was run by Scottish patricians following Culloden (the dukes of Argyll initially after the Union, then in later years the Dundas family). There was no attempt to hinder capital accumulation or investment in Scotland. Scots found their way to the highest echelons of the British state, and they were at the cutting edge of the building of the British Empire.

In terms of industrial development there was little to choose between Britain and Ireland in the 1780s. In both countries there were strong pockets of rural textile industries. However, the Act of Union destroyed much of Irish industry as it was opened up to English imports. Ireland went backwards economically and socially, culminating in the horrors of the Great Famine.

The potato blight which triggered the famine in Ireland occurred in the Highlands too. Interestingly, government intervention and public charity prevented starvation, unlike in Ireland, where it was seen by much of the British ruling class as a godsend sent to remove a surplus rural population of inferior stock.

The difference between Scotland and Ireland's position within the United Kingdom could be summed up thus. During her long reign Queen Victoria only visited Ireland on four occasions, whereas after 1848 she spent the autumn of each year at Balmoral. Gladstone, whose later career was dominated by the Irish Question, visited Ireland just once, but represented Midlothian in parliament and was a frequent visitor to Scotland.

The one area of industrial growth in Ireland, round Belfast, was closely tied to Clydeside (and Merseyside too in the case of shipbuilding), with Scots providing technology, investment and skills plus Ayrshire coal which provided power. Scotland's industrial economy did become trapped into dependence on the fortunes of British imperialism, but that was even more true for the north of Ireland. Britain's long economic decline hit Scotland hard. It hit Northern Ireland for six.

Scotland's industrialisation

Scotland's transformation in the decades after Culloden was dramatic. It was able to catch up with England economically in a matter of decades to become one of the wealthiest regions of the United Kingdom. It created the Scottish Enlightenment of the late 18th century, which took Scotland intellectually from the periphery of Europe to the centre. The Scottish Enlightenment was accompanied by rapid industrialisation: 'Scotland packed into about 30 years of crowded development between 1750 and 1780 the economic growth that in England had spread itself over two centuries'.[5]

The motor forces of this change were apparent to all:

Agriculture (especially in the Lothians) became a pioneer of new techniques. The Ayrshire coal owners found themselves in a position to become major suppliers to the Irish market. Glasgow's favoured position on the North Atlantic shipping route quickly secured it the bulk of the American tobacco trade. And, although there was no great growth in the industries selected for special subsidy under the terms of the 1707 Act (linen and fishing) and Border wool production was soon drawn into the orbit of the Yorkshire market, there was a remarkably rapid and successful response to the opportunities opened up in the 1770s and 1780s for cotton and iron manufacturing on an industrial factory basis.[6]

The year 1759 had seen the launch of the Carron Iron Works outside Falkirk. In successive waves Scotland saw industrial expansion.

The end of the American War of Independence saw the cotton industry displace linen in the west as employers made use of cheap labour and plentiful water. Initially the cotton industry was centred on new factories in rural areas where best use could be made of water power—most famously New Lanark but also Spinningdale, Deanston, Blantyre, Newton Stewart, Ballindalloch and Catrine. Then in the 1820s the cotton industry moved into the towns and cities of the Glasgow region as the number of power looms in the country rose from just 2,000 at the start of the decade to 10,000 at the close. The iron industry also developed in the 1820s. In the 1860s shipbuilding grew and grew along the Clyde, and then the 1880s saw the birth of the steel industry.

In the west of Scotland, Scottish capitalists were quick to draw on industrial innovation in England. By the early decades of the 19th century Scottish capital had moved ahead with a series of technological innovations.

Demographically, between 1770 and 1820 the population rose by a half. In 1755 just over half of Scotland's population lived north of a line from the Firth of Clyde to the Firth of Tay. By the 1820s it was down to just two fifths. Half of all Scots now lived in the central belt. Between 1755 and 1821 Glasgow's population increased by more than four times to 147,000, overtaking Edinburgh. Paisley's population increased by six times, Greenock's by five times.

These were the years which saw the creation of Scotland as we know it today. This was not the Scotland portrayed on countless shortbread tins but the Scotland of grim mining, steel and textile towns, of the slums of Glasgow, and of immigration from the Highlands and Ireland and later still Lithuania, Italy, Poland and much later Bengal.

Scottish culture and identity

The abruptness of this change was what lay at the centre of the Scottish Enlightenment. The philosopher David Hume commented:

> Is it not strange that at a time when we have lost our Princes, our Parliaments, our independent Government, even the Presence of our chief nobility, are unhappy, in our Accent and Pronunciation speak a very corrupt Dialect of the Tongue which we make use of; is it not strange, I say, that in these Circumstances, we should really be the People most distinguished for Literature in Europe.[7]

If there was an element of exaggeration in Hume's claims it is not surprising. As T C Smout points out:

> With men like Hume, Smith, Burns, Scott, Black, Watt, Telford, Robert Adam and Hutton in the first rank; with Ferguson, Millar, Reid, Robertson, Allan Ramsey Junior, Raeburn, William Adam, Rennie, Bosewell and Hogg in the second rank; and a third rank crowded with talent as diverse as that of William Symington, who invented steam navigation, and Francis Jeffrey, who founded the *Edinburgh Review*, the cultural performance of Scotland between 1740 and 1830 was of dazzling virtuosity.[8]

What was central to the Enlightenment was a sense of recent, sudden historical change which underwrites the writing of David Hume, Adam Smith and Walter Scott. In just a generation Scotland had gone from a backward feudal country which was highly militarised and carried strong folk memories of witch burning and religious wars to being a thrusting bourgeois society which was a powerhouse of new ideas and inventions within Britain and Europe.

Culturally, the most popular figure before Scott was Robert Burns. In Burns' poetry there is a powerful invocation of nationalism with repeated reference to Wallace and Bruce. 'Scots Wha Hae' was penned by him in 1793. But this can only be understood within the context of Burns' pro-Jacobin sympathies. This was the 'springtime of the nation' when Scottish sympathisers with the French Revolution, searching for champions of liberty, would look back into history and legend for figures to identify with as diverse as Brutus, William Tell or James Macpherson's partially forged Gaelic saga, *Ossian*.

The dominant cultural figure in shaping the new Scotland was the novelist Sir Walter Scott. He was a man of apparent contradictions: a Tory in British politics but one who openly expressed his pride in nationalist terms; a realist novelist celebrated by Balzac and the Marxist philosopher George Lukács but who helped spawn the Kailyard (cabbage patch) culture which blighted Scotland for the next century and more.

In five brilliant novels—*Old Mortality*, *Rob Roy*, *The Heart of Midlothian*, *Waverley* and *Red Gauntlet*—he charts the crucial years in the transformation of Scotland, from a backward feudal society on the periphery of Europe through to the point just before its industrial takeoff and its integration into the new, Atlantic economy.

Scott had a real grasp of the historical change which had occurred within living memory. His characters often take second place to the historical narration—but what narration! The centrepiece of *The Heart of Midlothian* is a brilliant reenactment of the Porteous Riots of 1736. A measure of Scott's impact is that in Edinburgh the monument erected to his memory dominates the east end of Princes Street while 40 miles west his column takes centre stage in Glasgow's George Square.

Scott himself was a complex figure. As a Tory he was vigorously opposed to parliamentary reform and saw democracy as destroying the British Empire. Yet he could also break into tears at a debate at the Faculty of Advocates in Edinburgh over the anglicisation of Scottish law and became impassioned about the loss of Scottish banknotes.

Above all Scott succeeded in creating a Scottish identity which was part and parcel of the new British state. The two identities could be combined by looking back into Scottish history to draw on the images associated with the Stuart Pretenders, now no longer a threat, and to a Highland society which at that very moment was in its death throes. Scott helped pioneer the recreation of a Highland 'culture', denounced in openly racist terms by Lowland Scots only a short time before, just at a time when Highland society was being destroyed. This image was central to British imperial expansion. Scott himself stage managed the 1822 visit of King George IV to Scotland, the first visit by a monarch in over a century, when the king donned the recently invented Highland dress, and gentry from across Scotland bought their 'historical' clan tartan from Lowland textile manufacturers.[9]

The Scottish as well as the British identity was forged in war, first against absolutist France, then revolutionary France and finally Bonapartist France. In a short time that identity could draw on new myths of Scottish military prowess gathered in the service of the British Empire and state. The symbols of middle class Scotland up until the 1950s and 1960s was one of the Scots Greys charging at Waterloo or the Thin Red Line at Balaclava. And this has continued into more recent times. Within my lifetime, for example, there was the lionisation of Lieutenant-Colonel Colin Mitchell, 'Mad Mitch', of the Argyll and Sutherland Highlanders in the late 1960s, following his attempts to suppress the independence movement in Aden. The SNP even tried to get him to stand as a parliamentary candidate, but he opted for the Tories.

Bourgeois Scotland was marked by the existence of a nostalgic Scottish nationalism alongside British imperialism up until 1918 and more markedly from the 1970s onwards. Neither were in conflict with one another. The novelist John Buchan, who became Governor-General of Canada, spoke at Westminster in 1932 warning Scotland was faced with 'losing its historic individuality... It seems to many that we are in danger very soon of reaching the point when Scotland will have nothing distinctive to show the world.' For the sake of Britain and the empire he implored it was necessary 'to intensify that consciousness of individuality and idiom, which is what is meant by national spirit... I believe that every Scotsman [sic] should be a Scottish nationalist'.[10] Buchan was invoking Scottish nationalism in a very different way from today's nationalists. This was the spirit of nationalism associated with war and imperial conquest. Similarly the new bourgeois Scottish culture would appropriate Jacobitism, now no conceivable threat to the British state. At Hampden Park or Murrayfield those images are still very much in evidence, from the military pipeband to the Glengarries and military kilts worn by supporters, and the lion rampant flag of the House of Stuart.

Scott's death marked the end of the of this extraordinary intellectual explosion centred on Edinburgh. Scottish literature took from him nostalgia, but it was bereft of any sense of historical change and contradiction. It succumbed into a folksy world of the Kailyard, glorying in a rural past which was a million miles away from the industrial world of the central belt.

In the century and more from Scott's death to the Second World War only three novels break from the Kailyard school: Robert Louis Stevenson's *Weir of Hermiston*, George Douglas Brown's *The House With the Green Shutters* and Lewis Grassic Gibbon's *A Scots Quair*. The first two highlight a darker side of Scots life and the dour grip of Calvinism. The latter, particularly in the first volume, *Sunset Song*, succeeds in recreating the doomed world of the agricultural labourers of Kincardineshire in the years up until the First World War quite brilliantly.

Industrialisation was to bring another change. It was to create one of the most class divided countries in Europe. And within the working class that developed out of immigration from the north and west there were powerful folk memories of clearances, famine and eviction in the Highlands and Ireland.

Prior to the end of the Napoleonic wars, Scotland was not regarded as more radical than England—far from it. John Wilkes in 1768 had railed against Scots as being opponents of liberty and supporters of despotism because Scots aristocrats were to the fore in edging forward George III to exercise royal power. As the Wilkes agitation swept London, Scotland provided a contrast:

A rising Scottish politician named Wedderburn observed smugly in 1768 that while the south of England was 'a great Bedlam under the dominion of a beggarly, idle and intoxicated mob without keepers, actuated solely by the word Wilkes', the north was frugal, sober and loyal. As to the Scots, another 'North British' politician could report that they detested Wilkes with 'the greatest unanimity'. The old picture was now stood on its head. London and the Home Counties could hardly be governed; Scotland gave no serious trouble at all.[11]

T C Smout points out:

There was...in Scotland no equivalent to the French revolutionary philosophers like Voltaire and Rousseau, to England's Tom Paine, or even to John Wilkes, John Cartwright, Thomas Spence and William Cobbett. Indeed, any of those Englishmen who fought with their pens and minds for what we now regard as the basic democratic rights of all British subjects would have raised an eyebrow to hear latter day Scottish historians boasting of the 'democratic intellect' of the north. William Cobbett was more realistic when he called upon heaven to protect him from the 'Scottish feelosophers'.[12]

This is perhaps too hard on Rousseau's friend David Hume or on the radical Thomas Muir of Huntershill, sentenced to deportation to Botany Bay by a kangaroo court only to be rescued by the French revolutionary regime. The year 1792 saw the creation of an Edinburgh based reform group, the Friends of the People, within which Muir, a Glasgow lawyer, led the radical wing. But the point Smout makes is valid.

Yet as late as 1830 Cobbett came to Scotland and specifically came north to examine why rural Scotland was so quiescent:

He had left the southern English counties in that year smouldering on the edge of social war, with ricks being burnt, new machinery destroyed, men transported and in a few cases executed for their part in in the destruction of property. This marked the culmination of a generation of intermittent turbulence in the south that had no parallel beyond the Tweed, even though farm workers in the same period were being subjected to the introduction of the same kind of highly capitalised farming with mechanical threshing which stimulated the maximum uproar in the south. Scotch bailiffs in command of English estates were boasting, to Cobbett's great wrath, of the obedience and orderliness of the rural workers in their native counties, even though industrial workers in Scotland had long ago been inclined to radical sympathies of a kind. Cobbett came to find out why the Scots were quiet while the English burnt the ricks.[13]

Repression destroyed the Friends of the People. In 1812 the best or-ganised group of workers, and the best paid, the Glasgow handloom weavers, had seen their strike broken by the employers. The handloom weavers began a lengthy process of immiserisation. But Scotland had no incidence of Luddism.

The 'Radical Wars'

The year 1820 saw the eruption of the 'Radical Wars'. Whereas the movements of the 1790s were led by sections of the middle class and involved artisans and small masters who were precursors of the modern working class, the events of the 1820s were of a different order. The centre of the agitation had moved away from Edinburgh and the east coast towns to the new industrial centres of the west. The background lies in an industrial recession which saw many jobless and growing demonstrations for reform in England culminating in Manchester's Peterloo Massacre in August 1819.

In Paisley, a key textile centre, a meeting of between 14,000 and 18,000 was held the following month on Meikleriggs Moor to protest at the massacre. Local magistrates tried to prevent people attending and banned the carrying of banners and placards:

As the meeting on Meikleriggs Moor dispersed, a section of the crowd marched down Paisley High Street, carrying their flags in defiance of the authorities. They were met by special constables lining both sides of the street, the magistrates and the Provost. The latter, determined to impose control, ordered the seizing of the flags. The ensuing scuffle developed into a violent confrontation, with the police being forced to concede con-trol of the streets, and the crowd breaking the windows of any building con-nected with authority. In this way began five days of conflict in which the streets were largely in the hands of the crowd, running battles devel-oped between the military and the working people, and the authorities were forced to escalate the extent of military support in order to regain control.[14]

Yet there existed an uneasy peace:

The formation of political unions, based on workshops and neigh-bourhoods, gathered momentum, and there is evidence of widespread arming among the weavers. That the initiative now rested with revolutionary Jacobins was indicated at a large Radical meeting in Johnstone on 1 November 1819, where pistols were fired and battleaxes prominently displayed, along with the revival of the symbolism of 'caps of liberty', presented by societies of female reformers. In December the authorities in Paisley arrested a local cutler, John Henderson, and discovered two pikes in his workshop and a number of gun barrels in the house of one of his neighbours.

The organisation of armed resistance centred around the weavers' shops of Maxwellton. According to John Parkhill, who was at the centre of these events, but who later adopted a disdainful attitude towards the Radical activity of this period, 'The preparations of the unions were...going on with great spirit. The casting of gun bullets was, at their leisure hours, a great occupation and the manufacture of cleggs became a great amusement.'

The Radicals undertook night drilling exercises, obtained lists of the names of the local yeomanry cavalry, so that their arms could be seized, and planned for the culmination of their activity in a general rising in the West of Scotland, coordinated with a similar rebellion in England.[15]

When it came the rising was abortive.

On 1 April 1820 a placard appeared on the streets of Glasgow calling for a complete cessation of work and an insurrection on 5 April. The government reacted by drafting troops into Glasgow. Despite this some 60,000 workers struck on the day. In Glasgow there was one clash between workers and troops, but no one was killed. A group of Glasgow Radicals had left earlier in the day intent on seizing the Carron Iron Works and obtaining arms. At Bonnymuir they were routed by the yeomanry and hussars. Three of their leaders were then hanged in Stirling. In Paisley four cotton spinners were tried for attempting to shoot their factory owner, who had pushed through wage cuts across the town.

The Radical Wars, as this episode became known, was part of a British wide upsurge. Tony Dickson makes the point that the resolutions passed at the Meikleriggs Moor meeting 'indicate the way in which the bulk of the Paisley Radicals saw their struggles as linked to a British context in which English reformers were called upon for leadership.' He concludes, 'Even in the insurrectionary phase of 1819-20, the assault on the British state was to to be led by the English working class'.[16]

The emergence of a militant working class movement

The emergence of a strong working class movement took time:

> Other groups too went down to defeat in the 1820s. Miners and cotton spinners both fought prolonged battles, essentially over trying to maintain some kind of craft-like control over their work processes. Who should be employed? Who should dictate the speed and pattern of work—the worker or the employer? Both groups lost out. The spinners union at least survived: the miners did not effectively reorganise until the 1840s.[17]

In 1837 the Glasgow cotton spinners' strike saw the workers go down to defeat after an epic battle. The defeat of the strike led Glasgow workers to look for political ways forward. In May 1838 some 200,000 attended the first Chartist demonstration in Glasgow. But Scottish Chartism was overwhelmingly of the 'moral force' wing. In Paisley 'there was little mass activity in the town in 1840' while the 1842 general strike call 'found no echo'.[18]

Following the demise of Chartism Scotland fell under Liberal hegemony. The Liberals dominated Scottish politics in the second half of the 19th century to such an extent that they did not feel under pressure to try and integrate and contain working class representatives. Eleven Liberal-Labour MPs were elected following the further extension of the franchise in 1884 but no Lib-Lab MP was ever returned in a Scottish seat: 'As a result Scottish trade councils were pressing for independent working class MPs even before the British Trades Union Congress endorsed this aim by creating in 1887 the Labour Electoral Association'.[19]

Scotland was excluded from the Liberal-Labour deal on parliamentary seats drawn up in 1905. Unlike England and Wales, Labour candidates were not given a clear run by the Liberals. The two Labour candidates elected in Dundee and Glasgow in the following year's general election did so in the face of Liberal opposition.

The Scottish Labour Party was founded in 1888 (and became a founding section of the Independent Labour Party in 1893). It pulled together the former miners' union official James Keir Hardie, the adventurer R B Cunninghame Graham, Christian socialists, converts from Irish nationalism and assorted other supporters. Hardie had stood earlier that year in the Mid-Lanark parliamentary by-election, but gained just 617 votes to the Liberal's 3,847 in a mining constituency.

When working class radicalism burst forth again with the New Unionism of the 1890s Scotland was largely peripheral. But within a few years changes were at work which would see Scotland leap forward from being one of the more backward regions in terms of working class struggle to being in its vanguard. That would lead to Red Clydeside.

Radicalisation and Red Clydeside

Recent years have seen a major assault on Red Clydeside from those who either want to deny its very existence or to incorporate it into the Labourist tradition. For socialists Red Clydeside was the crucial moment in the history of the Scottish working class, one of the high points in British, and indeed European, class struggle. In Scottish history this marked the challenge of the working class to the bourgeois order of Edinburgh's New Town and of Glasgow's industrialists.

The west of Scotland went through another period of rapid industrialisation in the years after 1870 with the rise of heavy engineering and steel shipbuilding. British ships carried a third of the world's freight tonnage and British yards built virtually all of the merchant fleet, with the Clyde building the most. After the 1860s production was shifted downstream, creating whole new working class townships. In north Glasgow Springburn changed from a semi-rural town into a key centre of locomotive production in the 1860s and 1870s.

Until the 1890s Clydeside was not regarded as a militant area. The high number of skilled workers helped create a clear social stratification:

A Partick shipbuilding worker would emerge from the solid tenements of Dumbarton Road on a clear morning to take the ferry across the Clyde to Govan or enter yards nearby. Below his housing were the less substantial dwellings reaching down to the waterside, whilst immediately above him were the elaborate stone flats of the artisans, foremen and small shopkeeping or professional people. On the crest of Thornwood Hill and in the Partickhill area were the mansions of shipbuilding dynasties like Stephens, who could gaze across at their Linthouse yard from the billiard room or turn to walk in the security of affluent Hyndland.[20]

Trade unionism was weaker north of the border:

Overall, the level of trade unionism in Scotland was lower than in England; the Webbs calculated the proportionate number of trade unionists in the United Kingdom in 1892 as 3.98 percent of the total population, but which for England and Wales was 4.55 percent and for Scotland 3.64 percent only.[21]

The growth of US and German competition led to two changes. The first was rationalisation and mechanisation of production. Previously skilled men had a degree of control over the work process. Now this was under attack:

> Employers were themselves trying to change the work practices and structure of authority in their own favour, distancing foremen from their customary links with trade societies and pressing them to implement unpopular policies against organised resistance.[22]

The second feature was the merger of companies. In the Vale of Leven the large textile dyeing concerns came together in the Turkey Red Company in 1890:

> The five Vale settlements employed over 6,000 workers, and were responding to changing market pressures in consolidating their interests at the end of the century. More effective and systematic management was reflected in the greater pace of industrial change and the formalisation of collective bargaining procedures with the male trade unions of craftsmen and machinists. Earlier methods of labour market controls over the young women at the dye plants, ranging from the system of enquiry lines to the importation of female labour from Ireland during the third quarter of the century, were also breaking down as the population stabilised and women became more resistant to male management authority. When in 1911 the National Federation of Women Workers joined with the Amalgamated Society of Dyers in recruiting the lesser grades of the Turkey Red workforce, matters came to a violent head. During the Great Colour House troubles and the setting up of disputes machinery at Leven in 1911-12, the employers complained of the conflicting pressures forcing them to assert managerial perogatives against rising resistance.[23]

The changing mood among the working class had already been demonstrated by the 30,000 who turned out on the 1909 May Day demonstration. In 1911 the dyers and women workers' unions brought out the majority of the unskilled and female workforce in a three week strike demanding a 10 percent wage increase, a 55 hour week and overtime rates for all. The strike won. Within two decades the Vale of Leven would go from an area with no record of working class militancy to one which would be dubbed 'Little Moscow'.

Another change was taking place among the industrialists. Gladstone's championing of Irish Home Rule led to a split in the mighty Liberal Party which affected the Glasgow bourgeoisie:

> Their traditional faith in Scottish Liberalism was badly shaken during the 1880s, when the growing influence of Lib-Labism and the disquiet over Gladstone's Irish policies crystallised in the Home Rule debate and the formation of Liberal Unionism. Industrialists were deeply divided over the issue, and such powerful families as the Tennants continued to uphold the Liberal cause, but a growing number of employers joined with traditionalist academics and professionals to fight the dismemberment of Empire. Among the Conservatives and Unionists who broke the Liberal domination of Scottish seats were shipbuilders such as Sir William Pearce of Govan who relied on imperial protection of overseas markets and massive naval expenditure to offset the notorious troughs of the shipbuilding cycle.[24]

On the one hand the employers were becoming more and more intransigent, while on the other the powerful tradition of skilled workers negotiating at a workplace level was throwing up shop stewards' organisation, just as engineering and shipbuilding were expanding in Glasgow as Britain armed in preparation for war with Germany.

But in terms of Marxist politics there were crucial weaknesses. Opposition to the reformist Independent Labour Party (ILP) was led by the Social Democratic Federation (SDF):

> By 1911 Glasgow was the strongest centre of the SDF outside London with six branches in the city and one in Govan, and John Maclean's classes in Marxist economics making him one of the best known Marxists in the region... It was these old SDF members that became the core of the British Socialist Party in Glasgow.[25]

Yet with its narrow emphasis on education and electoral campaigning the BSP offered little way forward:

> Before the war even Marxist socialists like John Maclean could not put forward a radically different socialist alternative because they still saw political struggle in similar terms to evolutionary socialists: the workers would take power through parliament and the trade unions. The only alternative perspective was that of the SLP [Socialist Labour Party], with their emphasis on industrial organisation at the workplace.[26]

The SLP limited itself to agitating round bread and butter issues, leaving its abstract approach to Marxist ideas outside the factory gate. Prior to the outbreak of the First World War, Maclean was committed to the SDF tradition. That makes his transformation into a revolutionary opponent of war even more important.

If a party had existed combining agitation and propaganda, economic, political and ideological issues, then the possibilities were enormous. Glasgow led the way in support for the great Dublin Lockout of 1913:

> From September 1913 to January 1914 the Glasgow labour movement devoted its energy to organising the largest city collection for the Dublin Lockout outside of Dublin. *Forward* [the Glasgow ILP paper] was the centre for the collection, raising £3,000 in a period when unskilled men earned 21 shillings a week and skilled men 35 to 42 shillings. Collections were taken at socialist branches, workshops, cinemas, football gates and in the street, quite apart from trade union branches. It was the ILP who organised demonstrations on behalf of the Dublin strikers, putting up speakers from the trades council, and had [James] Larkin speak at their large Sunday night meetings...
>
> The Govan Trades Council's efforts soon included collections inside virtually every local shipyard and factory, and in the area's tenements, the United Free Church and at Ibrox, the Protestant football club.[27]

The outbreak of war brought matters to a head. Unrest first broke out on the Clyde in February 1915, with 10,000 engineering workers walking out in support of a two pence per hour increase. Wages had been held down but prices had exploded as the war fuelled inflation. The government, anxious to keep arms production going, took a far more conciliatory line than the employers, especially hardliners like Sir William Weir. Eventually a return to work was secured with the promise of government arbitration.

But two issues were emerging which would affect both shipbuilding and engineering workers and their families—dilution (the deskilling of work) and rents and housing conditions. Added to this cocktail was the effects of the Munitions Act which forbade strikes and tried to place negotiations in the hands of union officials committed to preventing strikes. This created the conditions in which politics and economics began to fuse together: 'There was a clear tendency for industrial resistance and social protest to converge'.[28]

The strong sectional organisation of the skilled workers, with its tradition of workplace control, created shops stewards' organisation. An employers' offensive, wartime measures and the support of union officials for the war effort, including upholding the ban on strikes, turned that into a shop stewards' movement capable of acting independently. As James Hinton says, 'The shop stewards' movement originated on the Clyde'.[29]

Finally this created an opening for socialists opposed to the war like John Maclean:

> Speakers such as Maclean were remarkably successful in their public speeches against the imperialist conflict, however much this ran counter to widespread patriotism, just as Maclean's educational classes on working class economics attracted shop stewards disagreeing with his revolutionary politics.[30]

The mood on Clydeside can be gathered from the *Partick and Maryhill Press*'s report on the 1915 May Day demonstration, which, it said:

> ...was organised on a larger scale than any previous occasion. Over 165 labour and socialist organisations took part...and Glasgow Green was crowded with thousands of spectators. There were 12 platforms. Among those represented were those of the Socialist and Labour Party, Internationalism, Glasgow Housing Committee, the Anarchist Group, Socialist Children's School and Women Trade Unionists.[31]

Pre-war Glasgow was already short of housing. The influx of munitions workers added to that and drove up rents. Reports of factors, who managed properties and collected rents for landlords, trying to force out the families of those men serving in the forces were also circulating. On Boxing Day 1914, women took part in a protest to the City Chambers called by the Govan and Glasgow Trades Councils. In February Clydebank Trades Council organised a protest march against rent increases. And in May a rent strike began in Govan when tenants refused to pay increases:

> The first rent strike took place in the Govan district of Glasgow in May 1915. The firm of estate agents which factored 250 tenement dwellings there informed the tenants individually that with effect from 28 May their rents would be increased by sums ranging from 12 shillings to 24 shillings per annum.[32]

By September rent strikes were taking place in Shettleston, Govan and Partick. In the same month 1,000 people, many women, marched through the city and then 2,000 people prevented the eviction of one of the rent strike leaders in Thornwood Hill:

On the same day, also in Partick, a 70 year old pensioner living alone was due to be evicted on a warrant issued by Sheriff Thomson for refusing to pay a rent increase. The old man barricaded himself in his tenement flat and a large crowd gathered outside in his support, making his 'castle' impregnable. Again no official showed his face, but the stories of these and other cases spread throughout the yards and engineering shops, causing considerable hardening of feeling against landlords, the factors and the authorities in general.[33]

Women played a central role in physically preventing evictions:

The women in each tenement close set a guard on a rota system... The warden on duty had a handbell, a racket such as used to be favoured by football fans, a tin badin and spoon—anything that would make enough noise to warn of the approach of a stranger or any other apprehended danger. Summoned by the noise, the housewives would hasten to the scene, armed for combat. The favourite weapons were small bags fitted with pease-meal, dry flour or whiting.[34]

The government became increasingly worried that this might fuel industrial unrest in the shipyards and armaments plants where dilution was coming to a head.

Maclean, John Wheatley of the Independent Labour Party, Harry Hopkins of Govan Trades Council, and other socialists were holding factory gate meetings at shipyards and engine shops. Workers at the giant Parkhead Forge threatened to strike against evictions. The convenor at Parkhead Forge, David Kirkwood, was instrumental in forming the Clyde Trades Vigilance Committee (shortly after renamed the Clyde Workers Committee) to organise shop stewards against dilution and controls imposed on workers under the Munitions Act:

The imposition of labour controls under the Munitions Act provoked massive resistance during the summer and autumn of 1915. The significance of the movement lay not in demonstrating the dominant role of the shipbuilding sector in wartime unrest, but rather in creating the conditions for cooperation between shipyard and engineering unions in opposing the government.[35]

By November 1915 some 25,000 tenants were on rent strike. That month 15 rent strikers were brought to court:

Thousands of people marched to the centre of Glasgow, with deputations from at least five main shipyards and one armaments works to represent the views of the workforce. While the crowds were addressed by an array of socialist orators and strike leaders...the sympathetic sheriff heard the testimonies of the industrial delegations in support of the defendants. Speakers from Govan, Beardmore's Dalmuir shipyard, and a spokesman from 'one of the principal engine shops on the Clyde' warned of the dire consequences which would follow the authorisation of eviction.[36]

The sheriff persuaded the landlord to drop the case. The government rushed through an act of parliament putting rent controls in place. It was a tremendous victory: 'Wednesday 17 November must rank as one of the high points in British working class history'.[37]

October 1915 had seen shop stewards come together to form the Clyde Workers Committee to oppose the terms of the Munitions Act. The threat of strike action forced the government to release from jail three shipwrights from the Fairfield shipyard who had led a strike against the sacking of two men for 'slacking':

> The Clyde Workers Committee originated in the failure of the union's executives, or district committees, to place themselves at the head of the militancy of a section of the Clydeside engineers. From the Fairfield's case the more militant of the engineers learned that if the Munitions Act was to be opposed root and branch, it must be opposed by an organisation and leadership able to act independently of the official trade union structures. The February 1915 strike had taught them that for this organisation to be effective, it must be a delegate organisation based directly in the factories. Out of this experience the militants formulated and clearly expressed, for the first time, the principles of independent rank and file organisation which were to constitute the basis of the shop stewards' movement: 'We will support the officials just so long as they rightly represent the workers, but we will act independently immediately they misrepresent them.'
>
> From October 1915 until April 1916, when the committee was smashed by the government, 250-300 delegates met every weekend in a hall in Ingram Street, Glasgow.
>
> The day to day work was done by a 'small leading committee' elected at the delegate meeting and meeting two or three nights a week. Two things characterised this leading group. Its members were all shop stewards at one time or other of the arms firms which had led the February 1915 strike and were to remain the backbone of the committee through 1915-16. And they were all socialists.

The Independent Labour Party, by far the largest socialist organisation on the Clyde, was of no great importance in the shop stewards'
movement. Only two of the leaders of the CWC, Messer and Kirkwood, belonged to it...

It was from revolutionary parties to the left of the ILP that the CWC
drew its leadership.[38]

This was true but socialists like Willie Gallacher, who chaired the
committee, had a fatal weakness. They were anti-war but, because of
their syndicalism, did not carry out political agitation in the workplace,
so they made no attempt to unite opposition to the war with opposition to the offensive on the domestic front against the working class.
John Maclean was critical of the CWC for not taking the lead in the
rent strike and was expelled from the CWC meetings for demanding
it take a clear position against the war.

Such was the opposition to dilution on the Clyde that Lloyd George,
the minister in charge of munitions, visited the area to try and face down
opposition. On a visit to key armaments plants, shop stewards agreed
to the CWC's call to refuse to meet him—though at Parkhead Forge
Kirkwood did meet the minister. On Christmas Day Lloyd George was
due to address armaments workers in Glasgow's St Andrew's Halls.
The CWC effectively took the meeting over. Lloyd George was heck-
led throughout before James Muir from the CWC addressed the 3,000
trade unionists. John Maclean's paper *Vanguard* commented:

> Seldom has a prominent politician, a leading representative of the gov-
> erning class, been treated with so little respect by a meeting of the
> workers. It is evident that the feeling of servility towards their masters
> no longer holds first place in the minds of the Clyde workers.[39]

Yet when shop stewards were prosecuted for leading a strike at the
Dalmuir gun mounting shop the CWC took no action. And when
conscription was introduced, which the CWC had seen as a major
attack and had pledged to meet with a strike call, nothing was done
beyond organising a demonstration to Glasgow Green.

In January 1916 special government commissioners arrived in Glas-
gow to push through dilution. The ILP paper *Forward* and John
Maclean's *Vanguard* had already been suppressed. On 2 February the
CWC paper, *The Worker*, was suppressed. Gallacher, Muir and the
printer Walter Bell were arrested under the Defence of the Realm
Act. John Maclean was arrested the same day:

The new offensive provoked an immediate and massive response. Within 18 hours strikes had broken out at Weir, Albion, Barr and Stroud, Coventry Ordnance Works and Dalmuir. Up to 10,000 workers downed tools. Under this pressure the court changed its mind about bail and the committee's leaders (though not John Maclean) were released on the morning of 9 February... By the morning of the 9th some of the strikers were returning and more were expected to go back on the 10th... The leadership, seeing the weakness of the strike, called it off, and at some cost to their own prestige, persuaded the more obdurate strikers to return to work. For the time being the committee survived, though its paper was gone and the threat of a long prison sentence hung over the heads of Gallacher and Muir.[40]

The commissioners scored a success when they got agreement from Kirkwood at Parkhead to implement dilution. On the advice of the local ILP leader John Wheatley he broke the CWC's united front. This did not stop a confrontation developing at Parkhead. Soldiers were introduced onto the shop floor despite Kirkwood's opposition. Then the owner, Beardmore, revoked Kirkwood's right as convenor to move freely about the works. On 17 March 1,000 workers struck. Four days later the strike spread to the North British Diesel Engine works in Scotstoun when workers refused to work on a job transferred from Parkhead. Two days later it spread to Dalmuir for the same reason.

On the Sunday the commissioners acted. Kirkwood and two Parkhead stewards were arrested along with two other CWC leaders, Messer and Arthur McManus. All were deported from Glasgow. This led to the extension of the strike. Two more Parkhead stewards and three from Weir's were deported, and 30 men were prosecuted and fined under the Munitions Act. Yet the strike involved just 4,500 workers at its height and did not involve the whole workforce even at Parkhead.

At a meeting of the CWC Gallacher ruled out of order a motion demanding the committee call a general strike across Clydeside. Gallacher and Muir then travelled to London to broker negotiations with the government. These were vetoed by Lloyd George. Later Gallacher would write, 'If I had gone to see the factory committees at several of the other factories instead of trying a piece of 'clever' intriguing in London, the situation might have been saved'.[41]

The CWC collapsed. And the ILP had played a key role in undermining it:

Yet the most powerful socialist party in Glasgow was the ILP, which had influential members in almost every working class organisation in the city. John Wheatley's own power base was in Shettleston, scene of the great Parkhead works and a centre of ASE [the engineering union] influence under David Kirkwood. According to *Forward*'s report of the Lloyd George visit to the Beardmore plant, the shop stewards presented a clear proposal to the minister for a radical dilution scheme, explaining that 'joint management is what we wanted—the state, the employer or organiser, and the works committee.' Such a clear expression of goals betrays the hand of Wheatley rather than the vocabulary of Kirkwood, and set the agenda for subsequent discussion of dilution in the socialist press...

In this respect, the ILP made the running in coming forward with practical arrangements for dilution at district and plant levels. It is true that John Maclean warned the CWC against such compromises and demanded an open political strike to end the war and defend working class living standards. It is also true that a conflict over Kirkwood's freedom of movement at Parkhead led to the crisis that ended in the deportation of activists and the crushing of the CWC...

Although the ILPers had a practical grasp of the procedures for overseeing dilution, they had assumed that the employers would accept a significant degree of workers' control—enforced by the shop stewards and underwritten by the continued bargaining power of the workforce. It soon became clear that the employers would tolerate no intrusion on their right to manage and that the state would support the established institutions of authority in any crisis.[42]

Revolutionaries like Gallacher failed to build an effective alternative to the ILP. In the end, while the ILP presence in the committee was small, it pulled the committee rightwards. Christopher Harvie points out that the confrontation on the Clyde came before the horror of the Somme brought home the reality of war: 'Perhaps the government was fortunate to break both the shop stewards and the anti-conscriptionists before the going got very rough'.[43]

Despite the defeat of the CWC the conditions creating radicalisation continued: 'Criticisms of the official leaders of the union and the Labour Party were sharpened as the state advanced towards military and industrial conscription in 1917-18'.[44]

But in the absence of a shop stewards' movement, of John Maclean and of any effective alternative party, the ILP was the main beneficiary of this radicalisation:

In 1917 began an expansion which took the ILP in Scotland from 3,000 members in 117 branches to 9,000 in 192 branches by September 1918. It was an expansion which happened nowhere else in Britain and left Scotland with a third of total British ILP membership.[45]

In Glasgow 'between 1917 and 1920 local membership virtually doubled from 1,370 to 2,641 with the fastest rates of growth in the artisanal communities of Govan and Partick, the heartlands of the 1915 rent strikes. In 1919, the peak year for membership, the Govan ILP totalled 306, a third more than the second largest branches in the East End wards of Bridgeton and Shettleston and ten times the size of the smallest ILP branches'.[46] The ILP, however, was not a homogeneous organisation. Its membership extended from revolutionaries who looked to the 1917 October Revolution to outright reformists.

The one abiding image of Red Clydeside is the red flag being raised above strikers massed in Glasgow's George Square. The 40 hour strike of January and February was a vital test for the developing revolutionary movement not just in Scotland but in Britain.

As soldiers began returning to civilian life with the close of the war, unemployment began rising. With such a concentration of armaments plants and shipyards Glasgow was quickly affected by the fall in orders. Unemployment in engineering rose to 11 percent by February 1919.

The snap general election called by Lloyd George in 1918 amidst the euphoria surrounding peace returned the Liberal-Tory wartime coalition government. Labour won just one seat in Glasgow Govan. In the Gorbals John Maclean was defeated by the sitting MP, a Labour member who backed the war and the coalition government. The mood grew among workers that they would have to look after their interests and could not rely on the politicians who had promised 'a land fit for heroes'.

Meanwhile the engineering union had secured a 47 hour week. In a national ballot this was accepted by 36,000 votes to 28,000. The choice offered was between 47 hours and the existing 54. But across the country shop stewards were championing a 40 hour week as the solution to rising unemployment. This gained added support when it was discovered that the 47 hour deal allocated no time for breakfast and a 9am meal break had been scrapped. Altogether there was little difference in the time engineering workers had to get up and when they got home. Furthermore, the union had conceded that there would be no drop in production with the reduced hours, so workers were expected to produce the same in less time.

On Sunday 5 January the 47 hour week was rejected and a committee of eight was elected to organise united action. Factory gate meetings were held and shops balloted on shorter hours. After another conference which gathered shop stewards from across Scotland a strike date was set for 27 January.

The strike call was opposed by the engineering union, which backed the 47 hour deal, the TUC, the STUC (which wanted it delayed), the engineering employers, the press and the government. But attempts to stop the strike failed. On the first day, 27 January, 40,000 workers were out. That grew to 100,000 on the Clyde and 14,000 on the Forth:

> The strike was by no means confined to Glasgow. Engineering and shipbuilding workers on both sides of the Clyde, in Dumbarton and in Paisley, were out on the Monday; 8,000 struck in the Leith shipyards, as did large numbers of engineering and printing workers in Edinburgh. The naval dockyards in Rosyth were severely affected, and 1,000 workers were out in Grangemouth. On 28 January a delegate conference of strikers was held in Glasgow. Delegates attended from as far away as Dumfries, Dundee and Alloa, as did delegates from Belfast, Grimsby and Rugby.
>
> In West Fife the miners in Cowdenbeath had struck on 23 January for the re-establishment of demobilised tradesmen. They were supported by Bowhill, Lochgelly and Glencraig pits. Over the weekend the miners' rank and file organisation, the Fife Miners Reform Committee, campaigned in the militant areas and the demand for a six hour, five day week was adopted.
>
> On 30 January a 10,000 strong demonstration of miners marched from the West Fife coalfield to Dunfermline to gain official support for the strike. But the local officials campaigned against the strike in East Fife, and in a ballot of all Fife miners there was a small majority for a return to work.[47]

In Lanarkshire, miners ignored the instructions from their own union and struck on 27 January. Mass pickets helped close down the coalfield. On the Wednesday 1,500 striking miners rallied in Hamilton and demanded that the executive of the Lanarkshire miners call a ballot. That evening there was a mass demonstration outside the executive's offices, which were occupied. The executive called a strike for the next day and 15,000 came out. They then called another strike on the Friday. But on Saturday they sloped off to Edinburgh and there voted for a return to work. The strike crumbled.

Mass pickets were also used by engineering and shipyard workers:

> The mass picket was first seen on the Monday [27 January]. After deciding to strike, 2,000 workers at the Albion Motor plant marched *en masse* to Barr and Stroud and pulled them out. At Dalmuir, Beardmore's was closed as a result of a mass picket. John Brown's in Clydebank was the next target on Tuesday. From the first day of the strike, workers in Dumbarton held mass meetings which decided which factories to picket. The organised unemployed also made their point by picketing factories still working, urging the men to come out.
>
> On the Tuesday in Dumbarton 5,000 marched through the town. As the local paper remarked somewhat apprehensively, 'No strike demonstration like it was ever seen in Dumbarton before.' The 5,000 formed a mass picket at Dennystoun Forge and at Babcock and Wilcox's tube works, closing both. By the Wednesday night the whole area was at a standstill.
>
> On the Thursday the strikers marched from Dumbarton up the Vale of Leven, blocking the tramways *en route*, to the munitions works at Alexandria which were still working. They too joined the strike...
>
> The picture south of the Clyde was no different. In Paisley mass meetings of strikers were held each morning at the cross. After hearing reports on the strike's progress, they decided where to picket that lunchtime. On the Wednesday they marched down Love Street, 'which for a time presented a spectacle such as may be witnessed on a Saturday when a big football match is on at St Mirren's Park'. Love Street was not the target, but the works in Inchinnan Road.[48]

Local strike committees ran the strike and held daily mass meetings. From those morning meetings a delegate reported to the central strike committee in Glasgow and returned with the news of decisions made there. These were carried in the central strike bulletin.

The high point came on Friday 31 January. On the Wednesday strikers had demonstrated outside the City Chambers in Glasgow's George Square demanding that the Lord Provost ask the government to grant their demands. He told them to come back at 12.30pm on the Friday to hear the reply.

Some 30,000 workers converged on George Square that Friday. The police demanded that tram lines be kept open and then launched a baton charge to clear the way for a tram. The strikers seized a lorry loaded with lemonade bottles and replied in kind. Willie Gallacher was batoned from behind as he remonstrated with the chief constable.

Eventually the strike leaders succeeded in getting the strikers to march off to Glasgow Green for a rally. This did not stop the police arresting Gallacher, David Kirkwood and Emmanuel Shinwell.

The next morning troops occupied Glasgow. Mass picketing ceased. Attacks on the strike by the press and union officials mounted. The engineering union suspended the entire Glasgow, Belfast and London district committees of the union—the three most militant areas. By the second week, with no strike pay available, the strike ended when the workers voted to call it off until national action could be called.

This was no pipe dream. Belfast had been rocked by just as militant a strike for shorter hours, and shipyard workers in Hull, Liverpool and Newcastle had walked out in support. But the key weakness was the engineering union and the lack of a national rank and file network to win backing for a 40 hour strike across Britain. The Glasgow strikers looked to spread the strike but did not have a mechanism to do so.

Red Clydeside was a product of the specific circumstances on the Clyde but it did not exist in isolation. It was tied into shop stewards' organisation in Sheffield, Manchester, Barrow, east London, Coventry and other engineering centres. Its leaders looked to create a national shop stewards' movement.

In *Revolt on the Clyde* Willie Gallacher wrote, 'A rising was expected. A rising should have taken place. The workers were ready and able to effect it'.[49] This was to overstate matters. But if instead of demobilising the strike the local leadership had maintained the mass picketing and sent out delegations to England, Wales and into the coalfields, victory would have been possible. And victory in 1919, a year of revolution in Europe, could easily have created a crisis in Britain.

James Hinton quotes the Italian revolutionary Antonio Gramsci thus:

> We say that the present period is revolutionary because we can see that the working class in all countries is tending to generate from within itself, with the utmost vital energy…proletarian institutions of a new type: representative in basis and industrial in arena.[50]

Those institutions existed in miniature on Clydeside. They provide a model that socialists can draw on today.

John Maclean—Scotland's greatest revolutionary

In John Maclean Clydeside produced an outstanding revolutionary leader. Working in virtual isolation, he made a series of impressive breakthroughs which echoed those of Lenin and the Bolsheviks.[51]

Firstly, he understood that the First World War was an imperialist war about repartitioning the world between the Great Powers and that it was likely to lead to another imperialist conflict. He saw that as being between the former world superpower, Britain, and the emerging global power, the US.

Secondly, he grasped how important the national liberation struggles in the colonies were in weakening imperialism and the British Empire in particular. That was demonstrated by his strong support for the Republican struggle in Ireland. In taking this clear anti-imperialist position, Maclean was breaking from the dominant position within the British socialist movement.

Thirdly, he broke with the SDF tradition of abstaining from economic struggles, placing the emphasis on propaganda and electioneering, without going over into syndicalism. As he told the court in 1921, 'I argued that the workers should not confine themselves to industrial action, but should take political action as well. Neither political nor industrial action would do separately'.[52]

It was these positions that formed the starting point for his call for a Scottish Workers' Republic. John Maclean was not a nationalist. He produced no equivalent of James Connolly's *Labour in Irish History*. Indeed, up until the class struggle entered a downturn in 1920 most of his activity during 1919 had been in England and Wales, organising opposition to any intervention by Britain against the Russian Revolution.

Maclean grasped that the class struggle was on the wane. Convinced that another imperialist war loomed, he believed a blow had to be struck against its chief instigator, the British Empire. Further, he thought that Scottish workers were more militant. So in November 1920 he stated:

> We on the Clyde have a mighty mission to fulfil. We can make Glasgow a Petrograd, a revolutionary storm centre second to none. A Scottish breakaway at this juncture would bring the empire crashing to the ground and free the waiting workers of the world.[53]

At the close of his life, in November 1923, he stated in his general election manifesto to the voters of the Gorbals:

> Russia could not produce the world revolution. Neither can we in the Gorbals, in Scotland, in Great Britain. Before England is ready I am sure that the next war will be on us. I therefore consider that Scotland's wisest policy is to declare a republic... The social revolution is possible sooner in Scotland.[54]

Underlying Maclean's support for a Scottish Workers' Republic was the centrality of class struggle. It was never presented in nationalist terms. In reality the downturn in class struggle was as severe in Scotland as it was south of the border. When the class struggle exploded again with the 1926 General Strike there was no discernible difference in militancy between Scotland, Wales or England. The Fife coalfield was one of the most militant and best organised but that was true of the north east of England too.

Ultimately Maclean's weakness was his failure to build a party which drew on his political strengths. While he broke with the whole SDF/Second International tradition, he still operated politically as an individual. Maclean himself unfortunately never met Lenin (who admired him greatly), and it is doubtful how much of Lenin's writings he read.

As Terry Brotherstone has argued:

> Maclean, subjectively a committed Bolshevik, never had the opportunity to study Lenin's conception of the relationship of theory to practice and the role of a democratic centralist party in establishing the link between Marxist theory and political organisation. He probably never read Lenin's *Left Wing Communism: An Infantile Disorder*, and we can certainly can never know what he would have made of the struggles which went on for the method underlying it during the early years of the Third International.[55]

The decline of Britain and the rise of Scottish nationalism

Prior to 1914 Scotland had headed the other regions of the UK in its overseas investment. Glasgow was the biggest exporter of steam locomotives in the world and produced 45 percent of the world's 'Siemens' steel; 70 percent of Britain's ships were built on the Clyde.

But the Scottish steel industry depended on shipbuilding, which in turn depended largely on British orders. Heavy engineering on Clydeside was closely tied to locomotive construction. All of these faced growing competition from the US and Germany. Britain had begun its long economic decline. The industries of the west of Scotland were to suffer enormously.

In the years following the First World War the giants of Clydeside industry—Beardmore's, Fairfields, Colvilles and the Steel Company of Scotland—were facing ruin. One response to a shrinking British economy was to accelerate the concentration of capital on a UK wide basis. The six Scottish railway companies and most of the Scottish banks had been merged into London based UK concerns.

The slump of the 1930s hit Scotland hard:

> The Scottish economy not only experienced the effects of the slump, but entered a a distinct and irreversible decline. Unemployment was the most obvious evidence: from 1.8 percent of the insured workforce (on the whole skilled men) in 1913 (the figure for London in the same year was 8.7 percent) it rose to a minimum of 10 percent between the wars and sometimes rose as high as 25 percent... In 1908 Scots industry had provided 12.5 percent of UK production; by 1930 this had fallen to 9.6 percent.[56]

The growth industries of the 1930s, car manufacturing and electrical engineering, were virtually absent from Scotland. Industrial recovery when it came depended heavily on rearmament. It was this background which created modern Scottish nationalism. Irish nationalism rose in opposition to British rule. Scottish nationalism was a response to imperial decline.

The National Party was founded in 1928. It was based largely on ex Independent Labour Party members—including its first chair and secretary, Roland Muirhead and John MacCormick—intellectuals, students and journalists. Among its founding members was the poet Hugh MacDiarmid, another former ILPer.

Initially the new party made little impact but in the 1929 general election it did win 15 percent of the vote in St Rollox, the centre of Glasgow's depressed locomotive construction industry.

The forces of nationalism received reinforcements from an unlikely quarter with a split in the Scottish Conservative Party. Among the petty bourgeoisie there was growing unease with economic and political centralisation on a UK level. The creation of a National

Government uniting the Tories with the Labour leader Ramsay Mac-Donald, his supporters and a section of the Liberal Party seemed another step in that direction. A section of the Tory party split away to form the Scottish Party and in 1934 that merged with the National Party to form the Scottish National Party (MacDiarmid was expelled for opposing this merger). The new party stood in eight seats in the 1935 election, polling an average of 16 percent.

Scotland in the post-war world had changed from a country which at the beginning of the century was among the most prosperous areas of the UK to one whose gross domestic product lagged behind the UK average: 'The growth years of 1954-60 saw UK industrial output expand by 23 percent, but for Scotland the figure was a mere 9 percent'.[57]

Despite the post-war economic boom, unemployment remained relatively high: 'If the the UK average in 1964 be taken as 100, then Scottish unemployment reached an annual average of 209.5 percent'.[58] By 1963 unemployment in the Vale of Leven stood at 7.5 percent.

Other problems remained: 'Of 300,000 slum houses identified in 1956 only 92,000 had been cleared by 1963. Housebuilding had seen virtually no rise since 1957 and overcrowding was chronic'.[59]

In Glasgow in 1965 a survey revealed:

> 85 percent of all dwellings were flats and only 12 percent houses. One third of all these dwellings contained only one or two rooms and 93 percent lacked an internal water closet; 90 percent had no bath; 11,000 dwellings were totally unfit, 75,000 were substandard and not fit for improvement at reasonable cost, 49,000 substandard but susceptible to improvement at reasonable cost.[60]

In this situation people voted with their feet. I can recall from my childhood the queue of people outside the office on Edinburgh's Princes Street where they could secure assisted passage to settle in Australia: 'Between 1951 and 1966, 476,000 people left Scotland: 89 percent of the natural population increase'.[61]

All of this underscored a growth in support for the SNP. In 1962 their candidate in the West Lothian by-election, William Wolfe, came second to Labour's Tam Dalyell. In March 1967 the SNP took 28 percent of the vote in the Glasgow Pollok by-election, allowing the Tories to take the seat. That was the prelude to a far greater shock. In November the SNP's Winnie Ewing took the solid Labour seat of Hamilton with 46 percent of the vote. A 16,000 Labour majority simply melted away. The sitting MP, a government minister, had given up the seat to take a well paid job as chair of the North of Scotland Hydro-Electric Board. The by-election coincided with a balance of payments crisis which forced the Wilson government to devalue the pound and cut back on public spending. The SNP took another safe Labour seat in spectacular style in Govan in 1973, when Margo MacDonald overturned a 16,000 majority. In the February 1974 general election the SNP polled 27.2 percent of the poll in the Vale of Leven and then rose to 33.7 percent in the October general election. Overall that election saw the SNP reach its high water mark, with the party taking 30.4 percent of the vote across Scotland, winning 11 seats, compared to Labour's 36.3 percent.

A pattern was developing. Scotland's plight was no worse than that of the north east of England (whose unemployment rate has been consistently higher), Merseyside or South Wales. But what was (and is) different was that as discontent with Labour grew there was a viable electoral alternative in Scotland, the SNP.

Discontent with New Labour is once again growing and fuelling support for the SNP. The May elections for the Scottish Parliament only saw the SNP return to the position reached in October 1974, but across the four major cities there was a swing to the nationalists of 10 percent. In those elections the SNP consciously adopted 'Old Labour' rhetoric and policies. Yet it shares with New Labour a common approach to solving Scotland's economic problems—attracting multinationals to invest on the basis of low pay. The SNP has made great play of the apparent success of Ireland's 'Celtic Tiger' economy. Yet the reality is that Ireland's much hyped economic growth (which in itself has not matched those of the Asian Tiger economies a decade earlier) 'has had the lowest investment rates in Europe during the 1990s'.[62] It also has the highest level of long term unemployment, low wages and high indirect taxation to balance the lowest corporation tax in Europe. These low tech, low paid jobs are the first to go in any recession, as multinationals close plants where investment is lowest.

Socialists have no problem with Scottish independence. The Scottish people have the right to self determination. We have no interest in maintaining the unity of the United Kingdom given its bloody record. But at the same time Scotland remains a highly divided class society with concentrations of great poverty and great wealth.

How are we to change that? For too many on the Scottish left and in the working class movement Red Clydeside belongs firmly to the past. Yet the record of the working class in Britain is that Scottish,

Welsh and English workers have fought together and lost together. Red Clydeside is one period when Scottish workers were more militant than their southern brothers and sisters, but this was tied firmly into a British wide upsurge.

The same is true of the industrial upturn of the early 1970s. The sit-in against the closure of Upper Clyde Shipbuilders sparked a massive wave of solidarity across not just Scotland but the whole of Britain. In the year long miners' strike of 1984-85 Scottish miners stood shoulder to shoulder with their English and Welsh comrades. When it came to the poll tax Scotland led the way with non-payment, but it was the greatest riot in a century in the centre of London that destroyed Thatcher and her hated tax.

Class unity is not an abstraction. Even with the creation of a Scottish Parliament it remains an everyday reality for hundreds of thousands of Scottish workers. When it came to opposition to the Balkan War in 1999 a united response was needed across Britain.

There is in Scotland a pessimism about the ability of working class people to fight back. The scars of the defeats of the 1980s remain. This has led many on the left to embrace nationalism. Yet, as we face the most pro-market Labour government ever, the case for a socialist alternative remains more urgent than ever. For us there is a tradition which runs from the Radical Wars of the 1820s, through the crucial years of Red Clydeside and John Maclean, through the militancy of the Fife coalfield in 1926 to the great industrial battles of the early 1970s, the fight against the poll tax and that at Timex in Dundee in the late 1980s and the 1990s. That tradition does not belong to the heritage industry. It is alive, pointing the way forward.

Notes

1   For a fuller explanation see G Bois, *The Crisis of Feudalism* (Cambridge, 1984), which concentrates on Eastern Normandy but provides a materialist explanation for this European wide crisis.
2   C Harvie, *Scotland and Nationalism* (London, 1977), p29.
3   A Calder, *Revolutionary Empire* (New York, 1981), pp423-424.
4   C Harvie, op cit, p72.
5   R Mitchison, *A History of Scotland* (London, 1970), p345.
6   J Foster, 'Capitalism and the Scottish Nation', in G Brown (ed), *The Red Paper on Scotland* (Edinburgh, 1975), pp146-147.
7   E C Mossner, *The Life of David Hume* (London, 1954), p389.
8   T C Smout, *A History of the Scottish People 1560-1830* (London, 1987), p470. The references are to David Hume, Adam Smith, Walter Scott, Robert Burns, the chemist and physicist Joseph Black, the inventor James Watt, the engineer Thomas Telford, the architect Robert Adam, the geologist James Hutton, the philosopher and sociologist Adam Ferguson, the geologist and writer Hugh Millar, the philosopher Thomas Reid, the historian and principal of Edinburgh University William Robertson, the painters Allan Ramsey and Henry Raeburn, the architect William Adam and the naturalist James Rennie, Samuel Johnson's biographer James Boswell and the writer James Hogg.
9   For a brilliant demolition job on the kilt and tartanry read H Trevor-Roper, 'The Invention of Tradition: the Highland Tradition of Scotland', in E J Hobsbawm and T Ranger (eds), *The Invention of Tradition* (Cambridge, 1977), pp15-41.
10 Quoted in T Nairn, 'Old Nationalism and New Nationalism', in G Brown (ed), op cit, pp34-35.
11 A Calder, op cit, pp676-677.
12 T C Smout, op cit, p475.
13 T C Smout, op cit, p303.
14 T Clarke and T Dickson, 'Class and Class Consciousness in Early Industrial Capitalism', in T Dickson (ed), *Capital and Class in Scotland* (Edinburgh, 1982), p38.
15 T Clarke and T Dickson, op cit, p39.
16 T Clarke and T Dickson, op cit, pp38, 41.
17 W Hamish Fraser, 'The Scottish Context of Chartism', in T Brotherstone (ed), *Covenant, Charter and Party* (Aberdeen, 1989), p66.
18 T Clarke and T Dickson, op cit, p49.
19 C Harvie, 'Before the Breakthrough, 1886-1922', in I Donnachie, C Harvie and I S Wood (eds), *Forward! Labour Politics in Scotland 1888-1988* (Edinburgh, 1989), p8.
20 J Melling, 'Scottish Industrialists and the Changing Character of Class Relations in Early Industrial Capitalism', in T Dickson (ed), op cit, p93.
21 J J Smyth, 'The ILP in Glasgow, 1888-1906', in A McKinlay and R J Morris (eds), *The ILP on Clydeside 1893-1932* (Manchester, 1991), p21.
22 J Melling, op cit, p79.
23 Ibid, p84.
24 Ibid, p94.
25 J Smith, 'Taking the Leadership of the Movement: The ILP in Glasgow, 1906-1914', in A McKinlay and R J Morris (eds), op cit, p74.

26 Ibid.
27 Ibid, p78.
28 J Melling, op cit, p124.
29 J Hinton, *The First Shop Stewards Movement* (London, 1973), p103.
30 J Melling, op cit, p126.
31 A and V Flynn, 'We Shall Not Be Removed', in L Flynn (ed), *We Shall Be All* (Glasgow, 1978), p22.
32 Ibid, p22.
33 J Melling, op cit, p112.
34 Ibid, p24.
35 J Melling, 'The ILP During the First World War', in A McKinlay and R J Morris (eds), op cit, p99.
36 J Melling, 'Scottish Industrialists and the Changing Character of Class Relations in Early Industrial Capitalism', op cit, p114.
37 A and V Flynn, op cit, p28.
38 J Hinton, op cit, pp119-122.
39 Quoted ibid, p135.
40 Ibid, pp147-148.
41 W Gallacher, *Revolt on the Clyde* (London, 1936), p111.
42 J Melling, 'The ILP During the First World War', op cit, pp103-105.
43 C Harvie, 'Before the Breakthrough, 1886-1922', in I Donnachie, C Harvie and I S Wood (eds), op cit, p23.
44 J Melling, 'The ILP During the First World War', op cit, p111.
45 R J Morris, 'The ILP, 1893-1932: Introduction', in A McKinlay and R J Morris (eds), op cit, p5.
46 A McKinlay, 'Strategy, Ideology and Organisation, 1918-22', in A McKinlay and R J Morris (eds), op cit, p138.
47 J Leopold, 'The Forty Hours Strike', in L Flynn (ed), op cit, p37.
48 Ibid, p38.
49 W Gallacher, op cit, p224.
50 Quoted in J Hinton, op cit, p17.
51 For an excellent brief account of Maclean's life and politics, see D Sherry, *John Maclean* (London, 1999).
52 J Maclean, *In the Rapids of Revolution* (London, 1978), p233.
53 Ibid, p220.
54 Ibid, p247.
55 T Brotherstone, 'Internationalism in the 20th Century: Some Comments Upon John Maclean', in T Brotherstone (ed), op cit, p111.
56 C Harvie, op cit, p112.
57 M Keating, 'The Labour Party in Scotland, 1951-1964', in I Donnachie, C Harvie and I S Wood (eds), op cit, p87.
58 A and V Flynn, op cit, p32.
59 Ibid.
60 Ibid.
61 F Wood, 'Scottish Labour in Government and Opposition: 1964-79', in I Donnachie, C Harvie and I S Wood (eds), op cit, p101.
62 D O'Hearn, *Inside the Celtic Tiger* (London, 1998), p84.

Chapter 2

Marxism and the national question

Alex Callinicos

Marxism is, in essence, an internationalist tradition. 'Workers of all countries, unite!' the *Communist Manifesto* declares. For Marx and Engels, the fundamental division in the world was that between classes, not nations. The conflict between capital and labour cut across national borders, uniting workers and bosses in struggle with each other.[1]

It is commonly believed that this internationalism renders Marxism unable to deal with the reality of national divisions. Thus the philosopher G A Cohen, the author of an influential interpretation of Marx's theory of history, writes, 'A certain cliché of anti-Marxist thought is probably true, namely that Marx misjudged the significance of religion and nationalism'.[2] Tom Nairn, sometime Marxist turned cheerleader for Scottish nationalism, went even further, declaring, 'The theory of nationalism represents Marxism's great historical failure'.[3] And certainly it is tempting to see the 20th century—with all its horrors of world war, Holocaust, and ethnic cleansing—as representing the triumph of national identity over class.

But when we consider the record of the Marxist tradition, we see that in fact it contains the resources both theoretically to understand and politically to respond to nationalism. It is true that in the *Communist Manifesto* Marx and Engels express the excessively optimistic belief that the development of capitalism as a global system would sweep away all national differences. Thus they write, 'National differences and antagonisms between peoples are daily more and more vanishing, owing to the development of the bourgeoisie, to freedom of commerce, to the world market, to uniformity in the mode of production and in the conditions of life corresponding thereto'.[4] (A similar belief is held today, with far less justification, by the boosters of 'globalisation'.) But it soon became clear that, far from being opposed to one another, capitalism and national identity go together.

Capitalism and the nation state

There are two fundamental reasons for this. First of all, the development of capitalism as a mode of production requires the construction of nation states. Economic and social historians have shown how the emergence of industrial capitalism in Britain, for example, depended critically on the formation of a large domestic market for the goods and services produced by the new capitalist entrepreneurs. This 'first consumer society' presupposed the political unification of a relatively large economic zone within which people, commodities and money could move fairly freely. At the same time the development of capitalism was fuelled by the military struggle among the European powers. Thus the overseas expansion of the British state in the 17th and 18th centuries won markets and investment opportunities for its capitalists; at the same time massive state expenditure on the main instrument of foreign conquest, the Royal Navy, increased demand for the products of the manufacturing industries. Finally intense inter-state competition encouraged rulers to begin to appeal to their subjects as members of the same national community in struggle with their foreign rivals. Thus British national identity was forged during the long era of wars with France between 1689 and 1815.[5]

There was nothing 'natural' about the nations which emerged from this process. Individual identities in pre-capitalist society were either much narrower (to locality and/or kin group) or much broader (to some version of a world religion) than those of the new nations. These existing allegiances had to be broken down or subordinated to that of nationality. The formation of national identity was a process of forcible incorporation and assimilation. As Ernest Gellner persuasively argues, for its effective functioning a modern industrial society with its unified labour market and bureaucratic state requires a single homogeneous culture.[6] Typically this involved the emergence of a single 'national' language shared by rulers and ruled. Which language and associated culture assumed this role was usually a result of the historical accident of the language and culture shared by the class which happened to control the state: the other languages and cultures were left to wither away by neglect or formally suppressed. As Eric Hobsbawm vividly put it, 'Dialects, as everyone knows, are just languages without an army and police force'.[7] The state bureaucracy and modern mass education provided powerful engines of cultural homogenisation.

Secondly, while capitalism developed as a world system, as Marx and Engels had predicted, it did so unevenly. This process of what Trotsky called uneven and combined development meant, among other things, that the first capitalist powers, concentrated in Western Europe and North America, could dominate the rest of the world. In the 19th and early 20th centuries this took the form of the formal incorporation of what is now called the Third World (Africa, Asia, and Latin America) into the European colonial empires. But the period since 1945 has seen the continued economic and military domination of Western capitalism (expanded to include Japan), despite decolonisation. The Marxist theory of imperialism explains this state of affairs as a consequence of tendencies inherent within the capitalist mode of production itself. Competition among capitals leads to ever greater concentration and centralisation, resulting in the emergence of vast corporations operating on a global scale and closely interwoven with their nation states. As a result, the economic rivalries between firms tend to take on the form of military and territorial conflicts among states. One consequence is inter-imperialist struggles such as the two world wars and the Cold War; another is a hierarchy of power on a global scale, as the major capitalist states pursue their interests by seeking to impose their will on the smaller powers.[8]

It is against this background that we must see the development over the past two centuries of nationalism as a political ideology. There are, in fact, two kinds of nationalism. The first is the imperialist nationalism of the dominant powers—American, British, French and German. This seeks to bind the working classes in the imperialist countries to their ruling classes, to unite exploiters and exploited against both the workers and bosses of other imperialist countries and the masses in those countries oppressed by imperialism. Secondly, there is the revolutionary nationalism of the oppressed—the ideology that serves to unite a people suffering the domination of an imperialist power in their struggle to break free. The clash between these different nationalisms is one of the great dramas of the 20th century that has unleashed huge struggles in countries as diverse as Ireland, India, Vietnam and Algeria.

Marx already had to confront the effects of one of these conflicts in Victorian Britain. He was forcibly struck by the division between 'native' British workers and Irish immigrants in the great industrial cities. The latter were driven by famine, poverty and unemployment in Ireland to do unskilled, low paid labouring jobs in Britain; they were also discriminated against because of their religion and nationality. British workers were encouraged by the ruling class to see their Irish fellow workers not just as an economic threat, liable to undercut their wages and conditions, but as racially 'inferior' (the Victorian popular press was full of revolting racial stereotypes of the Irish). Marx believed this division between 'native' British and Irish workers to be 'the secret of the impotence of the English working class'.[9] He argued that to counter the ruling class's strategy of divide and rule it was necessary to win the British labour movement to supporting the struggle for Irish self determination. Only by identifying with the nationalism of the oppressed could the hold of the nationalism of the oppressor be broken amongst British workers.

Lenin on the national question

Lenin, benefiting from the experience of building a socialist party in the multi-national Russian Empire and from the debates over the national question within the international socialist movement before and during the First World War, generalised Marx's approach. He argued that it was the duty of revolutionary socialists to support the right of self determination of oppressed nations. His reasons for taking this position did not appeal to abstract moral principles, but were rather strategic: support for the national self determination of the oppressed was a means of achieving the international unity of the working class.[10]

Lenin's approach involved the following key elements:

(1) *Against imperialist nationalism*. For Lenin, the 'cardinal idea' in his approach to the national question lay in 'the distinction between oppressed and oppressor nations'.[11] Following Marx, he believed that the only way workers in the imperialist countries could be won away from national chauvinism was if they were to identify with the struggle of those nations oppressed by their ruling class. Thus he argued that in the Tsarist 'prison house of nations' it was essential for workers belonging to the dominant Great Russian nation to support the demands of, for example, the Polish people for national independence. This position did not, as we shall see below, imply an endorsement of Polish nationalism, or indeed of any form of nationalism. Rather Lenin expected that, by coming to see the justice of oppressed nations' claims,

Russian workers and their counterparts in other imperialist countries could be won to revolutionary internationalism.

Lenin was here challenging an abstract conception of internationalism influential among some Bolsheviks and also to some extent even on the great Polish revolutionary Rosa Luxemburg. This equated internationalism with ignoring national differences; often it went along with the mistaken belief that capitalism was abolishing national divisions. Since imperialism was in fact accentuating these conflicts through the domination of the Great Powers over the rest of the world, this abstract internationalism could easily turn into its opposite: pretending national differences didn't exist could slide into, in effect, colluding with a system that perpetuated national oppression. Given the capitulation of the main parties of the Second International to the imperialist war in August 1914, this was no mere abstract possibility (Luxemburg was, of course, an unflinching opponent of the war). Paradoxically, genuine internationalism required supporting one kind of national struggle—that of oppressed peoples—against another— that of the imperialist powers. Lenin wrote:

> In the internationalist education of the workers of the oppressor countries, emphasis must necessarily be laid on their advocating freedom for the oppressed countries and their fighting for it. Without these there can be no internationalism. It is our right and duty to treat every Social Democrat of an oppressor nation who fails to conduct such propaganda as a scoundrel and an imperialist.[12]

(2) *For oppressed nations against imperialism.* Thus far Lenin merely applied generally, and in typically sharp and polemical form, what Marx had argued in the case of Ireland. But he went beyond Marx in recognising the potential for the struggles of oppressed nations to weaken, not merely individual Great Powers, but indeed the entire imperialist system. Thus he was very quick to see how the Irish Republican movement could, particularly during the First World War, undermine British imperialism. He fiercely denounced the sectarianism of those Bolsheviks who dismissed the 1916 Easter Rising in Dublin as a mere 'putsch' by petty bourgeois nationalists:

> To imagine that social revolution is conceivable without revolts by small nations in the colonies and in Europe, without revolutionary outbursts in the colonies and in Europe, without revolutionary outbursts by a section of the petty bourgeoisie with all its prejudices, without a movement of the politically non-conscious proletarian and semi-proletarian

masses against oppression by the landowners, the church, and the monarchy, against national oppression, etc—to imagine all this is to repudiate social revolution... So one army lines up in one place and says, 'We are for socialism,' and another, somewhere else, says, 'We are for imperialism,' and that will be a social revolution!... Whoever expects a 'pure' social revolution will never live to see it.[13]

Lenin saw that the crisis of imperialism produced by the First World War and its aftermath would involve more than the 'pure' conflict between capital and labour. Other social forces—in oppressed nations, all the classes suffering from the effects of imperialist domination—would be driven to rebel against the existing order. Their struggle could combine with that of the working class to weaken and ultimately to destroy the entire system. Thus, in the 'Draft Theses on the National and Colonial Questions' presented to the Second Congress of the Communist International (Comintern) in July 1920 Lenin wrote:

World political developments are of necessity concentrated on a single focus—the struggle of the world bourgeoisie against the Soviet Russian Republic, around which are inevitably grouped on the one hand the Soviet movements of the advanced workers in all countries, and on the other hand all the national liberation movements in the colonies and among the oppressed nationalities, who are learning from bitter experience that their only salvation lies in the Soviet system's victory over world imperialism.[14]

(3) *The limits of nationalism.* But, at the same time as he envisaged an alliance between communist workers' movements and national liberation movements, Lenin was careful to emphasise that the two movements had different class bases and therefore should not merge. Thus the 'Draft Theses' stress:

The need for a determined struggle against attempts to give a communist colouring to bourgeois democratic liberation trends in the backward countries; the Communist International should support the bourgeois democratic national movements in colonial and backward countries only on condition that, in these countries, the elements of future proletarian parties, which will be communist not only in name, are brought together and trained to understand their special tasks, ie, those of the struggle against the bourgeois democratic movements within their own nations. The Communist International must enter into a temporary alliance with bourgeois democracy in the colonial and backward countries, but should not merge with it, and should under all circum-stances uphold the independence of the proletarian movement even if it is in its most embryonic form.[15]

Behind this call was the Marxist analysis of the national question outlined above. A fundamental gulf separates even the most revolu-tionary nationalism and revolutionary socialism. They are the ide-ologies of different classes. Nationalism is a bourgeois ideology not in the sense that all or even most of its adherents are capitalists but rather in the sense that it always articulates the interests of an actual or aspirant capitalist class. Revolutionary nationalism is usually the ide-ology of an aspirant capitalist class. Imperialist domination tends to impede the development of indigenous capitalism in oppressed coun-tries. The impetus for the nationalist movement is typically provided by middle class intellectuals. More often than not they are, as a social layer, the product of the imperialist order—brought into being by its need for bureaucrats familiar with its language and culture and capa-ble of acting as its intermediaries with the oppressed masses. Caught up in this intermediate position, close enough to the imperialist power to appreciate its power, but still part of the oppressed nation and there-fore despised and humiliated by their masters, these intellectuals form the idea of a political movement that can create a new nation state with the power to promote a capitalism under their own control. (Even where an indigenous bourgeoisie did develop under imperial rule and support the national cause—for example, among the industrial-ists of Bombay and rich Catholic farmers in Southern Ireland—the movement was still led by intellectuals like the barrister Gandhi, the Harrow and Cambridge educated Nehru, the postal clerk Collins, and the schoolteacher Pearse.[16])

Faced with the refusal of the imperial power to make concessions, the nationalist leaders are forced into a strategy of confrontation, based on different combinations of mass action and armed struggle. This requires the construction of a broad national movement seeking to unite all the classes of the oppressed population—workers, peasants, intellectuals and capitalists—against the oppressor. This process in turn involves the ideological construction of a national community where shared identity transcends class divisions: typically this is achieved by the projection into the pre-colonial past of a largely mythological history of a nation whose past glories will be restored and its present suffering redeemed once independence is secured.[17]

But, however great the confrontation with imperialism, and however heroic the sacrifices it involves, every nationalist struggle ends in compromise. This reflects the class nature of revolutionary nationalism: since its aim is to carve out a new capitalist state, ultimately it must come to terms with the system of capitalist states and the dominant powers within that system. The compromise may betray some of the basic objectives of the movement; it always denies the more radical hopes generated in the course of the struggle. We can see this historically—for example, when the Irish struggle for independence led to the 1922 treaty that set up the Northern statelet and sparked off civil war within the Republican movement, or in the ambiguous triumph of Indian nationalism in 1947, with Congress inheriting the structure of power created by the Raj and the sub-continent subjected to the agony of partition. But the same pattern is present in more recent movements. Three of the major national liberation struggles of the past generation—South Africa, Palestine and Northern Ireland—have been apparently 'concluded' in agreements that to a greater or less extent deny their basic aspirations.

There thus comes a point in the history of every nationalist movement where the leadership seeks to restrain the mass movement it had previously mobilised. The tasks of the struggle are replaced by those of 'nation building'—of constructing a new state in which the old revolutionary leadership presides as part of a new capitalist state. The conversion of Robert Mugabe from political leader of the guerrilla war which freed Zimbabwe from minority white rule to the figurehead of a corrupt and increasingly despotic regime at war with its own people is a recent example of this process.

Permanent revolution

Lenin grasped very clearly that the class nature of revolutionary nationalism made it essential that the communist parties in colonial and semi-colonial countries should retain their political and organisational independence and build strong working class movements. He did not, however, resolve the problem of how the demands of the nationalist struggle against imperialism—bourgeois democratic demands, since they could, in principle, be met without overthrowing capitalism—related to those of the specifically working class struggle for socialism.

After Lenin's death in 1924, as Joseph Stalin came to dominate the Bolshevik regime, the Comintern adopted what came to be known as a stages strategy. On this view, revolution in the colonies had to go through two stages—first the bourgeois democratic struggle for national independence, and then the working class struggle for socialism. The first stage required a broad alliance of all the classes with an interest in achieving national liberation—'national' capitalists as well as workers, peasants and intellectuals. During this phase the working class should subordinate its distinctive interests to those of the nationalist coalition, and avoid pursuing demands and struggles that might alienate the capitalists and the petty bourgeoisie of small property owners.

The Chinese Revolution of 1925-27 was the first of many cases that showed that this strategy led to disastrous consequences.[18] As Trotsky pointed out at the time, the key problem was the 'national bourgeoisie'. Because capitalism involves a process of uneven and combined development, capitalists in the less developed countries tend to be weak and dependent on imperialism. This means that they are unlikely to support a consistent struggle against imperialism. They also tend to fear mass mobilisations since they may get out of control and develop into a struggle against all property owners, local as well as foreign.

Thus the Chinese Communist Party (CCP) sought to restrain the struggles of workers and peasants for fear of antagonising the 'national bourgeoisie'. Even basic land reforms were ruled out since Chinese capitalists were usually closely linked to the landowners. The CCP concentrated on doing what one Comintern official called 'coolie work' for the nationalist Guomindang (GMD) by mobilising mass support for its military campaigns. When their usefulness was over, the GMD leader, Jiang Kaishek, seeking to ingratiate himself with foreign and local capital, turned on the Communists and slaughtered thousands of them. The same story was subsequently to be repeated again and again in many parts of the Third World. One of the most striking cases came during the Iraqi Revolution of 1958-59, when the Communist Party supported Qasim's 'progressive' military regime, demobilising an immense mass movement of workers and urban poor and thereby opening the door to a CIA backed coup whose eventual outcome brought the Ba'ath nationalist party and thus eventually Saddam Hussein to power.[19]

The Stalinist stages strategy represented the triumph of nationalism over socialism, and therefore the negation of Lenin's insistence on working class independence. Trotsky's theory of permanent revolution provided the basis of an alternative strategy based on the experience of the Russian Revolution of October 1917. Uneven and combined development in Tsarist Russia led to the creation at the end of the 19th century of enclaves of advanced industry within a predominantly peasant society. The capitalist class, dependent on the state and foreign capital, shunned any determined struggle to rid Russia of the Tsarist autocracy. The working class based on the new industries, though only a minority of the population, therefore took on the leadership of the entire democratic movement. But the logic of the workers' struggle drove them beyond purely democratic demands to fight for their own class interests. In October 1917 this process culminated in the workers seizing power under the Bolsheviks' leadership and with the acquiescence of the peasant majority.

Trotsky argued that the same process of permanent revolution was at work in the colonial and semi-colonial countries. In countries like China the working class could lead the oppressed and exploited majority—peasants, unemployed and the like—in a struggle which would combine the demand for national independence with the effort to break the hold of capital. As the example of Russia also showed, however, socialist revolution, especially in an economically backward country, could only succeed if it spread by winning the support of workers in other countries. As a world system, capitalism could only be broken on an international scale. In the absence of global revolution, capital would reassert its power either by directly organising a counter-revolution to destroy the workers' state or through the effects of economic and military pressure in encouraging the emergence of a Stalinist bureaucracy within the isolated socialist regime.

Thus the very processes of uneven and combined development that give rise to revolutionary nationalist struggles against imperialism in the first place also ensure that these struggles can only succeed if they develop into socialist revolutions that triumph on an international scale. The only way in which the grip of the capitalism world system on individual countries can be broken is if that system is itself destroyed. And no national struggle can achieve this—only an international class, the working class, can remove that system and replace it with a world in which different peoples and their cultures can flourish in all their diversity.

The national question today

The Marxist approach to the national question, mainly developed by Lenin, seems to me the best available. It grasps the revolutionary dynamic of nationalist movements—their capacity to destabilise even the greatest imperialist powers. The Indian and Irish struggles undermined British imperialism; the Vietnamese epic imposed a humiliating defeat on the greatest of all imperialist powers, from which in many ways the US ruling class has yet politically to recover; nationalist rebellions in the Caucasus and the Baltic played a crucial part in the disintegration of the Soviet Union in the late 1980s. At the same time, Marxism highlights the limits of nationalism: the trajectory of even the most heroic nationalist movement is to carve out its own space within the capitalist world system and therefore ultimately to make its peace with that system.

This analysis allows us to avoid the two characteristic errors committed by the left towards nationalism. One is to demonise it; the other is to capitulate to it. The former reaction has been very common since the collapse of the Stalinist states at the end of the 1980s. Many left intellectuals have reacted to the fall of regimes in which they often harboured illusions by portraying a world succumbing to a wave of barbaric and irrational nationalisms. The wars in the former Yugoslavia and on the peripheries of the old Soviet Union encouraged this attitude. What this view missed out was the essential ambiguity of nationalism. The warring Serbian and Croatian nationalisms that ripped Yugoslavia apart in the early 1990s were indeed based on chauvinist mythologies justifying bestial atrocities. But this did not alter the fact that different nationalisms served as the umbrella under which tens of millions of people in the Baltic and Caucasus rose up against an oppressive Stalinist regime in the late 1980s.

The ambiguity of nationalism reflects its class nature. The same ideology that legitimises a struggle against oppression can also be used by a new capitalist class to justify its consolidation of state power by seizing territory from and denying elementary rights to those now stigmatised as aliens. This is why every nationalist movement has to be judged concretely, on the basis of the particular political effects that its actions have in a specific context. When the Vietnamese liberation armed forces rolled up the American client army during their march on Saigon in the spring of 1975 they were completing a great struggle for national liberation. When they invaded Cambodia nearly four years later they were asserting the claim of the Vietnamese state to dominate Indochina by its military might.[20]

The opposite error to demonising nationalism is closely related. It consists in capitulating to a particular nationalism by depicting it as inherently progressive. This was common on the Western left in the 1960s and 1970s, when Third World national liberation movements were celebrated as being in the vanguard of socialism. Thus many student radicals went beyond solidarity with the Vietnamese struggle against US imperialism to uncritical support for the ruling Vietnamese Communist Party. But when Vietnam went to war with two other 'socialist' countries, Cambodia and China, in 1978-79 the result was enormous confusion and disillusionment. Exactly the same error is made—of giving what Lenin called 'communist coloration' to bourgeois nationalist movements—but with far less excuse by those socialists who today regard the Scottish and Welsh nationalist parties as leading a struggle against imperialism.

The distinctive feature of the Marxist approach to the national question, as elaborated chiefly by Lenin, is that it is concerned primarily with the specific political impact of a given nationalist movement. Michael Löwy puts it very well:

> From the methodological point of view, Lenin's principal superiority over his contemporaries was his capacity to 'put politics in command', that is, his obstinate, inflexible, constant, and unflinching tendency to grasp the political aspect of every problem and every contradiction... On the national question, while most other Marxist writers saw only the economic, cultural or 'psychological' dimension of the problem, Lenin stated clearly that the question of self determination 'belongs wholly and exclusively to the sphere of political democracy', that is, to the realm of the right of political secession and the establishment of an independent nation state... His aim was democracy and the international unity of the proletariat, which both require the recognition of the right of nations to self determination. What is more, precisely because it concentrates on the political aspect, his theory of self determination makes absolutely no concession to nationalism.[21]

Thus from a Marxist point of view the significance of a national struggle lies in the social conflicts it expresses and, in particular, the political consequences it has. Where the latter include the weakening of imperialism and strengthening of the international unity of the working class, socialists should support its struggle; where they do not, socialists should not support it. Of course, this is a general approach which must be applied with care to particular circumstances—for example, to the different national questions within the borders of the United Kingdom, in the North of Ireland, Scotland, and Wales: other essays in this collection address the specific question of Scottish nationalism. But it should now be clear that the national question is not the rock on which Marxism founders. On the contrary, the Marxist tradition can both explain the nature of national conflicts and offer a strategy for dealing with them.

Notes

1   This essay is based on a talk given at Socialism in Scotland, Glasgow, 20
    November 1998. A much fuller Marxist analysis of the national question will be
    found in C Harman, 'The Return of the National Question', in *International
    Socialism* 56 (1992), reprinted in A Callinicos et al, *Marxism and the New
    Imperialism* (London, 1994).

2   G A Cohen, 'Reconsidering Historical Materialism', in A Callinicos (ed),
    Marxist Theory (Oxford, 1989), p162.

3   T Nairn, 'The Modern Janus', *New Left Review* 94 (1975), p3.

4   K Marx and F Engels, *Collected Works*, vol VI (London, 1976), p503.

5   See especially M Mann, *The Sources of Social Power*, vol 1 (Cambridge, 1986),
    pp483-485; J Brewer, *The Sinews of Power* (London, 1989); and L Colley, *Britons*
    (London, 1994).

6   E Gellner, *Nations and Nationalism* (Oxford, 1983).

7   E J Hobsbawm, *The Age of Empire* (London, 1987), p156. For an interesting
    account of these processes at work in the formation of the modern British state,
    see M Hechter, *Internal Colonialism* (London, 1975).

8   See A Callinicos, 'Marxism and Imperialism Today', in A Callinicos et al,
    Marxism and the New Imperialism, op cit.

9   K Marx and F Engels, *Selected Correspondence* (Moscow, 1965), pp236-237.

10 There are good discussions of the debates in the Second International and of
    Lenin's solution in C Harman, op cit, pp202-222; and in M Löwy, 'Marxists and
    the National Question', in M Löwy, *On Changing the World* (New Jersey, 1993).
    There is an anthology of the main contributions to the debates in G Haupt et
    al, *Les Marxistes et la Question Nationale* (Paris, 1974).

11 Lenin, *Collected Works*, vol XXXI (Moscow, 1964), p240.

12 Ibid, vol XXII, p346. Until the Russian Revolution, Marxists generally called
    themselves 'Social Democrats'.

13 Ibid, vol XXII, pp355-356.

14 Ibid, vol XXXI, p146.

15 Ibid, pp149-150.

16 Some of the social and ideological tensions involved are brought out in a recent
    study of a leading Irish Republican of the era of the Black and Tans, and Civil
    Wars: R English, *Ernie O'Malley: IRA Intellectual* (Oxford, 1998). Unfortunately
    much interesting material is marred by English's leaden prose style and his
    adhesion to a particularly crass version of the anti-Republican 'revisionist'
    ideology now apparently dominant in Irish historiography.

17 See E J Hobsbawm and T Ranger (eds), *The Invention of Tradition* (Cambridge,
    1983).

18 H Isaacs, *The Tragedy of the Chinese Revolution* (Stanford, 1961).

19 H Batatu, *The Old Social Classes and the Revolutionary Movements of Iraq*
    (Princeton, 1978).

20 See G Evans and K Rowley, *Red Brotherhood at War* (London, 1984), for an
    account of how national interests predominated in relations between the
    Indochinese Communist Parties after the Vietnam War.

21 M Löwy, op cit, pp71-72.

Chapter 3

Scotland's bourgeois revolution

Neil Davidson

When was the Scottish bourgeois revolution?[1] And what form did it take? These questions have not received a great deal of attention from the left in Scotland—or indeed the left anywhere in the world. This is partly because politically engaged work on Scottish history tends to divide along British Unionist or Scottish nationalist lines, with the central issue being the impact of the Treaty of Union. Both positions have had supporters on the left, but with the general growth in Scottish national consciousness since 1979 it is nationalism—or what might be called 'Scottish national populism'—that has become dominant. Within this ideology, Scottish history, at least for the period before industrialisation, tends to be presented in terms of national conflict, particularly conflict with England. What tends to be ignored is not only whether Scotland could seriously be described as a 'nation' in, say, 1707, but also the class nature of the states involved and the class divisions within them. The theory of bourgeois revolution, which is centrally concerned with these issues, has, however, only rarely been invoked as an alternative approach. Indeed, some Marxist historians of Scotland have declared that it is impossible to discern whether or not a bourgeois revolution took place, and others have declared that one definitely did not.[2] There are two reasons why Marxists should treat the question of the Scottish bourgeois revolution rather more seriously than this.

The first is theoretical, and has as much to do with the general validity of historical materialism as it has with Scottish history. The theory of bourgeois revolution, like all Marxist concepts, has come under increasing attack since the fall of the Stalinist regimes in 1989-91, although in this case the attacks began much earlier, during the first Cold War. Defence of the theory depends not just on proving its relevance to the 'classic' English and French examples—whose own revolutionary nature has of course persistently been denied—but by using it to explain difficult cases which do not fall into these more obviously 'revolutionary' patterns of historical development. Since Scotland has clearly been dominated by the capitalist mode of production longer than anywhere else outside the Netherlands and England, to concede that a bourgeois revolution was unnecessary to that outcome is theoretically to surrender to the anti-Marxist consensus. Scotland cannot be an exception to the theory of bourgeois revolutions without the theory itself being put into question.

The second is practical. Marxists do not defend their theoretical tradition merely to prove its intellectual superiority over rivals, but in order to guide their political activity. Scotland is entering a period of intense political change, in which arguments over history have direct political implications, most obviously in relation to whether or not Scotland has been subject to national oppression at the hands of England. If Scotland did not experience a bourgeois revolution in the process then it could be argued that some of the supposed 'tasks' of that revolution—notably national independence—remain to be accomplished. Knowledge of the terms under which Scotland first entered the capitalist system and became part of the British state is clearly central to entering this debate.

Marxists and the Scottish Revolution

It will be useful to begin this discussion by briefly reviewing the positions taken by the few Marxist writers and historians who do accept the existence of a Scottish Revolution. Generally speaking, they have adopted one of two interpretations, neither of which is satisfactory.

The first claims that the revolution took place in the form of a struggle between two geographically distinct societies, the capitalist Lowlands on the one hand and the pre-feudal Highlands on the other.[3] Victory for the former (in alliance with capitalist England) is said to have occurred after the suppression of the last Jacobite Rebellion of 1745. This is plausible, but several problems remain. It assumes the Jacobite Rebellions between 1688 and 1746 were political manifestations of Highland clan society. Although a popular view, reproduced most recently in the Jacobite section of the new National Museum of Scotland, it is wrong: Jacobitism was as much a Lowland movement as a Highland one. Moreover, if the transformation of the Highlands after the '45 is the key episode in the Scottish Revolution, then the central process must be the Highland Clearances. But the majority of these—certainly the majority of forcible clearances—took place between 1815 and 1860, long after Scotland had established itself at the summit of world capitalist development. The timing is simply too late. Finally, for Lowland society to effect this change in the Highlands, it must also have experienced a bourgeois revolution beforehand. But when? Focusing on the Highlands leaves the central question unanswered.

The second interpretation appears to resolve these difficulties. There are two variants. In one, the Scottish bourgeois revolution takes place in the Lowlands at the same time as in England, between 1638-60 and 1688-89.[4] In the other, the Union of 1707 becomes the missing Scottish bourgeois revolution, allowing the 'structural assimilation' of Lowland Scotland into England.[5] (Both variants revert to the first interpretation regarding the fate of the Highlands after their respective closing dates for the end of the revolution in the Lowlands.) The problem here is that Scotland—including Lowland Scotland—was not dominated by the capitalist mode of production either after 1689 or immediately after 1707. All the economic indicators show that the transformation of Lowland Scotland along capitalist lines took place in the second half of the 18th century—over 50 years after the Treaty of Union was signed. Furthermore, between 1707 and 1746 Scotland was the base for four counter-revolutionary risings against the British state, all but one of which were combined with actual or potential foreign invasions. And these risings were by no means confined to the Highlands; indeed, the '15 was almost entirely a Lowland affair. Two of these risings, in 1708 and 1719, were of little consequence, but the other two, in 1715 and 1745, led to civil wars which, in different ways, had the potential to undo not merely the Union, but the English settlement of 1688 whose transference to Scotland the Union was supposed to have concluded.

The nature of bourgeois revolutions

One way of approaching the problem of periodisation is to define more precisely what we mean by a bourgeois revolution. I view them here in general terms as a series of social and political upheavals which removed institutional barriers to local capitalist development, before going on to establish independent centres of competitive accumulation within the framework of the nation state. This definition neither requires bourgeois revolutions to take a particular form, nor indeed for them to be carried out by the bourgeoisie, but focuses instead on the construction of a state system where each component part is geared towards the accumulation of capital.

Each bourgeois revolution is to be seen as a process, rather than a single 'event'. All occurred within their own epoch, which only began when three objective conditions were fulfilled.[6] First, an organic crisis of the feudal system. Such a crisis was general in late medieval Europe, but outside some of the Swiss cantons, feudalism nevertheless re-emerged at the end of the 15th century, transformed but still dominant. A second condition is therefore required: a potentially capitalist solution to the crisis. This does not simply mean the existence of capitalist production. The epoch of the Italian Revolution, for example, did not begin with the establishment of capitalist production in the city states of the 12th century, when feudalism itself had been consolidated as a system for little over 100 years, but at the end of the 18th century, by which time capitalism, and the classes associated with it, had developed sufficiently to dominate the national economy and society. The second condition suggests, in turn, a third: the existence of social forces capable of imposing the capitalist solution. Each individual epoch of bourgeois revolution ended only when capitalist property relations were irreversibly installed and could only be threatened by a class still more advanced than the bourgeoisie, which is to say, the proletariat. The conjunction of crisis, solution and agency could, of course, exist for a period of time without the situation being resolved. The epoch of the German Revolution, for example, was not restricted to the years between 1862 and 1871 when unification actually took place, but can be dated, like the Italian case, from the late 18th century. Pre-Bismarkian attempts at revolution, notably that of 1848, failed not because the objective conditions were unripe, but because of a subjective failure on the part of the bourgeoisie themselves.

Does the notion of an epoch not substitute a 'gradualist' view for that of revolutionary transformation? Only if we assume that bourgeois revolutions take the same form as their proletarian successors—that is, a frontal assault on the state apparatus. But with the exceptions of the English and French absolutist regimes, the feudal states against which the bourgeois revolutions were directed differed in several ways from later capitalist states, most significantly in that they were not all unitary machines against which such an operation could be mounted. Some revolutions, such as the Swiss and the Dutch, took the form of extended wars against foreign dynasties, gradually liberating territories where the capitalist mode of production was already dominant. Others, such as the German and the Italian, took the form of unification movements incorporating different regions at varying levels of development within the most advanced. In both cases the establishment of a state committed to capital accumulation can be the result of a prolonged period of transformation and the process still be classified as a revolution.

What were the social forces that brought about these revolutions? From Engels onwards, Marxists have tended to divide the bourgeois revolutions into two distinct cycles, lying on either side of the year 1848, each of which were accomplished by different types of agency. The bourgeoisie themselves were certainly present in the leadership of the first cycle of revolutions—notably in the Dutch Revolt and the early stages of the French Revolution. The driving force tended, however, to be the petty bourgeoisie, whose aims by no means coincided with those of their greater brethren, not least because, in some cases, they would be individually undermined or collectively expropriated by the triumph of the latter. Although these revolutions generally involved an alliance 'from below' of small producers against the absolutist state or its colonial extensions, even they contained elements of revolution 'from above' and 'from outside', most notably in the activities of the New Model Army during the Protectorate and the French armies during the Republican and Napoleonic periods. Even during the episodes of maximum mass involvement, bourgeois revolutions are minority affairs, whose ultimate achievement is to establish a new ruling class, albeit one with a broader basis than feudal absolutism. During the second cycle the role of existing state power became more marked. In all these cases a fraction of the existing ruling class, under pressure from nation states that had already undergone their bourgeois revolutions, simultaneously restructured the existing state from within, and expanded its territorial boundaries without through conventional military conquest. Popular involvement in these revolutions, although present in the Italian Risorgimento and, to a lesser extent, the American Civil War, only appears as a subordinate element in a process otherwise directed from above.

The epoch of the Scottish Revolution

When, then, was the epoch of the Scottish bourgeois revolution? The chronological boundaries must be set within the first cycle of revolutions, since Scotland—considered separately from Britain for the moment—was a leading capitalist nation long before 1848, or even 1789. Yet the type of 'revolution from below' characteristic of this cycle is largely absent. The answer lies in the fact that revolutions are not made by acts of will, but according to the availability of social forces capable of carrying them out, and these forces are themselves the products of prior economic development. The weakness of bourgeois elements within Scottish society, let alone those classes further down the social structure, meant they were never capable of over-turning feudalism on their own. Considered as a self contained political entity, Scotland therefore has no completely independent revolutionary epoch. The possibility of transcending feudalism could not in fact arise until the last manifestation of that system had been destroyed in England. For this reason we can date the opening of the Scottish revolutionary epoch with the completion of that process in 1688, after which the English state and the class which it represented potentially became allies for Scottish capitalism.[7]

That the Scottish Revolution took another 60 years to complete can be explained by the fact that it was neither conducted against a centralised absolutist state, nor against a foreign occupation. Instead, it took place against the feudal nobility of a pre-absolutist Estates monarchy where social power was territorially dispersed throughout the kingdom and central state power had been temporarily dissolved after the Union of 1707. The events surrounding the Treaty of Union must therefore be seen as an episode in the revolutionary process, and by no means the final episode. That only occurred when the threat of counter-revolution was finally dispelled in 1746, with the suppression of the last Jacobite rising. The Scottish Revolution concluded, not in the construction of a capitalist nation state in Scotland, but by confirming the fusion of Scotland with an existing capitalist nation state, England, to form yet another: the United Kingdom of Great Britain. The remainder of this essay will attempt to explain the process that led to this unique outcome. In doing so I hope to dispel some of the misconceptions—about the nature of Highland society, the extent of Lowland capitalist development, the class forces behind the Union and the social basis of the Jacobite movement—that have hitherto prevented a proper understanding of this crucial period in Scottish history.

There were four decisive moments in the revolutionary process; the revolution of 1688, the economic crisis of the 1690s, the Union of 1707 and the last Jacobite rising of 1745. To place these events in context, however, we must first examine the nature of Scottish society on the eve of the first.

Late feudal Scotland

As late as 1767 the pioneer of political economy, Sir James Steuart, wrote of his native Scotland that he imagined it to be 'less or more, the picture of Europe 400 years ago'.[8] This was an exaggeration by that date, and would have been so even in 1688. Nevertheless, it contains an important kernel of truth. In 1688 Scotland was not merely less economically developed than England, but dominated by a different mode of production—feudalism. This had two distinguishing features.

The first was that the main source of income for the landowning class was appropriated in the form of rent from the surplus produced by the peasantry, rather than from the work of slaves or wage labourers. Although serfdom had disappeared from peasant life in Scotland long before 1688, rent was still mainly collected in kind, supplemented by the even more backward method of labour service.

The second was the process by which the surplus was extracted. Since the peasants had effective possession of the means of production (land, tools, animals), and would not have handed over part of their produce without external pressure, the relationship between lord and peasant was inevitably coercive, involving either the threat or actual application of force. As a result, the political and judicial institutions through which this pressure was exerted were inseparable from economic relations, and must be included in any definition of the system. Key amongst these institutions were territorial jurisdictions through which the local lord could bring tenants to his own court of law.

In Scotland these took two forms—baronies and regalities—which differed in terms of size and the powers which they conferred, but in both cases were private, hereditary and unalienable. By the time the jurisdictions were finally abolished in 1747, there were a total of 16 hereditary sheriffdoms, 200 regalities and 1,000 baronies in Scotland. As the title suggests, a barony corresponded to the domain of the local baron and accompanied the granting of land from the crown. A baron court could try all criminal offences except treason and the 'four pleas of the crown'—arson, murder, rape and robbery. A regality was a larger unit, often comprising several baronies, and usually in the possession of a lord with greater status than a mere baron. As an index of his superior position, the lord of a regality could try all criminal offences except treason, which remained the preserve of the crown. Where fines were imposed on offenders, the revenues went directly to the feudal superior—the implications of which, given the parlous state of most noble finances, it should not be necessary to labour. Neither type of court was, however, concerned solely or even mainly with crime, but with the management of the estate and enforcing the duties of tenants, and neither the crown nor its appointed sheriffs had any right to interfere with the lord within his own jurisdiction. Indeed, many sheriffdoms were themselves hereditary and the property of men who were already lords of regality. The penalties that the jurisdictions made available to the lords extended to the death penalty. 'Every laird [of note] hath a gibbet near his house', noted Thomas Kirke, an English visitor in 1679, 'and has power to condemn and hang any of his vassals; so they dare not oppose him in anything, but must submit to his commands, let them be never so unjust and tyrannical'.[9] One consequence was that they could force their tenants to take up arms on their behalf. Indeed, in some parts of the country tenure specifically involved a commitment to bear arms. McDonald of Keppoch, questioned as to the size of his rent roll, simply replied, 'I can call out and command 500 men'.[10] This form of military tenure, called wardholding, is usually associated with the Highlands, but it could also be found in the Lowlands, particularly in the north east, as late as the end of the 17th century.

As this suggests, the Highlands and the Lowlands had more in common than is often assumed. The first misconception about Scottish development is that by 1688 the two regions were radically different from each other in socio-economic terms. In fact, the Highlands were not as backward as is usually thought and neither were the Lowlands as advanced: both social formations were dominated by the feudal mode of production. What then were the differences between the two?

The most obvious was the existence of clanship in the Highlands, yet the nature of the clans is frequently misunderstood. The original Scottish clans were similar to those that existed everywhere before the rise of class society, but these had evolved feudal structures by time the kingdom was unified in 1057. The 14th century crisis of feudalism brought the Scottish state to a point of virtual disintegration and, as a result, seems to have produced a resurgence of clannic *political* forms in the Highlands, but under new feudal *economic* conditions. The local lords developed defensive political structures in which they adopted the role of 'chief' and, because of geographical inaccessibility and the scattered nature of landholding, these structures tended to cut across territorial superiorities. Thus a lord might be feudal superior to one group of peasants (his 'vassals'), but also chief to another who nominally bore his name (his 'clan'). The overlap between these two groups might be total or non-existent, but if the clan members were not his vassals then they would surely be those of another lord. The peasants may have placed themselves under the protection of a clan chief and taken his name, but clan organisation was not only compatible with, but also entirely dependent on, their exploitation. Where else could the relative wealth of the chiefs have come from? The clan system must therefore be understood as part of the political superstructure of Scottish feudalism—it corresponded to no other mode of production. Given the claims that are made for the distinctiveness of the Scottish Highlands there is some irony in the fact that by 1688 the majority of clans had organised themselves on the classic military-feudal lines that had been superceded everywhere else in Europe, except Poland. Many Lowlanders did indeed feel themselves to be distinct from the Highlanders and hostile towards them, but there is no indication that this had anything to do with clanship as such. Highland 'difference' was in fact a product of three factors.

The first factor was a consequence of the relative backwardness— in feudal terms— of the area beyond the Highland line. Scotland was a poor country in any case, but the greater degree of poverty in the Highlands, and the breakdown of order during the 14th century, gave both incentive and opportunity for some of the warriors to engage in large scale plundering, particularly of cattle, from the more settled Lowland communities. These onslaughts resembled more the lordly marauding typical of the feudal epoch in its formative years than normal conditions in the early modern period. And although they were not directed solely at the Lowlands, but also at other Highland communities, the Perthshire peasant, watching his herd being driven off by armed clansmen, was scarcely likely to give this fact consideration. These incursions would not, however, in themselves have fixed the division between the two Scotlands.

The second factor was language. The *Gaidhealtachd* (the area in which Gaelic was spoken) once dominant across the entire territory of Scotland apart from the south east, had been retreating since the 11th century before its main rival, the Scots vernacular. Whether one regards the latter as a separate language from English or not, it was at any rate comprehensible to those who spoke the English language of trade and administration. The extent of the *Gaidhealtachd* at the end of the 17th century cannot be exactly defined, not least because of the way in which it shaded into areas on its south and eastern border where both Gaelic and English were spoken, often by the same people. What is clear from this is that the *Gaidhealtachd* was increasingly syn-onymous with the geographical Highlands of Scotland. Yet without a third and final factor, it is unlikely that the hostility between Lowland and Highland would have reached the extent that it did.

This third and final factor was religion. The Reformation failed to make permanent inroads beyond the Highland line until late in the 17th century. Indeed, one reason for Lowland opposition to Gaelic was that it prevented the Highlanders from being converted to the Calvin-ist version of Christianity practised by the Church of Scotland. By 1688 only a minority of Highlanders remained Catholic, the major-ity having converted to Protestantism, but of the Episcopalian rather than the Presbyterian variety—and in the eyes of many Lowlanders Episcopalians were little better than Papists.

From the 14th century onwards, therefore, the behaviour, language and, in a minority of cases, religion of the Highlanders led Lowlanders to compare their neighbours not to themselves, but to the native Irish and the settlers who had over the centuries been assimilated to that culture. In particular, all the negative characteristics that the Lowland mind identified with the Highlands appeared to be confirmed by the close links that existed between Ulster and the western Highlands. The political implications of these connections were made clear during the civil wars. The British colonists in Ulster who came under attack in the Irish rising of 1641 largely consisted of Protestant Scots from the Lowlands, while in Scotland itself some of the clans, led by the roy-alist commander James Graham, Marquis of Montrose, leagued with the Irish Confederacy, led by Alasdair MacColla, in support of Charles I, the Scottish MacDonalds fighting alongside the Irish MacDonnells.

The divisions that opened up between the Highlands and the Low-lands in the late 14th century continued to widen down to and beyond 1688. Those Scots who were beginning to acquire a proto-national consciousness through hostility to the English state and identification with their native church were exclusively in the Lowlands. The divisions between Highland and Lowland prevented the extension of such a consciousness across the entire territory of the Scottish state. Highlanders thought of themselves as Scots only in the sense of being notionally subject to the Scottish crown. Indeed, they saw more similarities between the Lowland Scots and the English than between Lowland Scots and themselves. The word 'sassenach', usually taken to be an abusive Scottish term for the English, is in fact derived from the Gaelic word for Saxon (*sasunnach*), and was originally used by Highlanders to describe all non-Gaelic speakers, Lowlanders as much as the English.

The majority of the Scottish ruling class on both sides of the Highland Line were uninterested in orientating themselves towards market relations, since this would have meant undertaking long term investment to which few could afford to commit themselves, particularly when the results would have been slow in making themselves felt. They were more concerned with maintaining a stable level of income and the social power that came from their traditional form of proprietorship. A conspicuous display of consumption, not an ascetic commitment to accumulation, was the mark of a great man in 17th century Scotland. Consequently, little progress had been made towards a monetary economy. Where market relations did exist in agriculture they were restricted mainly to areas of the south east that served the capital, Edinburgh, and the English export market. More important still, the market in land was virtually non-existent. This is not to say that capitalist production had made no inroads into the Scottish economy, merely that it remained subordinate to feudalism. Take, for example, the coal industry.

In the vast majority of cases, coal mining was organised by the landowners under whose estates the coal lay. Yet for them the sale of coal merely generated a supplement to their main income from feudal rent; it did not at this stage lay the basis for capital accumulation. It is true that after 1707 some owners began to import the most advanced technology and techniques from England and Belgium, but at the same time the labourers who worked in the mines were literally serfs, at a time when even the Scottish peasantry had risen above that status. To explain such contradictions we require the concept of combined and uneven development, where the backward neither merely repeat the experience of the advanced, nor find their progress to advanced status blocked by earlier developers, but adopt advanced economic techniques and organisational methods within an overall socio-economic structure still characterised by archaism. In certain circumstances it is possible through this process for a hitherto backward economy to equal or even surpass those previously in advance of it (and the transformation of the Scottish economy after 1746 is a classic example of this process), but in the absence of such circumstances combined and uneven development also has a downside which affects the very organisation of production itself. 'The [backward] nation', wrote Trotsky, 'not infrequently debases the achievements borrowed from outside in the process of adapting them to its own more primitive culture'.[11] Hence there was a coal industry in which the most advanced forms of imported English technology were operated by men enserfed through feudal labour law and then disciplined by the heritable jurisdictions.

The failure of revolution before 1688

In the political sphere, too, Scotland was less advanced than other feudal states. With some notable exceptions, the most important again being Poland, absolutism had by 1688 replaced the Estates monarchies of military feudalism to become the typical state form across most of Europe. The social upheavals which might have pushed the Scottish lords into supporting and strengthening the monarchy instead of exploiting its weakness never emerged. Since peasant revolts were unknown in Scotland, at least until after 1660, there was no need for a more highly centralised state to suppress the direct producers. And the weakness of the urban sector meant that there was no burghal support system for rural insurrection, even had one been set in motion by the peasant masses. But if the peasantry was largely quiescent, the individual lords retained a local weight unparalleled elsewhere in Western Europe. It is unsurprising, therefore, that the attention of the monarchy was fixed less on suppressing the direct producers than on subduing their noble exploiters. The Stuart monarchy did, in fact, attempt on seven different occasions between 1455 and 1662 to legislate out of existence the jurisdictions on which noble power rested. Had they succeeded in doing so it would, in the short term, have massively increased the authority of the state, and their failure is in itself eloquent testimony to the real balance of power between the nobility and the crown. Instead of creating a centralised authority to control the nobility, the crown strategy became one of supporting particular territorial lordships, such as those of Gordon in the north east and of Argyll in the south west, in order to maintain local stability and act as counterweights to each other. The effect was, however, to help create the alternatives to royal power which it was intended to avoid. In this respect the territorial expansion of the earls of Argyll, both as feudal superiors and as chiefs of Clan Campbell, is only the most extreme example of a general process.

If internal pressure towards absolutism was missing, however, external pressure was not. From the invasion of 1296 that began the Wars of Independence, down to the beginning of the Reformation in 1559, this threat had always been from the most obvious source: England. The result of the English threat was not, however, the emergence of a native absolutism but reliance by the Scottish monarchy on that of another: France. The 'Auld Alliance' between Scotland and France meant, above all, that the strength of the French state was employed, at various crucial points in the long struggle with England, as a substitute for absent Scottish military might and diplomatic influence. Absolutism in Scotland could only ever be an external imposition, and on two separate occasions the nobility successfully led coalitions that prevented this imposition taking place.

The first of these was at the Reformation of 1559. The Scottish nobility adopted Calvinism for the same reason that the Dutch bourgeoisie did, not because there is anything intrinsically 'capitalist' about it, but because Calvinism sanctioned—indeed, demanded—the overthrow of the existing state, if that state refused to allow the church freedom from its control. Calvinism gave ideological legitimation to the struggle against France, and it was this quality which endeared it to the Scottish lords, who might otherwise have been attracted to the Lutheranism adopted by the German princelings to whom they were otherwise quite similar.

Calvinism was, of course, more than simply a flag of convenience for a faction of the nobility. A layer of ideologues, linked by adherence to what Hugh Trevor-Roper calls 'the Calvinist International',[12] had been at work in Scotland since the 1520s, winning converts among sections of the merchant and artisanal classes. At best, however, they remained a large minority among the population as a whole, and after 1547 their leaders were forced completely underground by a repression which resulted in their future leader, John Knox, being sent as a slave to the French galleys. An attempt by the French queen regent, Mary of Guise, to allay fears of French domination led to a partial lifting of religious repression after 1554, with the result that in some of the burghs, 'privy kirks', or secret congregations of believers, were established. If Edinburgh is in any way typical, these included representatives of most the urban classes of the time, from members of the merchant and craftsman guilds to the journeymen apprentices who laboured for them. The urban poor in particular had a direct material interest in seeing church revenues redirected towards poor relief. In so far as the contemporary vernacular classic *The Complaynt of Scotland* can be taken as an accurate representation of plebeian grievances, it indicts, through the character of the Labourer, the lords as much as the Catholic church:

> My two brothers, nobles and clergy, who should defend me, are more cruel to me than my old enemies, the English...The war is cried against England, but the war is carried out against the labourers and it consumes their miserable lives.[13]

When a minority of the nobles first banded together on 3 December 1557, as the Lords of the Congregation, the forces at their disposal were few beyond their own vassals and the radical minority in the larger burghs. In the end they had their hand forced by a series of local insurgencies planned and put into effect by Protestant militants in the main burghs during May 1559. Had Mary of Guise succeeded in crushing this rebellion French control over Scotland would have been assured; the lords therefore had to intervene or see their hopes buried. In the process they allowed local protestants, where they were organised into 'privy kirks', to take control of local churches and town councils. The resulting civil war saw the lords declaring themselves to be acting in the interest of the Scottish realm, and Mary of Guise declaring them to be in rebellion against the French crown, but neither side was capable of forcing the issue to a decisive conclusion. Just as the 'privy kirk' congregations could not have seized power on their own behalf locally without the lords, neither could the lords seize power nationally without outside intervention. By the end of 1559 the contending forces had reached a stalemate in which the French forces were firmly installed in the port of Leith along the Firth of Forth while the lords conducted a rather ineffective siege from neighbouring Edinburgh. In the end it was the English state which resolved the matter.

Elizabeth I acceded to the English throne in November 1558 and allowed the need for a Protestant ally in the north to overcome her unwillingness to encourage a rebellion against royal authority. On 23 January 1560 the English fleet cut the French supply lines between

Leith and Dunkirk, although this was not in itself enough to dislodge their forces. Had the French state been able to supply reinforcements they might still have recovered the situation, but the outbreak of the French Wars of Religion on 17 March signalled the opening of the French Calvinist (Huguenot) bid for power and prevented the Guises from relieving their forces in Scotland. The simultaneous intervention of English troops on the side of the lords forced France to concede defeat. It is indicative of the extent to which Scotland had become a pawn in the struggle for European hegemony that the Treaty of Edinburgh, which brought the war to a close, was signed on 6 July by representatives of the French and the English states, not those of the opposing Scottish factions.

A large minority among the ruling class had established their own faction in power, broken with French control and made an uncertain alliance with England based upon the introduction of Protestantism as the new state religion. Two aspects of this reformation, neither of which would be fully realised until the following century, are important for our purposes. One was that the rapprochement between Scotland and England allowed the Stuarts to successfully press their claim to succeed the Tudors as the ruling dynasty in England (and Ireland), thus providing a base for their absolutist ambitions in all three kingdoms which Scotland could not have provided. The other was the establishment of the Church of Scotland, the institution which was to provide the focus for popular resistance to those ambitions until they were permanently thwarted at Culloden.

The theological doctrines and organisational forms of the new kirk were still relatively fluid for several years after 1560. Presbyterianism was first advocated in 1574 by Andrew Melville, who was influenced by his experience of Calvinist Geneva, but it was adopted by the Scottish Parliament only in 1592, and even then on a temporary basis. In essence, Presbyterianism involved two principles.

First, the church and state should be separate and exercise authority over distinct spiritual and secular domains. The state should not seek to interfere in the structure and doctrine of the church and, in return, the church would not participate directly in politics. Had this principle been applied, it would have led to the withdrawal of the entire Clerical Estate, represented by the bishops, from the Scottish Parliament.

Second, ministers were equal; neither the activities of existing ministers nor the admission of new ministers to the profession should be supervised by anyone other than themselves. This supervision would be exercised through the hierarchy of church courts, which ascended from kirk sessions for the parishes to presbyteries for the districts and synods for the regions before reaching the General Assembly for Scotland as a whole. In other words, the existence of bishops as a distinct layer of clerical bureaucracy was incompatible with Presbyterian church government.

Neither of these principles endeared themselves to the rulers of Scotland after 1560. Far from wishing to separate church and state, they wanted to subordinate the former to the latter. The bishops were a key instrument in achieving this end. The period after 1572, and particularly after 1603, therefore saw a struggle for control between an increasingly Presbyterian majority of the kirk ministers determined to assert their independence from the state, and a crown determined to make the kirk an arm of that state. The result was an unstable compromise in which congregation-elected Presbyterian elders in the parishes coexisted with crown-appointed bishops in church offices. By the time James VI of Scotland (and I of England) died in 1625 this had shifted decisively towards an Episcopalian settlement. But while the Presbyterian ideal was being simultaneously developed and subverted at the apex of Scottish society, Protestantism was becoming ever more entrenched at its base. By 1625 the kirk had assumed the role of 'state within a state' at the parish level. As a result of the gradual supremacy of Episcopalianism within the kirk, some congregations at least began to worship at unofficial prayer meetings or conventicles, often in the open air, unconstrained by Anglican or Popish innovations. Thus the kirk was guaranteed to be both a participant and prize in any future social crisis.

The second great noble-led coalition arose in 1637 around the National Covenant. At the time of his accession in 1625, Charles I introduced an Act of Revocation to the Scottish Parliament, signalling to the nobility that an English monarch had at last gone onto the offensive against them. The act, as amplified by the Decrees Arbitral of 1629, contained a complex set of proposals, the heart of which gave the crown the power to compulsorily buy up the heritable jurisdictions—at values massively reduced by inflation—upon which the social power of the lords depended. Charles had embarked on a classic absolutist strategy of building up the third estate as a bulwark against magnate insubordination. Yet any credit that Charles might have gained among the lairds or burgesses by this measure was wiped out by increases in taxation, which fell as much on them as the nobility. The final provocation leading to open revolt was, however, the attempt by Charles to impose uniformity with Anglicanism on the kirk. Given the interpenetration of religion with all forms of social and political life in the 17th century, this was not and could not have been simply a theological issue. Many of the ministers were either first or second generation offspring of parents who were small landowners or larger tenants, but in addition to producing feelings of class solidarity, the intrusion of bishops threatened to remove their local influence of the kirk sessions and set unelected appointees above them in place of the presbyteries.

What kind of movement was the National Covenant? In one sense it was entirely typical of European revolts during the first half of the 17th century. All shared one underlying political cause: opposition to the construction of absolutisms whose innovations threatened the lords both in terms of their local power (by transferring it to the central state) and their income (through increased taxation to fund the work of centralisation). In this sense, the Covenanting movement was driven by the same desire to resist absolutist encroachments onto their feudal powers as the Frondeurs in France or, in a British context, the Northern Earls who rebelled against Tudor absolutism during the previous century. What gave the Covenanting movement greater significance than a wholly reactionary revolt like that of the Northern Earls was that opposition to Charles was diffused not only throughout the Scottish Estates, but beneath them in the subordinate classes, whose developing national consciousness—in the Lowlands at least— had been aroused by the innovations which they perceived to be of English, rather than royal, origin. The effect of this temporary coincidence of interests was to obscure different class interests within an outward show of unanimity.

Scotland therefore conformed to a general European pattern; it was England that did not, for it contained a class which was not concerned to defend the pre-absolutist order, but move beyond it. Unlike England, however, the bourgeois interest in Scotland was not strong enough to separate out and articulate a programme of its own. Although the Covenanters originally entered the first 'English' Civil War on the side of parliament, the class differences between them and the Independents—let alone the Levellers—could not be permanently submerged. For the increasingly moderate majority among the nobles, the radical turn in the English Revolution (indicated by the explosion of sectarian groupings and the Leveller movement within the army) was beginning to make an alliance with Charles seem a more attractive prospect, although one which would be on their terms. The Engagement signed on 26-27 December 1647 allowed for Presbyterianism to be established in England, initially for three years, while Scotland would be permitted to participate in the English colonial trade. In return the Scots were to invade England with the intention of restoring Charles. Significantly, the vast majority of the nobles supported the Engagement, but the lairds and the burgesses split down the middle, and the ministers were almost totally opposed. Argyll, the Scottish commander David Leslie and other members of the ruling class who opposed the Engagement were isolated voices within the state. Yet they were soon vindicated. Without Leslie or the experienced leaders who had previously led it to victory, the Scottish army was smashed by Cromwell at Preston between 17 and 19 August 1648. In fact, the Engagement merely saw the nobles take up a position of support for the crown which, had they been English, would have been theirs in 1642. Its failure, however, allowed something previously unknown in Scottish history to occur: the entry of the oppressed onto the historical stage on their own behalf, rather than at the behest, or in support, of their oppressors. For the first time a movement arose which was not only independent from the nobles but also actively opposed to them. Some extreme Presbyterians from the south west had formed a quasi-military organisation called the Western Association. The Association had already fought pro-Engagement forces on Mauchline Moor on 12 June while resisting conscription into the army; now they rose in a force numbering 2,000 and on 5 September descended on Edinburgh for the event known to Scottish history as the 'Whiggamore Raid'.

Cromwell arrived in Edinburgh on 4 October 1648 to find that the Engagers had been overthrown by the Western Association and replaced by a new coalition known as the 'Kirk Party'. This comprised Argyll, the few other nobles who had refused to accept the Engagement, the ministers and a host of the lesser lairds who now sat in parliament as commissioners in place of the discredited nobles. An uneasy agreement was struck between Cromwell and Argyll that allowed the New Model Army to return to England for the final act in the Civil War. Part of the agreement was that all those who had participated in the Engagement (the 'Malignants') were to be purged from the state apparatus—the General Assembly of the kirk, parliament, army and judiciary.

In so far as there is an episode of bourgeois revolution 'from below' in Scottish history, then it is to be found in the year 1649. A survey of the legislation passed by the new regime confirms its anti-feudal nature, but also points out the contradictions inherent in its social composition. The Act of Classes [ie classes of offender] passed on 23 January 1649 banned all those who had been Engagers, supported Montrose, failed to condemn the Engagement when they had the chance, or who were guilty of immorality or neglect of family worship from local or national office. Seven days later the General Assembly argued for the abolition of patronage by the lords in the selection of ministers, a demand which passed into law on 9 March and provoked a walkout by several of the landowners who thought—correctly— that it was aimed at removing one of the pillars of their local authority. On 1 March an Act Anent the Poor was passed which established that where voluntary contributions to parish funds were insufficient to provide for the poor, taxes would be collected by the state to raise the necessary funds, the greater proportion of which would be levied from landlords who had contributed to local poverty by setting excessive ('unjust') levels of rent for their tenants.

Instead of a dictatorship of the army, for which England was shortly destined, Scotland had a dictatorship of the clergy. Yet even as the ministers forced the nobles onto the Stool of Repentance for their sins, fined them or seized their estates, they also waged a godly crusade against the plebeians from whom they themselves had risen. If this was heralded in that section of the Act of Classes which classified moral offences on a par with political betrayals, it was brutally revealed throughout 1649 in the most intensive outbreak of witch hunting yet seen in Scotland. And in a theocracy this made perfect sense. God had passed judgement on Scotland and found it wanting, as was clear from the tribulations that had now befallen it. His wrath could only be assuaged by an assault on sin—from whatever quarter. The regime, in short, looked back to the millenarian Hussite or Taborite movements of pre-Reformation Bohemia rather than across to the Independents or the Levellers. The essential problem was that the social base did not yet exist to replace the nobility. 'The worst thing that can befall a leader of an extreme party', wrote Engels, 'is to be compelled to assume power at a time when the movement is not yet ripe for the domination of the class he represents and for the measures which this domination implies'.[14] This observation, made of Thomas Munzer during the German Peasant Revolt of 1525, is also relevant to the collective leadership of the Kirk Party regime, for they had been able to take power only because of the political vacuum at the heart of the Scottish state. *Militarily*, the regime could rely on the clannic and feudal levies at the disposal of Argyll in his domains, although even these had been reduced by ten years of war. *Socially*, outside the ministers themselves, its support lay almost solely among the 'slashing communicants' of the south west and a slightly more widespread scattering of lairds elsewhere in the southern Lowlands. Given time, the reforming legislation introduced between January and March might have gained support among the plebeians and the 'middling sort', but in the short term—which was all it had—the social repressiveness of Kirk Party rule impacted far more directly, with the result that popular support throughout the population as a whole was muted at best.

The execution of Charles on 30 January 1649 indicated the limits of such radicalism as the Kirk Party possessed. It instantly moved to proclaim Charles II as king, not merely of Scotland, but of Great Britain, Ireland and (according to that quaint custom then still in place) France: this was a direct threat to the Republic which was shortly to be declared in England. Had the Scots even restricted themselves to proclaiming Charles king of Scotland, it is possible that Cromwell might simply have declared the Union of Crowns dissolved and left the Scots to their own devices, but to openly put Scotland at the centre of counter-revolution in Britain as a whole left him with no alternative. Cromwell had never wished to invade or conquer Scotland. As late as August 1650 he wrote to the General Assembly of the Kirk, 'I beseech you, in the bowels of Christ, think it possible you may be mistaken'.[15] To no avail.

Total defeat for the Scots at the Battle of Dunbar divided the Kirk Party in two. The radical wing (the 'Remonstrants'), based on the western bonnet lairds and their ministers, withdrew from the regime and declared, logically enough, that an even more full blooded purge of the army must be imposed to instil godly discipline and restore godly favour. The moderate wing (the 'Resolutioners'), including Argyll, the remaining nobles and the majority of the lairds, had Charles crowned on 1 January 1651 and allowed all those willing to fight to do so—regardless of their position over the Engagement—provided they were not actually opposed to the Covenant; but since Charles himself had taken the Covenant with both fingers firmly crossed behind his back, this was no impediment to any but the most scrupulous. The last vestiges of the Kirk Party regime were buried on 2 June with the repeal of the Act of Classes. A final desperate attempt by the official [ie Resolutioner] Scottish army to restore Charles to his English throne received no support in England itself and was decisively defeated at Worcester on 3 September 1651. Thereafter Cromwell turned back to the north and began the mopping up operations against both the western radicals and the northern royalists that took until the fall of Dunnottar Castle on 26 May 1652. But by then the bulk of Scotland was not only under English rule but had effectively been incorporated into the English state.

The revolutionary role of Cromwell and the New Model Army is actually demonstrated more clearly in Scotland than either England, where they were challenged from the left by the Levellers, or Ireland, where they were responsible for imposing a colonial regime of notorious savagery. In Scotland, however, they stepped into a social vacuum and undertook one of the purest examples of bourgeois revolution 'from above and outside' until the Republics established by the Directory and Napoleon after 1795. Prior to the conquest, English radicals had hoped that Scotland would follow the same path as England of its own accord. As one supporter of the Levellers wrote in their paper, *The Moderate*:

> When once the light breaks forth in this Kingdom (and I think the sun is near rising) it will warm and heal apace, but the clouds must be broken first, the foundation of the old fabric must be shaken; and when the poor, blind, dead people shall see the light and feel the warmth of the sun (sweet liberty) to redeem them out of their present slavery, then the strugglings of Scotland will be as great as those of England, which hath overcome a few of these, but not yet gotten to the top of its glory.[16]

Now it was clear to both military administrators and intellectual supporters of the Protectorate that they needed to take the measures that the Scottish people had been unable to take for themselves. The first attempt was made in the legislation that announced Scotland's place within the Commonwealth. On 28 October 1651 the English Parliament issued *A Declaration Of The Parliament Of The Commonwealth Of England, Concerning The Settlement Of Scotland*, which noted, 'Many of the people of Scotland who were vassals, or Tenants to, and had dependency upon the Noble-men and gentry (the chief Actors in these invasions and wars against England), were by their influence drawn into...the same Evils.' These innocent victims were to be pardoned and, more importantly, 'Set free from their former dependencies and bondage-services, and shall be admitted as Tenants, Freeholders and Heritors, to form, hold, inherit, and enjoy from and under this Common-wealth, proportions of the said confiscated and forfeited Lands, sundry easy Rents, and reasonable conditions, as may enable them, their Heirs and Posterity, to live with a more comfortable subsistence than formerly, and like a free People, delivered (through God's goodness) from their former slaveries, vassalage and oppression'.[17]

Cromwell and his officers repeatedly expressed their belief that Scotland could only be raised to the same godly heights as England by crushing the power of the nobility. And until 1660 the nobles were displaced from their traditional social dominance. Yet this did not mean that a new bourgeoisie arose to replace them, or even that the nobles themselves began the transition to capitalist production. The second misconception about Scottish history is that Cromwell made possible the development of Scottish capitalism. This cannot seriously be supported from the available evidence. Demographic collapse and the resulting shortage of the most important means of production—human labour—after years of civil and national war meant that many of the most productive agricultural areas reverted to waste. The export of raw materials and manufactures declined with the closing of trade links with Europe, partly as a result of the various wars fought by the Protectorate and Commonwealth regimes with states which had been Scottish markets (like the United Netherlands), partly because much of the Scottish fleet had in any case been destroyed. Money which could have been spent on investment was siphoned off in taxation (to pay for the occupying army) and fines (as penalties for supporting the Stuarts).

It was not in the economic but the social sphere that the Cromwellian regime brought to Scotland the advantages of a society more developed in capitalist terms, not least by suppressing the obscenity of witch burning. But social progress from the barrel of a musket had the effect of stimulating proto-national feeling against the very idea of the Commonwealth, particularly since the permanent factionalism of the kirk had led the military regime in 1654 to abolish the last remaining embodiment of proto-national consciousness, the General Assembly of the Church of Scotland. This was the first, but certainly not the last time that such a dilemma would confront a bourgeois revolutionary regime. The Napoleonic armies which invaded Spain in 1809 were clearly the bearers of a more advanced social system than the Bourbon monarchy they sought to overthrow, but the fact that change was being imposed at bayonet point provoked a popular resistance which ultimately aided the reactionary alliance against France. A similar mood, if not actual opposition, was present in Cromwellian Scotland. Given time, this might have been overcome, but time was something which the Commonwealth did not have.

In England the Restoration was a *reaction* within the boundaries of what the English Revolution had achieved; in Scotland the Restoration was a *counter-revolution* which swept away even the limited gains made by the various Covenanting regimes and the Commonwealth. One of the conditions that the English Parliament placed on Charles before agreeing to the Restoration was that he confirm the abolition of feudal tenures. In 1662 parliament duly passed Act 12 Charles II c 24. The effect of this legislation should not be exaggerated: it merely confirmed in juridical terms the balance of class forces bequeathed by Cromwell. It is in stark contrast, however, to the Act Rescissory, passed on 28 March the previous year by the Scottish Parliament, which repealed all legislation enacted since 1633. Nothing better illustrates the distance between Scotland and England in socio-economic terms than these respective enactments. The nine years of Commonwealth rule were not long enough to allow the conditions for an indigenous Scottish bourgeoisie capable of completing the revolution on its own account to emerge from the wreckage of the Scottish economy. Yet without such a development, the withdrawal of the English military presence in 1660 allowed the surviving members of the existing ruling class to return to their previous positions. As a result of the wars and the economic collapse which accompanied them, most of the legislation which might have contributed to the development of capitalism remained little more than indications of the direction in which the more advanced sections of the ruling class wished to go. Nevertheless, had these enactments remained in force, then under certain conditions they might have supported the efforts of those sections of Scottish society that wished to embrace the market, wage labour and the rest. Their removal was emblematic of the fact that it was not merely the king who had been restored, but the jurisdictional rights of the lords. English absolutism had been like a dead skin, sloughed off by a social body that had outgrown it; Scottish feudalism was still like a suit of armour, confining the social body and preventing further growth.

Charles II obtained the temporary acquiescence of the nobility for three reasons. First, virtually the entire ruling class had opposed the

House of Stuart at one time or another between 1637 and 1647. They had much to make amends for and, although Argyll was the only noble to be executed for his actions, the penalty for treason could theoretically have been exacted from virtually any that had not risen with Montrose. Second, the Restoration monarchy was the only institution capable of re-establishing the lords' economic position. Or more precisely, it was the only institution capable of restoring to them the social power by which they could regain their economic position. Third, like many other ruling classes in history, the Scottish nobility had incautiously unleashed popular discontent during an internal dispute and as a result sustained the first concerted attack on lordly wealth and power from below in Scottish history. Their attitude was not only based on their recent experience, however, but on events during the Restoration period itself. For the second time in Scottish history the great missing element that had made absolutism unnecessary to the lords, a peasant movement—or more precisely one centred among the 'bonnet lairds'—rose to challenge their power.

The bonnet lairds were the most obvious contenders to become a rural capitalist class orientated on production for the market. For several reasons they were exceptional in the Scottish social structure They were subject to the legal jurisdiction of the lords through the feudal superiorities, but were not economically bound to them, since for all practical purposes they had heritable tenure. Like the lords, they had effective possession of their land; unlike the lords, they did not live off the rent of tenants. Like the tenants, they worked their own land; unlike the tenants, they did not pay rent. They had an incentive to produce for the market that was denied either the lordly proprietors above them or the tenant farmers below them, whose insecurity left them ill suited for the role of leading the rural masses against their landlords. Resentful of the social power of the lords and with enough economic independence not to be completely cowed by it, the bonnet lairds were a class comparable to the English yeoman, the independent small farmers who had earlier formed the core of the Cromwellian Independents, and were described as such by contemporaries. The problem, however, was that only in the south west, in Dumfries and Galloway, and areas of Strathclyde south of Glasgow, were they numerous and concentrated enough to mount any kind of collective action in defence of their religious principles or material conditions. These areas were distinguished by uniquely high levels of bonnet laird occupancy and were the site of an intense but isolated peasant insurgency, exploding first in the risings of 1648 and 1650, and then in an intermittent guerrilla struggle between 1660 and 1688.

The trigger for the latter rebellion lay in the religious settlement. The Stuart monarchy and its noble supporters correctly saw the religious doctrines and organisational principles of Presbyterianism as subversive of the state, not simply at the highest reaches where the kirk presumed to have authority over the monarch himself, but at the local level where the election of ministers had, since 1649, removed the power of the lords to patronise 'suitable' nominees for the position. A succession of acts passed during 1662 restored the bishops, while they banned the signing of covenants, attendance at conventicles, or the meeting of presbyteries and synods, unless they had prior approval from the Episcopate. Patronage returned, and even sitting ministers who had taken a position since 1649 were required to seek presentation from the patron and confirmation by the bishop—in effect to re-submit to the authority of the landowners and the religious arm of the state. By 1 February 1663 over 270 ministers, out of a total ministry of 952, had refused to do so and were consequently forced out—the biggest expulsion in Scottish history up to that point. As might be expected, the area with the highest number of excluded ministers was the south west. In the synod of Galloway only three out of an original total of 37 ministers were left in their posts at the end of the purge. The problem here for the state was not only that the ministers assigned to take the place of the expelled were often met with empty churches or even violent reception committees designed to prevent them from occupying the manse. It was also that in many cases elders and congregations followed the departing ministers to resume worship in the very conventicles that had been declared illegal. Resistance came in two main waves.

The first followed the outbreak of the second Anglo-Dutch war in 1665. The war saw Scotland, which had been forced to follow England in international relations, lose one of her main trading partners. The decline in trade, together with an increase in taxation to pay for the war, produced a severe economic downturn. In the south west and parts of Fife, this was exacerbated by military attempts to suppress conventicling and enforce church attendance through the imposition of fines. A proclamation of 11 October 1666 established that proprietors were responsible for their tenants, masters for their servants and magistrates for the activities of the burgh community. Such were the tensions in the area that an attempt to fine one laird in 1666 provoked a rising of nearly 1,000 men, mainly lairds and tenant farmers. The Pentland Rising—so called because Rullion Green, the scene of its defeat on 28 November is at the foot of the Pentland Hills—confirmed what was already apparent at Mauchline Moor and in the Whiggamore Raid, that the radicalism of the Covenanting movement had passed to the lowest levels of the landowning classes and the tenantry. The aftermath of their defeat saw 35 participants hanged and dozens more transported for life to the Caribbean. By the end of the decade the state attempted to follow not merely a policy of repression, but one of conciliation, enacting the first of two Declarations of Indulgence on 15 July 1669 (the second followed on 2 September 1672). The effect of this was to allow expelled ministers who had not been convicted of conventicling to be reappointed to their original parishes or appointed to newly vacant parishes—but not to conduct services or pastoral functions outside them. Their political conformity with the state was the price of their religious nonconformity with the established church. Fully 136 ministers—or just over half of those expelled in 1662 accepted the Indulgence. The desired result was clearly to divide the clerical leadership of the movement by drawing off the more moderate faction and their congregations. The impact on the conventicling movement, however, was minimal. If anything, the numbers attending the preachers who remained in the fields, and the newly ordained who replaced the indulged ministers, began to grow again by the mid-1670s.

The second wave of open resistance was sparked by the murder of James Sharp, Archbishop of St Andrews, by Covenanters on 3 May 1679. The heightened level of repression that followed brought a much larger response. Conventicles had grown to such proportions that one, on Skeoch Hill at Irongray parish in Dumfries consisted of 14,000 people. And they were armed. John Graham of Claverhouse led the royalist forces to defeat at Drumclog on 1 June, but rather than make military preparations to build on their victory, the triumphant Covenanters set up a camp at Bothwell Brig and devoted three weeks to a debate concerning the future direction of the movement, much of it concerned with their attitude towards the indulged ministers. Two clear factions emerged, one prepared to cooperate with those who had accepted indulgences, which in effect wanted as far as possible to unite the Presbyterian movement, the other influenced by the minister Richard Cameron, which reacted with sectarian hostility to any compromise with the state. In the event, no conclusions were ever reached, since a superior force led by the Duke of Monmouth defeated the rebels at Bothwell Brig on 21 June. Defeat broke the Covenanters as a mass movement until the very eve of the revolution of 1688. The intransigent faction led by Richard Cameron, whose name they took, could not have had more than a few hundred adherents at most. Yet their declarations of war against church and state, invariably posted on the market cross of some south western town, fuelled an increasing level of repression throughout the 1680s, climaxing in a period between August 1684 and the revolution of 1688 which has become known, after the Presbyterian historian Robert Wodrow, as the 'Killing Times'.

The Scottish central state had traditionally been one of the weakest in Europe, but after the accession of James VII of Scotland (and II of England) to the throne in 1685 it was openly strengthened by an external absolutism. The intention, as in 1625-37, was to restrain noble power in Scotland as a prelude to confining the now considerably more developed capitalist interest in England. The vast majority of the nobles took an instrumental view of absolutism. Ideally, their monarch should be little more than a figurehead for their own continued ascendancy; if that was not possible, as it had not been possible after 1660, their conversion to the virtues of absolutism was equally calculated to further their material interests. Charles II had kept to this arrangement, at least until the closing years of his reign, but almost as soon as James acceded to the throne it became clear that he did not, undermining his support among the nobility in two crucial areas.

One was that the politicians he chose to administer his regime were increasingly drawn from the narrow group who shared his Catholic faith. This was despite the fact that there were no more than 2,000 Catholics south of Inverness, most of these being in the north eastern areas of Aberdeenshire and Banffshire, with perhaps another 12,000 to 14,000 in the Highlands proper, mainly concentrated in the Hebrides and western Highlands. Given that only a minority of these belonged to the dominant noble class, it did not constitute a social base large enough from which to build popular support for a revitalised absolutism. Taken together with Catholic dominance on the Privy Council, however, it was enough to cause suspicion among the Scottish nobles that James was planning to bypass them, the traditional rulers of Scotland, for a small group of religiously reliable court appointees. Yet their alienation from James went deeper than distrust of his Catholicism.

The other area was one in which the state had previously fallen short of the European model of absolutism to which it aspired: the 'military revolution', particularly that aspect concerned with the establishment of a professional and centralised standing army. Charles was content to leave internal control in the hands of local militias run by politically trustworthy magnates. One of the first acts passed after the accession of James was designed to run down the militia system; and since this move was accompanied by an increase in the size of the regular army from 1,000 to 3,000 men, the lords correctly inferred that James wanted no countervailing source of military power and was withdrawing from the bargain struck between the British monarchy and the Scottish ruling class in 1660.

The nobles were the only class in Scotland with the necessary social and ideological cohesion to lead resistance to James, yet despite their unhappiness with developments in the state, they would be the last people to do so, for fear of the unintended consequences. They did not challenge James, even as he began constructing the apparatus of the absolutist state with which to overcome them, because the only way to do so would have been to go down the same road as in 1637, with all that implied in terms of possible external conquest and internal insurgency. They refused, for example, to support the abortive rising led by John Campbell, Ninth Earl of Argyll, in May 1685 (which was timed to coincide with that of the Duke of Monmouth in the West Country of England) precisely for this reason. It took the English Revolution of 1688 to relieve them of their dilemma.

1688

On a superficial assessment, the Glorious Revolution in Scotland appears to be more radical than that of England. There was certainly a far higher level of popular involvement. Across the Lowland burghs the crowds rose to attack the symbols of Catholic worship which had been increasingly displayed since the accession of James VII. Edinburgh, where this process had gone furthest, was the scene of a notable riot directed at the Chapel Royal at Holyrood. Yet the anger of the crowd was directed more at the symbols of Catholic worship (and occasionally the persons of Catholic worshippers) rather than the realities of class power. Indeed, the Privy Counsellors present in Edinburgh had endorsed the sack of the Chapel Royal, and local dignitaries led the onslaught. Once the targets of popular hostility had been destroyed, the crowds tended to lose a focus for their activities and disperse of their own accord.

Religious issues also ostensibly motivated events in the rural south west, yet what made them more significant than the destruction of Catholic iconography was that they did not have similar approval from local elites. From Christmas Eve 1688 a coordinated operation was mounted by the Presbyterian sects to eject the Episcopalian ministers imposed by the Restoration regime in 1661. To evict a sitting minister was to cross the will of the local lord, through whose patronage the ministers would normally have been first appointed. Nevertheless, once the initial aim of driving out the curates had been achieved, the disturbances ceased. The tenants had challenged the right of the lords to choose a minister for the church in which they worshipped, not the right of the lords to own the land on which they laboured. Nor was the movement genuinely in competition with the existing state. The apparatus was momentarily powerless, not as the result of popular action, but of external events which had allowed it to take place, namely the invasion by William of Orange and his mercenary army. Scotland was not in a state of social or political collapse as it had been in 1648 at the time of the Whiggamore Raid, or the Presbyterian challenge might have fed into a more generalised revolutionary movement, as might the riots in Edinburgh and the other burghs. In the absence of such conditions, however, both stopped with the attainment of its formal goals. The ruling class seem to have realised this, since a majority of the leading lords and burgesses, despite their evident unhappiness with the situation, felt confident enough to decamp *en masse* for London and stay there for three months—an unlikely course of action had they feared an insurrection in their absence.

No revolution, even one as limited as this eventually proved to be, could hope to succeed by observing the legal framework established by the existing regime—a framework by definition designed to prevent radical change from taking place, although the English revolutionaries pretended to believe that this was what they had done. Accordingly, in the elections for the Convention of the Scottish Estates scheduled to meet on 14 March, the Presbyterian lords who initially took control of the Privy Council proclaimed—quite illegally—that the loyalty oath to the absolutist regime, the Test Act, be set aside, and that all Protestant freeholders and burgesses were allowed both to vote and stand for election. The intended objective was secured: in place of a body completely submissive to James, the Convention became one in which the sides were numerically more evenly matched, particularly outside the noble Estate.

On 4 April the Convention agreed, with only five opposing votes, that James had 'forfaulted' the crown; on 11 April it adopted a document entitled the Claim of Right which explained why. The Claim of Right, unlike the English Bill of Rights on which it was based, had no place for the polite fiction that James had 'abdicated' the throne by virtue of leaving the country. On the contrary, it makes it quite clear that he had forfaulted the crown because of the nature of his regime: 'The Estates of the Kingdom of Scotland, find and declare, That King James the Seventh, being a professed Papist...hath by the Advice of Wicked and Evil Counsellors, invaded the Fundamental Constitutions of this Kingdom, and altered it from a Legal Limited Monarchy, to an Absolute and Despotic Power'.[18] Two days after this declaration, on 13 April, a further document called the Articles of Grievances was approved by the Convention, and William and Mary were proclaimed joint monarchs.

The Scottish nobility rejected James and embraced William and Mary for reasons different—indeed, diametrically opposed—to those of the English revolutionaries. Certainly, the almost casual dismissal of the Stuart dynasty that had ruled Scotland for over 300 years does not suggest an over-reverent attitude to the Divine Right of Kings, but if this was a class opposed to absolutism, it was on grounds far from the bourgeois constitutionalism that predominated in England. In fact it represented the traditional belief of the Scottish nobility that they were entitled to dispose of any monarch who threatened to undermine their rights and privileges. As with their earlier opposition to Charles I, their newly discovered opposition to James was from the position of a pre-absolutist feudal nobility, not a post-absolutist capitalist bourgeoisie. Any attempt to assimilate events in Scotland to those in England because of superficial similarities renders subsequent events incomprehensible. The year 1688 in Scotland represented a *political* revolution which changed some personnel among the feudal ruling class, but left that class as a whole intact: the chessmen moved around, but were not swept off the board; 1688 in England saw the conclusion of a *social* revolution that confirmed the new capitalist ruling class in power and established a state geared to the accumulation of capital. That state had still to undergo several subsequent transformations, largely to accommodate the process of industrialisation and the classes that it produced, but there was no longer any question of a retreat to feudal economic relations or absolutist political rule.

This was why the counter-revolution in Scotland was of little consequence compared to that in Ireland; it was totally unnecessary for the vast majority of the ruling class. John Graham of Claverhouse, First Viscount Dundee, and the man at the forefront of repressing the Covenanters during the 'Killing Times', attempted a counter-revolutionary rising but was unable to raise support from any source other than the small and middling clans based at Lochaber and the Western Isles. And they were far more concerned with protecting themselves from the legal and military interference which could be expected from the Williamite regime than with the Divine Right of James. The largest force that Dundee was able to raise was only 2,600. This relatively small force was able to win a convincing victory over a numerically stronger but largely inexperienced government army at the Battle of Killiecrankie, on 27 July 1689, through the tactic known as the 'Highland charge'—a success that could have opened up the whole of the Lowland plain to the Jacobites had they taken the opportunity. They failed to do so for two reasons.

One was the death of Dundee, who was shot in the very hour of his victory. With the exception of Sir George Murray during the '45, Dundee was the only capable military leader the Jacobites were ever to have and, unlike Murray, he had also been their political leader. Without him at their head, the clan forces began to fragment. This in itself indicates the weakness of the contemporary Jacobite cause; a movement whose forces were primarily concerned with their own tangential interests, and which stalled on the death of its leader, was not a serious contender for power. This, however, was not immediately apparent.

The other reason was that the Jacobites were confronted with a regiment of ideologically committed volunteers recruited from among the most militant of the Presbyterian sects—the Cameronians—who were sent to defend the Perthshire town of Dunkeld and block the advance of the Highland army towards the southern Lowlands. On the morning of 21 August, the Highland army attacked the Cameronian force of 1,000 with four times as many men. The personal conviction and collective courage of the defenders would not have ensured their victory in every circumstance, but their position in Dunkeld was precisely one where these qualities would have the greatest effect. The Highland charge of their opponents, on the other hand, was of limited use in taking a town where practically every house had to be fought for, often in hand to hand fighting and under threat of sniper fire. After four hours of fighting in which the town was virtually destroyed (most of the inhabitants had already fled before the approach of the Cameronians), the Jacobite army, overconfident after Killiecrankie, and without the stomach for the losses needed to destroy Dunkeld and its defenders, began to disperse back to the Highlands.

In retrospect, it can be seen that the rising did not in itself pose any threat to the new monarchy, but this was far from clear at the time, given the continuing war in Ireland and the possibility of a French landing which would both reinforce and reunite the clans. Nevertheless, the relative lack of social weight behind the Jacobite cause at this time suggests that even if Dundee had lived, and Dunkeld gone the other way, the risk of a Stuart restoration was small. Neither the left wing of the revolution represented by the Cameronians nor the counter-revolution embodied in the Jacobite clans had succeeded in mobilising more than a small minority of the population, and in both cases from a highly restricted regional base. What then was the final balance sheet of the Glorious Revolution in Scotland? The settlement had two consequences of major significance.

First, it saw the re-establishment of the Scottish Parliament as the main arena for the ruling class to resolve its internal disputes. The Revolution Government had forced William to dissolve some of the apparatus through which his predecessors had kept control of parliament. This did not mean, however, that it was free from all crown interference. Although still a separate state, Scotland remained part of the composite British monarchy whose interests in Scotland were represented by the full time bureaucracy known as the Officers of State. These were a handful of officials—the Lord Commissioner, the High Treasurer, the Lord Justice Clerk, and so on—nominated by the crown. The paradox of the Scottish Parliament was therefore that, while it no longer suffered from the constraints of absolutist rule, the Scottish political system turned out to have no constitutional safeguards such as those imposed on the crown by the English Parliament during and after the supposedly more conservative English Revolution. Nevertheless, whatever controls the court still exercised, between 1689 and 1707 parliament was for the first time the centre of political life.

Second, it permanently settled the religious question in Scotland on a Presbyterian footing, removing the kirk from the role it had hitherto played both as a catalyst and focus for wider social discontents.

It was here that the Revolution Parliament displayed the greatest radicalism. It abolished Episcopalianism, restoring Presbyterian church government from parish kirk sessions up through regional presbyteries and provincial synods to the ultimate governing body of the General Assembly. It confirmed both the forcible expulsion of the Restoration ministers and the positions of those who had taken their place. It passed the Act Concerning Patronages of 1690 which established the right of small landowners and elders of a parish to buy out for 600 merks (£32.50) the right of an existing patron to present ministers to vacant ministries. There were certainly limitations of this legislation from the point of view of the congregations for, although they could refuse to endorse a nominee presented by heritors and elders, they could not nominate or elect a minister of their own choosing. Even when this qualification is taken into account, however, the passing of this act was the most radical decision since the disregard of the Test Act. Above all, it was the only enactment of the revolution to flout the rights of the lords to dispose of religious arrangements on their property as they saw fit. Why did such a conservative parliament consent to this measure?

The primacy of politics was absolute here. The majority of the ruling class were no more opposed in principle to Episcopalianism in religion than they were to absolutism in politics. But, if William had been forced to concede greater freedoms to the parliament because he needed its support against France, then the parliament would be forced to make concessions to the Presbyterians outside because it needed their support against the counter-revolution inside Scotland—and Episcopalianism was at the heart of the counter-revolution. The General Assembly of the kirk met in November 1690 for the first time since 1653. A purge was instituted and two commissions, one based north of the Tay and the other to the south, were set up to free the kirk of the remaining Episcopalian cadre once and for all. The southern commission, operating in favourable territory, did its work so well that only 24 ministers from the post-1661 intake remained after the purge was completed. The evictions often took place in circumstances comparable to those of 1688-89. Only the survivors of 1661 and their anointed were completely safe in their appointments, since they alone had never compromised with James. The northern commission, however, worked to little avail; the purge of Episcopalians had foundered on the rocks of noble intransigence and, in some areas, popular support. The latter is a factor of some significance, particularly in the western Highlands where Presbyterianism was associated with Clan Campbell and the Argyll interest. The final result of the religious settlement was not therefore a kirk restored to Presbyterianism, but one that was irrevocably split into two unequal parts. The legally established church was now thoroughly Presbyterian, and in that respect probably corresponded to the wishes of a majority of the population south of the Tay, but this geographic limitation meant that the position it enjoyed as a national church was actually less than in more compromised days, when there was nevertheless but one church.

For the vast majority of those who had supported the Covenanting movement during the Restoration, their aims had been achieved. Of course, the kirk had not achieved equality with the state, still less attained supremacy over it. The settlement had not even fully removed the state veto on its decisions, neither had the congregation been allowed an unrestricted right to choose their minister; but the General Assembly had been restored, the congregations could at least challenge the nominees they were offered rather than have them imposed and, most significantly, the recognition of Presbyterianism by the post-revolutionary regime—albeit under duress—allowed a reconciliation between former rebels and the state. The immediate effect of this was to eliminate the Covenanting movement as a meaningful participant in the struggle to reorganise Scottish society. Not only was their military wing incorporated into the proto-British army as an organisation, but many of the young men of the south west, who would have become bonnet lairds in their turn, were siphoned off the land to fight in its ranks. A similar process of incorporation also took place at the parochial level with the Cameronian ministers being received back into the Church of Scotland after giving assurances of their conformity.

Nevertheless, two groups remained unsatisfied with the settlement: one that looked, however uncertainly, forwards to a capitalist future, the other, far clearer in their objectives, back to the absolutism which had just been vanquished.

Four different interests stood in actual or potential opposition to existing society. All of the groups embodying these interests had different aims and, even where they were not in contradiction with each other, there was no unifying faction or ideology that might have brought them together in opposition to the existing order.

The first was that of the Glaswegian 'new' merchants, trading with the same areas of North America and the Caribbean that had made the fortunes of their English counterparts in the first half of the century. The precariousness of this trade may have contributed to the relative openness of the Glaswegian merchant elite, since they were subject to a far higher proportion of failures, and consequently bankruptcies, than were their less intrepid brethren on the east coast. The English merchants, and the state that they had helped to fashion, were unwilling to share the source of their wealth with a new set of interlopers, particularly when they belonged to a different nation. Despite the navigation laws and the risks involved in breaking them, these merchants continued to trade illegally with the new world and looked for ways of legitimising their activities.

The second was that of the lawyers. Their social position was still ambiguous. An advocate might be—indeed was almost certain to be—wealthier and enjoy higher status than many who held burgher status within urban society, but was excluded from standing for political office in the burgh, not only by surgeons—who were at least of comparable social status—but by such plebeian types as skinners and bonnet makers. Lawyers therefore had excellent political reasons for wishing to overthrow feudal obstacles to their advancement in burghal government. But status group closure was not their only reason for complaint. The universalisation of legal norms was blocked by a barrier that ran across almost every part of Scottish society: the existence of the heritable jurisdictions. Not only were the lords still entitled to apply 'law' within their own domains, they were themselves in some respects outside its reach. As late as the 1740s the Earl of Cromarty was avoiding bankruptcy by one simple expedient: no one could sue him in his own baron court. The expansion of their profession across all areas of civil society was therefore dependent on removing alternative sources of legal authority.

The third was that of the ministers of the Church of Scotland. One result of the wars and political revolutions between 1637 and 1651 was that the higher social layers who had previously filled the profession were replaced by the 'middling sort' from lower down the social scale. The attitudes of the new ministers tended to be hostile to the landowning classes and consequently less likely to preach acceptance of the existing order to their congregations. Ministers were highly educated men, not only compared to their parishioners—many of who were illiterate—but to the landowners who had the power of patronage over clerical appointments. The necessity to make oneself acceptable to intellectual inferiors, to whom one already felt a strong class antipathy, bred resentment among the parish clergy—particularly among those most committed to pastoral care, who did not see their role as announcing rent increases from the pulpit on behalf of the laird. There was another reason why the existing state of Scottish society was unsatisfactory to the ministers. In a situation analogous to that of the lawyers, who were prevented from practising in areas where the heritable jurisdictions held sway, the ministers were excluded from preaching across whole areas of the Highlands by the physical remoteness and the inability of the Scottish state to fully exert control over the region. But now they no longer had to compete only with pockets of Catholicism and the remnants of ancient superstition, but with a vastly greater number who had retained the Episcopalianism enforced during the Restoration, and many of these were in the north eastern Lowlands.

The fourth and final interest was that section of the great landowning nobility who aspired to the same levels of wealth as their English equivalents. To achieve this they would have not merely to 'improve' their estates in the technical sense, but also alter the relations of production that prevailed on them. Only those already in receipt of relatively high levels of income from their feudal rents had sufficient financial reserves to undertake the type of long term investment involved.

Far more coherent were the three interests intent on restoring feudal absolutism.

The first was that of the dispossessed Episcopalian clergy. Their political militancy was based on the material consequences of the religious settlement. The Episcopalian laity could have privately adjusted to the disestablishment of their church organisation but their clergy, for reasons of material self preservation, could not. As a proto-Marxist analysis from first century Palestine, with which they were no doubt familiar, has it, 'For where your treasure is, there will your heart be also'.[19] The victims of the purge were expelled from their livings without redress or, for the first time in Scottish history, compensation. Even those who accepted a compromise with the Presbyterianism in church and state knew that their ultimate security depended on a change of regime and a reversal of the religious settlement. It is no accident, therefore, that the 5,000 to 6,000 Episcopal clergy became the ideologues of Jacobitism in Scotland.

The second was that of another, lesser section of the feudal landowning class. The Act Concerning Patronages caused considerable discontent among those based in the southern Lowlands where—since the heritors and elders were generally of the independent 'middling sort' and consequently closer to the views of the congregation as a whole— it was more liable to be put into effect, while in the north east and the Highlands it both increased noble suspicion of Presbyterianism and— since the northern lords had more power over the laity—often confirmed their control over clerical appointments. The lords whose clerical nominees had been expelled recognised this as an attack on their social control and power and frequently employed many of the dispossessed Episcopalian clergy as private tutors or chaplains. Although too fragmented to be described as a church in any organised sense, their clergy nevertheless had the ear of significant numbers among the lower levels of the ruling class disaffected with developments since the revolution, and for whom religion, whatever its other consolations, had a functional character.

The third, and more significant in material terms than either clerical dissidence or noble hostility, was that of the alienated Highland clans. After Dunkeld, the Highland War had effectively degenerated on the Jacobite side into large scale robbery and cattle rustling. The Massacre of Glencoe of 1692 effectively forced the submission of those clans which remained in the field, but in the long run it did more to boost the Jacobite cause than any prior event, showing, as it apparently did, that neither William, nor the central government, nor the Campbells could be trusted. Clan interests had been partially protected by James for his own reasons, but that memory was heightened by these events.

All three groups were excluded from the revolution settlement and prepared to act respectively as the ideological, political and military wings of Jacobitism when it eventually emerged as a serious movement. This is usually dated from 1688 but, in fact, the date has little except formal significance in Scotland since Jacobitism served no purpose for any significant section of the Scottish ruling class at this stage.

The majority of the feudal nobility and their allies among the traditional merchant class still had hopes of establishing their nation as an independent player within the state system. It was only after that turned to ashes that Jacobitism, and the historical reversal of relationships between England and France that it would necessarily have involved, became an option. The fact that the Scottish and English states—founded on different principles and presiding over societies at different stages of development—were still harnessed together in a multiple kingdom was to contribute significantly to the crisis of Scottish society during the next decade.

The crisis of the 1690s

Social relations in Scotland remained essentially feudal and, consequently, the economy remained trapped within the twin track of subsistence agriculture and raw material exports. In the 1690s a threefold crisis, of appalling social cost, brutally revealed these limits to Scottish development.

First, the involuntary surrender of long established trade links at the behest of the British monarchy showed the political constraints acting on the ruling class. Scotland had no serious colonies, and the tariff barriers that her exports faced were not restricted to the manufactured goods which formed the lesser part of national output, but extended to the raw materials which formed the greater. The later Stuarts had provided one service for the Scottish ruling class: their admiration for and, more to the point, financial dependence on the French monarchy prevented the inevitable systemic conflict between England and France for as long as they sat on the throne. Thus, although Scottish trade with the United Netherlands was disrupted by enforced participation in the various Dutch wars of the Restoration period, the dependent nature of aspirant Stuart absolutism meant that Scotland was not involved in a far more disruptive war with its major trading partner. With the accession of William, and the immediate outbreak of the long delayed hostilities, even this advantage was lost. The Wars of the British and Irish Succession lasted from 1688 to 1697 and would in any event have had a generally disruptive effect on trade, but the outbreak of hostilities led to the cessation of all commercial relations with France. The impact of war was also felt in two other areas. Scottish shipping was now exposed to attack from French privateers and had little chance of protection from an English fleet which was instructed to treat the task as very low down on its list of priorities. Nor were there any Scottish frigates that could provide self protection until 1697, the last year of the war, and the Scots had to buy even these from England. Similarly, conscription removed Scottish men, particularly skilled mariners, from economic activity and exposed them—already in proportionally higher numbers than those of England—to the threat of death or mutilation. The Anglo-French struggle had temporarily come to an end with the Treaty of Ryswick in 1697, but this had no benefit for Scotland. Apart from the immediate problem caused by now unemployed officers and men returning to a country which could not feed its existing population, the expected upturn in trade did not transpire. Between 1697 and 1702 France banned the import of Scottish wool and fish, and imposed heavy duties on coal, as did the Spanish Netherlands. Most seriously of all, however, was the decline in trade with England, trade which had become increasingly significant during the 17th century and, unlike trade with the European mainland, was not liable to disruption by France. Yet between 1698 and 1706, the value of Scottish exports fell by 50 percent, from an average yearly figure of £114,000 in 1698-1700 to £54,000 in 1704-06. One figure reveals the extent of national economic weakness at the end of the 17th century: the Scottish exchequer raised at most £110,000 per annum; yet £66,000 was required for the pay of the army alone under its 1692 establishment of approximately 3,000 army officers and men, to which must be added the cost of clothing and equipment.

Second, the failure of the agricultural sector to cope with a massive subsistence crisis revealed the socio-economic constraints on production. A downturn in global weather conditions had significantly increased the incidence of harvest failure throughout the early 1690s, and by 1694 this had already led to famine in France and Sweden. In August 1695, the Scottish harvest failed for the first time since 1674, and by December it was obvious that the country was on the verge of a famine which was to last, with peaks in 1696 and 1699, until normal harvests resumed in 1700. We will never know the full extent of population loss across the country as a whole, since not every area had comparably accurate statistics. The overall figure cannot, however, have been less than 5 percent and may have been as high as 15 percent; that is to say between 50,000 and 150,000 people. The famine did not result simply from climatic changes whose effects could not have been anticipated beforehand or countered once they had begun, as demonstrated by the comparable—and in some cases considerably greater—levels of mortality elsewhere in Europe. 'Natural causes' cannot be invoked here any more than to explain more recent famines in sub-Saharan Africa. Rather than causing their respective crises, natural events triggered them by exposing the underlying weakness of existing socio-economic relationships. In the case of Scotland, these relationships were the still dominant forms of feudal tenure which had prevented the commercialisation and increased productivity of agriculture that might have prevented the actual level of devastation. It is worth considering that while some countries did indeed suffer even greater loss of life than Scotland (Finland lost perhaps as many as a third of its population), two others suffered a sharp increase in food costs but no actual starvation. It is perhaps unnecessary to add at this stage in the argument that they were the two that had either broken through to commercial agriculture (England) or whose trading and banking activities provided the resources to buy food (the United Netherlands). The main long term economic effect of the famine was to further retard development by forcing tenants to devote whatever surplus they produced towards paying off rent arrears accumulated during the 1690s.

Third, and finally, an attempt to transcend these boundaries by opening up new colonial markets was to expose the underlying weaknesses of the state itself. In 1695 the Scottish Parliament tried to legislate a way out of the economic impasse. Two acts were passed; one For Encouraging Foreign Trade and the other allowing the formation of joint stock companies with the power to undertake both colonial and trading activities. The creation of the Company Trading to Africa and the Indies was the result, but under the pressure of the crisis, the nature of that venture changed from being a trading endeavour to something quite different: the launching of a colony at Darien on the Panamanian Isthmus. The precedents in Scottish history for such a project were not propitious. From the first attempted colony in Newfoundland during 1617 to Stuart's Town in South Carolina during 1684-86, all Scottish imperial ventures were intermittently maintained, poorly resourced and small scale compared to the English ventures in the same continent. Nevertheless, high hopes accompanied the five ships and 1,200 people who left the Port of Leith on 18 July 1698. Yet the colony they established had collapsed within a year of them setting sail, and two subsequent attempts fared no better. Final abandonment of the project came with submission of the last colony to the Spanish on 30 March 1700. The balance sheet reveals the loss of 2,000 people—although this was a drop in the ocean compared to the thousands dying of starvation at home—and something between a fifth and a half of the national capital, money that was now unavailable for any more achievable end. Why did it fail?

Darien was part of the declining Spanish Empire, which could be expected to oppose any intrusion by another power, but it was no means destined to be successful—Spanish forces were beaten at Tubuganti by the second expedition and Native American allies as late as 15 February 1700. Spanish hostility was therefore unwelcome, but not necessarily decisive.

A more plausible reason might be found in the actions of the English state. The company had originally received investment from English merchants, but under pressure from the East India Company, William had forced them to withdraw. Despite this, the colonists might at least have expected to receive protection from the existing English colonies in the Caribbean. According to the very act that founded the company, England would have to protect the Scottish fleet from foreign (ie Spanish) interference. Even in their negotiations with Spain after armed struggle had broken out, the colonists continued to play on the supposed fact of royal support. There was only one difficulty in this respect: England was allied to Spain. The Scots had blundered into the complex web of international alliances which characterised Europe as it awaited the death of Charles II of Spain and the impending struggle for the Spanish succession between France, Bavaria and Austria. William was not prepared to allow their ambitions to upset the power balance against Louis and, in particular, to jeopardise Willam's manoeuvring over the Spanish succession, which he was anxious to prevent Louis obtaining at any cost—thus, no help was forthcoming from English colonies elsewhere in the Americas. For William the maintenance of the anti-French alliance took first place, the wishes of the more powerful of his English subjects second and those of his Scottish subjects—however powerful—a very poor third.

The attitude of the English government was not, however, decisive. Leaving aside the inherent absurdity of complaining that a project which was supposed to establish Scotland as a trading nation independent of England failed from the lack of English help, such a perspective ignores the fact that English hostility had not stopped the Glaswegian merchant class from earlier establishing trading links elsewhere in America, when they were faced not only with lack of support but illegality. In fact, the principal reason for the failure of the colony was neither military intervention by the Spanish Empire nor diplomatic opposition by the British crown, although these certainly compounded the difficulties experienced by the colonists. Both could have been coped with, had either the Scottish state or civil society been resilient enough to sustain the venture. Were they?

In fact, the Scottish state threw the sole responsibility for organising, financing and defending this crucial project onto civil society. It is a measure of the frustration, perhaps even the desperation, of the bourgeoisie that they were prepared to take the enormous gamble involved in the company to break through the developmental barriers at one bound, but it was quite beyond them. Supplies for the colonists failed to appear from famine ridden Scotland, and they had insufficient money to buy more provisions. And in any case, from whom would they have bought them? The company had failed to appoint factors in New York or the Caribbean who could have arranged for provisions to be sent. Nor did matters improve later. Among the cargo of the third expedition were 4,000 periwigs (to trade with the Native Americans) and 1,500 copies of the English bible (for the edification of the colonists, the majority of whom were Gaelic speaking Highlanders). After setting sail it was discovered that only six months stock of provisions had been laid in instead of the expected nine, and as the bread was mouldy it would not in fact be enough to keep the colonists for three months.

Contrast this debacle with the one successful colonisation in Scottish history, that of Ireland. The Scottish colony in Ulster was initiated by the composite monarchy that emerged from the Union of the Crowns in 1603 for two purposes. The first was to remove disruptive elements from Scottish territory; on the one hand committed Presbyterians who refused to accept compromise with Episcopalianism, on the other displaced Border reivers (outlaws) squeezed out by the combined pressure of the Anglo-Scottish repression. The second was to use the colonists as agents of regal power over the native inhabitants; in that sense we can speak of a 'British' Empire taking shape in Ireland over a hundred years before 'Britain' itself came into existence. But the colony was ultimately guaranteed by the English state. The Scottish settlement in Darien had no such support and consequently lacked military capacity. Given that the crown had no intention of protecting the company, this therefore meant that the state had thrown the sole responsibility for this crucial project onto a civil society that was incapable of accomplishing the task.

Shortly before surrendering to the Spanish, the besieged colonists attempted to negotiate. Hidden among the ensuing bluster is a passage which, in its quiet way, is one of the most tragic in Scottish history: 'We have sent herewith the Act of Parliament, letters patent under the great seal of the Kingdom of Scotland, one in English, and another in Latin, whereby you may have a clear and full view of the just ground of our settlement, and great powers and privileges granted to us'.[20] There is something desperately moving in the picture of these bedraggled colonists, disease ridden, dying, exhausted, outnumbered and abandoned, waving aloft these bits of paper giving notice of their 'great powers and privileges', as if the words of the Scottish Parliament could substitute for the power that the Scottish state so evidently lacked.

The loss of between 50,000 and 150,000 people, and between a fifth and a half of the available national capital, was not an accidental diversion from an otherwise unbroken upward progression, but the inevitable result of failing to break the existing mould of society. The effect was paradoxical. On the one hand it raised popular hostility to the supposed English source of national humiliation, and to those among the Scottish elite who appeared insufficiently supportive of the endeavour. On the other hand, the ruling classes were made aware that, whatever solution was adopted, the existing situation could not continue.

1707

On 16 January 1707 the Scottish Parliament ratified a Treaty of Union with England by a majority of 110 votes to 69, thus uniting the two kingdoms in the new state of Great Britain, which formally came into being on 1 May with the opening of the first British Parliament. The Scottish Parliament adjourned on 25 March and was dissolved by proclamation on 28 April. What lay behind this event? The third great misconception about this period in Scottish history is that the Union represented a deal between the Lowland bourgeoisie and the English bourgeoisie to exploit jointly the British Empire. It was not.

First, as we have seen, the Scottish bourgeoisie neither directly nor indirectly controlled the Scottish state and consequently were in no position to do deals with anyone. The voting record clearly shows that the nobility were the Estate most in favour of ratification:[21]

	For	Against
Nobility	42	19
Barons	38	30
Burgesses	30	20
Total	**110**	**69**

Second, most members of the Scottish bourgeoisie were not only opposed to the Union—on the eminently materialist grounds that exposure to free trade with England would see their manufactured goods swamped by more competitive English rivals—but were also responsible for mobilising popular opposition against it.

Third, the empire was not an issue during the treaty negotiations and only became important to the Scottish ruling class in the second half of the 18th century.

The issues here are extremely complex. Marxists generally accept the decisive nature of the Glorious Revolution in England. Yet there is a difficulty in unreservedly accepting this judgement—not because the revolution failed to correspond to some abstract model, but because of the international context in which the English state found itself. Any revolution that introduces a new type of society is liable to be overturned by a mixture of external pressure and internal subversion as long as it remains isolated in a world where a different and hostile system prevails. Only when the cumulative impact of several revolutions has established a new social system can safety be assured. Was this the case after 1688 for the bourgeois revolution in general and its English manifestation in particular? We should not make the mistake of confusing the existence of pre-existing components of the capitalist system—money, wage labour, commodities—for the system itself, where these are combined in the process of competitive accumulation. Capitalist relations of production, although still largely subordinate to feudalism, were indeed present in Western Europe and colonial America, but only in a handful of territories had they separated out and become dominant in their turn, and none of the states founded on these relations were secure.

If we exclude the United Netherlands, which was already entering its decline, England was by 1688 the only surviving source of a systemic alternative to feudal absolutism. Was it safe from overthrow? The finality ascribed to the Revolution of 1688 above is only possible, in fact, if events in England are treated in complete isolation both from the other nations of the British Isles and from the wider struggle with France for European and colonial hegemony. And of course this is not possible, as the English ruling class themselves were only too well aware at the time. The War of the Spanish Succession, like the War of the British and Irish Succession which it continued, was an intersystemic conflict between a still insecure capitalist order centred on England and a still dominant feudal absolutist empire centred on France. If Louis XIV succeeded in pressing his claim to the Spanish crown then, whatever the formal terms of the ensuing settlement, the territories of the Spanish monarchy would simply be absorbed by

France, with decisive consequences for future European development. The English ruling class faced the prospect of its greatest rival presiding over a world empire which stretched from the manufactories of Flanders to the gold mines of the Americas, well positioned to seize the English colonies and so cut off one of the main sources of English ruling class wealth. The nature of the external danger was therefore clear.

Was there also an internal threat? There was, but danger of counter-revolution lay not in England itself (nor in Ireland, which had been quiescent since the Treaty Of Limerick in 1691), but in Scotland. It is here that the difference between the English and Scottish revolutions of the 17th century is most significant. For the failure of the Scottish bourgeoisie to break the bounds of existing society meant that the state was potentially an ally of France in its competition with England. The oft stated desire of the Stuarts to reclaim all of their previous kingdoms, combined with the French need to remove their opponents from the international stage, meant that the English ruling class were faced not only with impoverishment, but also with a threat to their continued survival as an independent class. It was therefore a strategic necessity for them to permanently block a Stuart restoration by continuing the joint monarchy after the death of William's sister in law and successor, Queen Anne. The Elector of the German state of Hanover was chosen for this role. How would the Scottish Parliament react?

The first Scottish Parliament to be elected since the revolution of 1688 assembled on 6 May 1703. It did not consist solely of feudal superiors and their nominees, but even the smaller lairds and burgesses who both embodied more advanced social relations and were free from the influence of the great nobles—a rare combination—were present by virtue of the existing feudal means of representation. Attempts by historians to superimpose the structure of English party politics at this time onto Scotland are therefore profoundly misleading. At one level Scotland appeared little different in political structure—electorates were small, elections infrequent and organisational apparatuses impermanent—but the Scottish and English parties were as different from each other as the parliaments in which they sat. There was no Whig party in Scotland in the sense there was in England, just as there was no Jacobite party in England in the sense there was in Scotland. What then was the nature of the Scottish parties?

In addition to the crown officers and their supporters ('the Court party') there was of course a Country party claiming to uphold the mantle of patriotism against the courtiers who were allegedly betraying Scottish interests—an attitude that carried a certain plausibility after Darien. It would be wrong, however, to imagine that these sentiments reflected anything comparable to modern nationalism. After 1689 the majority of Country members had tended to be nothing more than a new set of courtiers in waiting, using the rhetoric of national emergency in order to propel themselves into the offices occupied by the existing Court party. In one respect, however, their 1703 incarnation was different and reflected the reality of the situation after Darien in which many of the leading members had lost heavily. They were set, therefore, not simply on becoming the Court party but a Court party that held the monarch under their control, rather than the other way around. This was, of course, the ancient goal of the Scottish nobility as a class, but as things stood in 1703 it could not be achieved while the monarchy remained in England, since it was precisely this arrangement which allowed William to thwart similar attempts at control during the period of post-revolution settlement. In short, the Country party represented an unstable alliance of factions. In particular, within the Country party was one faction—and at 20 strong they had perhaps a third of the total membership—which did represent the intention to control the monarchy for the 'national' interest rather than for the purposes of noble convenience. This was the faction around Andrew Fletcher, the one exception to the general non-Whiggism of Scottish parliamentarians referred to above.

A man often unjustly maligned by socialists, Fletcher was committed to a programme of radical reform of the Scottish state and society which would have reduced the role of the monarchy to a virtually ceremonial one and to the same degree strengthened the power of parliament. The core of his programme can be found in his 'limitations'—the 12 points by which he argued the Scottish Parliament could resist the imposition of arbitrary rule. Ironically, in the light of the position which he was shortly to take in opposition to Union with England, Fletcher had been one of the few Scots to declare himself in favour of such an arrangement during the Revolution of 1688, but his support for a union was on the assumption that it would be with a truly revolutionary England. His politics were therefore comparable to the extreme Whigs or Commonwealth Men who were defeated in the English Convention Parliament. Consequently, when it became clear that William intended to agree to the most conservative settlement possible, the very reason for seeking union disappeared and the possibility of achieving his goals within Scotland alone became his main project.

Finally, there were the Jacobites (who, appropriately enough, referred to themselves as the Cavaliers), with around 70 members. Like Fletcher, the Jacobites had a definite solution in mind to the Scottish dilemma: a restoration of the Stuarts that would also have resulted in Scotland coming under the domination of France. It is worth bearing this in mind when reading their protestations of concern for Scottish sovereignty. Hypocrisy aside, however, it is possible to view the Jacobites as being nearer to the modern notion of a party than either of their competitors—not in the sense that they possessed a permanent organisation, but that they had a clearly defined programme, ideologically distinct from the inchoate shifting between Court and Country typical of the ruling class as a whole.

The parliament passed two acts in August 1703. The Act of Security provided for the Scottish Parliament choosing the next monarch of Scotland, the only criterion being that whoever was chosen could not at the same time hold the crown of England unless certain conditions—which had still to be decided—were met. In the meantime all eligible males were to be trained to resist foreign invasion from an unspecified quarter. The Act Anent War and Peace additionally moved that only the Scottish Parliament could declare war on behalf of Scotland. These acts were the result of factional moves by different sections of the opposition rather than an agreed strategy. The Jacobites wished to abort the Hanoverian succession in favour of the Stuarts and saw the acts as a step in that direction. The radical minority of the Country party around Fletcher saw them as the beginning of parliamentary independence from monarchical control. But the majority of the Country party, who represented what might be called the mainstream of Scottish ruling class thought, saw them as a bargaining counter to secure the Hanoverian succession on more favourable terms; they wanted the advantages of trade with England and English military protection, but without surrendering in return any of their privileges or freedom for political manoeuvre. Fletcher pointed out their folly in a speech which his present day admirers rarely quote:

> For prerogative-men [ie both the Jacobites and the Hanoverians] who are for enslaving this nation to the directions of another court, are courtiers to any successor; and let them pretend what they will, if their principles lead necessarily to subject this nation to another, are enemies

to the nation. These men are so absurd as to provoke England, and yet resolve to continue as slaves of that court. This country must become a field of blood in order to advance a papist to the throne of Britain. If we fail we shall be slaves by right of conquest; if we prevail, have the happiness to continue in our former slavish dependence.[22]

The analysis is flawless. To accept the Hanoverian succession would leave Scotland in exactly the same predicament as it had been under William. To oppose it would almost certainly involve accepting the return of the Stuarts and being forced into war with the English state in response. Yet what does he propose as a solution? A set of paper limitations which, in the absence of any material force to back them up, would have been as successful in confining the powers of the crown as the letters patent (under the Great Seal of the Kingdom of Scotland) waved by the Darien settlers had been in stopping the bullets of their Spanish opponents.

Nevertheless, Fletcher was right about the consequences of provoking the English. The English ministry chose to regard the acts as a straightforward rejection of the Hanoverian succession and decided that their security lay in an incorporating Union. The first step which the English Parliament took to help induce 'voluntary' acceptance of the proposed union was to pass a piece of legislation known as the Aliens Act, but whose purpose is better revealed in its full title—'An Act for the Effectual Security of the Kingdom of England from the Apparent Dangers that May Arise from the Several Acts Lately Passed in the Parliament of Scotland'. This deprived Scots of the privileges of English citizenship, forbade all Scottish imports and, most importantly, decreed that all estates in England held by Scots were to be confiscated, unless the Hanoverian succession was accepted by Christmas Day 1705. Some of the lords had estates in England but, more generally, what the Aliens Act offered was an uncertain economic future in which they would be excluded from English markets for the goods produced on their estates. Of no less importance, they would also be denied the prospect, however slight it might have been, of betterment, or at any rate escape from the confines of Scotland through the avenues of the marriage contract or military service. Yet an alternative to this dismal prospect was also on offer. The act containing a clause appointing commissioners to negotiate a union between the two kingdoms had passed both English Houses of Parliament. The document eventually signed by the Scottish and English negotiators in July 1706 had 25 articles covering three sets of issues.

The first set dealt with Scottish representation in the British Parliament. These were the most obviously unsatisfactory for the Scottish political elite. Articles 22 and 23 established that there would be just 45 members (30 for the shires and 15 for the burghs) in the House of Commons—only one member more than the 44 who sat for Cornwall—and 16 peers in the House of Lords. There were at the time 513 English MPs and 185 peers, so the Scots were being asked to accept between an eleventh and a twelfth of the English representation. The number of Scottish representatives was effectively a compromise between economic and demographic measures, since the Scottish population was then a fifth of the English, but the income which the Land Tax in Scotland was expected to raise for the Exchequer was calculated at less than a fortieth of that raised in England.

The second set dealt with existing Scottish institutions. Article 19 ensured the continuation of the main component of the Scottish state outside parliament itself, the legal system—although it said nothing about which body would constitute a final court of appeal, the implication being that it would be the House of Lords (not a gathering renowned for comprehending the complexities of Scots law). Article 20 specifically retained the Heritable Jurisdictions—a point to which I will return. The 'Rights and Privileges' of the royal burghs were preserved by Article 21. Contrary to what is sometimes supposed, the education system is unmentioned in the treaty. Of far greater significance than this, however, was the fact that it also remained silent on the position of the Church of Scotland.

The third set dealt with economic issues. Article 4 conferred freedom of trade on Scotland. This was a considerable concession—although probably an unavoidable one—for the English ruling class, since they had been refusing precisely this measure for the previous 100 years. But the corollary of equal access to English markets was of course equal contributions to the British Exchequer, as detailed in Articles 6, 7 and 8. Whatever the enthusiasm, or lack of it, for free trade, these measures were always going to be unpopular. On the other hand, Article 9 set the level of the Land Tax, limiting Scotland to paying £48,000 per annum as opposed to England's £2,000,000. In other words, a ratio of one to 42, or less than £50 per every £2,000 paid by England. Article 15 established the Equivalent, nicely calculated at £398,085 10s, for taking a share of the English National Debt. It specifically included compensation for losses incurred by the adoption of the English coinage and, more importantly, to repay Darien stockholders for their losses in the sum—again nicely calculated—of £232,884 5s $^2/_3$d.

As soon as the terms of the treaty became known, Scotland exploded in generalised opposition to its ratification by parliament. Daily demonstrations took place outside Parliament House. Petitions were submitted, signed either by the inhabitants of a particular parish or burgh, or by delegates to a particular institution like the Commission of the Assembly of the Church of Scotland or the Convention of Royal Burghs. Less frequently, the Articles of Union were publicly burned. On two occasions, once in Edinburgh and once in Glasgow, demonstrations turned into serious riots. Finally, in an extraordinary conjunction, an armed rising uniting the Presbyterian sects of the south west with the Atholl clans of the central Highlands was set in motion, although never actually launched. What was behind this explosion of popular activity? And why did it fail to prevent ratification of the treaty?

References to nationalism get us little further forward, unless we believe—as some modern nationalists evidently do—that it is a natural phenomenon requiring no further explanation. The inhabitants of the Scottish Lowlands were indeed beginning to develop a sense of national *consciousness*, but the transformation of this form of consciousness into a political nationalism was never fully achieved while the Scottish state was in existence. Nationalism involves at the very least some level of identification of the 'people' with the state, but such an identification was impossible for the vast majority of Lowland Scots. The Scottish state had failed miserably to achieve the goals it had set itself in Darien, and the functions that it did perform to any degree of efficiency were those of a feudal apparatus geared to aiding their exploitation. The crowds were provoked rather by a concern for the Scottish society in which they experienced not only oppression, but also the things that made their lives halfway bearable. Their 'nationalism' was in reaction to the two specific ways in which the treaty threatened their conditions.

The first was the undermining of the kirk. The ominous lack of any reference to its constitutional position—in contrast to the guarantees offered to the legal profession—led many to suppose that Presbyterianism was once more under threat from English bishops. The kirk was the only institution over which the plebeians exercised any democratic control. The ministers shared their concern, although in their case for reasons that had also to do with the preservation of their clerical benefices. The second was that, for the classes below the no-bility and the merchant elite, the Union offered, above all else, higher taxation and, although it was not mentioned in the treaty, it was quite clear that a more rigorous customs and excise regime on the English model was to be imposed. This could only be to thwart the smuggling operations that provided illegal employment for many along the east coast and access to cheap goods, especially wine, elsewhere. Agitation over both issues was, however, defused before the final vote on the treaty was held.

An Act for Securing the Protestant Religion and Presbyterian Church Government, although separate from the treaty itself, must be considered as integral to it. The kirk ministers were not thereby won over to the idea of union with English Episcopalians, but the protec-tion which the act offered them effectively defused their opposition to the extent that they ceased agitating and started grumbling in-stead. The concern over taxation was met by a series of amendments to the treaty, whose importance has rarely been recognised. The vote on Article 8, dealing with Scottish exemption from English salt taxes, was the only serious defeat suffered by the court throughout the entire ratification process. Why this issue, above all others? If taxes on Scot-tish salt were kept lower than on English or other imported salt, then it would remain affordable for the mass of the population, for whom it was a necessity both to preserve food during winter and to render their regular diet more edible throughout the year. It would be inad-visable to dismiss these as merely base material concerns. Given the highly circumscribed lives of most people at this time, a worsening of their material conditions in these areas was a serious matter.

The combined effect of the guarantees offered to the kirk and the amendments which withdrew, at least temporarily, the economic cost of incorporation seem to have removed these immediate concerns. The majority of people did not, of course, become enthusiasts for the Union as a result, but they were more prepared to tolerate it. There was, however, another reason for the decline in opposition to the treaty—a realisation that it was opening up the way not for an 'in-dependent' Scotland, but a Stuart restoration. Naturally, this point was rammed home by pro-Unionists: 'Men are known by their friends', noted one pamphlet (probably written by Daniel Defoe) published after the Glasgow riots and the attempted rising. 'All the Jacobites are in League with you, the Papists are on your right Hand, the Prelatists on your left, and the French at your Back...on what account do these people join with you?'[23] Propagandist in intent though these remarks were, they touched on a real problem. Indeed, a Scottish *anti*-Union pamphleteer, James Hodges, had to remind his countrymen who were contemplating the return of the Stuarts of what, in his view, were the reasons behind the revolutions of 1559, 1637 and 1688: 'Can you think an Arbitrary and Absolute Monarch a fit Assessor and Supporter of Your Rights and Liberties as a Free People?'[24] For the Presbyterian sects of the south west in particular, to support a rising in conjunction with the Jacobite clans would have been like the Bolsheviks siding with Kornilov against Kerensky in September 1917. They were neither so unprincipled nor so unthinking as to imagine that the restoration of an absolutist regime, supported externally by Catholic France and internally by the Episcopalian clans, would benefit them in either religious or social terms, and it must be supposed that similar considerations operated elsewhere in Scotland.

Was the opportunity to trade with England the main reason for acceptance of the treaty? The fact that Article 6 on free trade had the most support of all the articles, with only 19 votes against, indicates that it was of some importance. The problem here is that it is necessary to be more specific about for *whom* free trade with England was a reason for accepting the treaty. The English market was far more important to lords like Banff, Cromarty or Seafield, who were landowners in the arable lands of the north east, than it was to urban manufacturing or rural extractive industries for whom the home market was key. Since the noble Estate gave proportionally the biggest support for the treaty, this might seem to resolve the issue. Unfortunately, matters are not so simple. The lord who would have benefited most from the continuation of free trade was the Earl of Galloway, on whose lands were raised the black cattle whose sale in 1703 amounted to 40.2 percent of the value of all exports to England; yet Galloway voted against the article on free trade and every other except Article 1. The lord who would have benefited least was the Earl of Wemyss who, exceptionally among his class, derived the majority of his income from the sale of coal extracted from his estates. Given the superior quality of English coal he would inevitably suffer from competition; yet Wemyss voted for every article of the treaty.

Does this mean that the Union was carried simply by coercion and bribery? The English ministry could only have contemplated an invasion as a last resort, but the question of bribery is, on the face of it, more plausible. The accusation was given memorable literary expression by

Robert Burns, who described those who voted for the treaty as 'a parcel of rogues' who arranged for the Scottish people to be 'bought and sold for English gold.' That the majority were a parcel of rogues is indisputable, at least from the point of view of the people over whom they ruled—although it is surely also true of those who voted against, since they did not become paragons of benevolence to their tenants, workmen and servants by virtue of preferring the House of Stuart to that of Hanover. The issue is surely not whether payments were made to certain individuals—this is undeniably the case—but first, whether they invariably voted the way they did as a result of such payments, and second, whether the votes secured in this manner were what carried the treaty. These issues are far less clear. Nevertheless, what is clear is that the biggest inducements offered to the nobility were simply the terms of the treaty itself: an astonishing series of concessions which effectively preserved many of the functions of the Scottish state. Indeed, if the English had been able to rely on bribery these would never have been included in the final treaty. Nor would concessions have been made over the kirk or taxation. Measures intended to gain the acquiescence of an entire social class (such as the preservation of the Heritable Jurisdictions) or a profession (such as the preservation of the Scots law more generally) cannot be treated as bribes. One might profitably contrast the guarantees offered to the Church of Scotland with the conditions imposed on the Catholic and Presbyterian Irish after the Treaty of Limerick in 1691, notably the suppression of the Roman Catholic church and persecution of its priests. Equally illuminating, however, are the conditions imposed on the Anglican landowning class that actually ruled Ireland on behalf of the English. They were not to be admitted into free trade with the colonial power, and the difference between their situation and that of the Scots was one of which the latter were all too painfully aware. The Protestant Irish ruling class wanted a union with England, and were far more united on this point than their Scottish equivalents had ever been.

The divisions within parliament had reflected divisions within the feudal ruling class themselves about how best to preserve their existing place within Scottish society. The English response to the Act of Security had made it apparent that the options available to them were considerably fewer than they had previously thought. Party allegiance, and consequently voting, was therefore determined, for the majority of the Estates, not by calculations of what would result in short term financial advantage to do so, but by a more long term assessment of what a union was likely to offer them and what the alternative was likely to be. From this point of view it makes as little sense to talk about the 'treachery' of one faction of the ruling class as it does to talk about the 'patriotism' of another. While Scotland certainly had formal sovereignty over its own affairs, what it lacked was the autonomy to put its sovereign power into effect. The entire ruling class opted to abandon sovereignty altogether for incorporation into a greater power that would protect what they had. Once it became clear that the option of a federal union with a different monarch from that in England was unattainable, the choice was more starkly posed between three alternatives; the Stuarts and France, Hanover and England on a voluntary basis, or Hanover and England 'by right of conquest', as Fletcher put it. The only option was which state they would choose to subordinate themselves to. Why did the majority choose England?

On the negative side, the return of the Stuarts could only occur under the same terms that parliament had rebelled against in 1689. At best they would become the comprador nobility of a French satellite, enduring absolutist encroachments on their social power and Roman Catholicism imposed on their church, not to speak of the revenge which James might be expected to extract for what he saw as past betrayals of his family. Furthermore, since a Stuart restoration in Scotland would inevitably mean war with England, the French option also held out the possibility of defeat and an English conquest that would reduce Scotland to the same condition as Ireland. Only the most desperate of the nobility could have contemplated this scenario. It is no accident that the commissioners who gave the most consistent opposition to the treaty were the barons at the bottom of the ruling class ladder: they had least to lose.

On the positive side, beyond personal bribery, beyond even the specific guarantees of institutional continuity and financial restitution, the treaty contained an overall commitment to preserve the existing structure of Scottish society—with all its contradictions—within the new state. In this respect the key clause in the treaty does not maintain the educational system, nor does it preserve the Church of Scotland, nor does it even enshrine Scots Law, although it is an aspect of that law. The key article in the treaty was number 20, which preserved the feudal superiorities and Heritable Jurisdictions. This article alone would explain the extent of noble support for the Union; indeed, the very term 'superiorities', which had been omitted from the original treaty, was added by an amendment to this article during the discussion on 6 January—obviously the lords were leaving nothing to chance. In this respect the juridical element was infinitely more important than the pedagogic or confessional ones to which it is usually linked; and not as the bearer of some transhistorical 'national identity', but as a means of exercising class power.

As this suggests, the English regime showed not the slightest interest in what could have been the real historical justification for union— the completion of the task that Cromwell had temporarily carried out 50 years before. Can this alliance of convenience between the Scottish and English ruling classes therefore be described as 'progressive' in any way? For Marxists, this term refers, in the context of the bourgeois revolution, to an event or process which leads either to the development of the productive forces or which heightens the political consciousness and organisation of the bourgeoisie—or indeed the classes below them in feudal society. In neither sense can the Union be said to qualify for such a description. It should be clear that it was, literally, a conservative measure for both the English bourgeoisie and the Scottish nobility. The very most that can be said for it is that, unlike the only realistic alternative, it was not actually reactionary in the sense of throwing society backwards.

The implications of the Union did not remain in neutral for long. Rather than the results of the English Revolution radiating northwards to the benefit of the Scots, as has been claimed ever since, the opposite took place: the unfinished business of the Scottish Revolution was transferred intact into the new British state, bringing into its territorial framework the very source of counter-revolution itself. This is the paradox that lay at the heart of the Treaty of Union. The intention of the English regime was to prevent a Stuart restoration in Scotland opening up a second front for France (or any other hostile power) on its northern border through incorporation into a new state. The consequence of incorporation was precisely to increase the chances of such a front being opened, not as a short term response to the immediate strains of adjusting to union, but as the result of a long term structural crisis in Scottish society. For Scotland did not enter the new state completely unchanged. The key difference was, of course, the absence of the parliament, but this had different implications for different social classes.

It is sometimes said that the removal of political representation from Edinburgh meant that the majority of the population without the vote now had no opportunity to influence the political classes through petitions, demonstrations or riots. Ironically, the greatest influence which popular pressure may have had on political outcomes was forcing through the amendments to the treaty that in the end made it more bearable, if not more popular. For the bourgeoisie too, parliament was a most imperfect instrument, filled with their most conservative elements. For the lords, however, the absence of parliament was decisive, and it is a measure of the crisis they felt themselves to be in that they consented to its dissolution by such a majority. For although their local power was left in place, and indeed preserved as their private property, they could no longer command national politics in the same way. Reaffirming their power at the socio-economic base of society, the Union removed it from the political superstructure. Henceforth, any attempt to influence events by any fraction of the nobility could only be violent and could only be conducted on an all-British basis. The period between the Union and the last Jacobite rebellion, when this threat was finally destroyed, is therefore the first British revolutionary epoch; and the site of this struggle was the territory which had once been the domain of the Scottish state.

The social basis of Jacobitism

The fourth misconception about Scottish history is that the Jacobite movement which arose after 1707 was based solely in the Highlands and represented the political expression of clan society. In fact, the material roots of Jacobitism must be sought throughout the Scottish social formation as a whole. Equally, those roots must be sought in a specific social class, not an undifferentiated Scottish 'nation'. Whatever their specific differences, all the Jacobite risings after the Union—1708, 1715, 1719 and 1745—were made possible by a combination of three distinct factors. The first was, of course, the exiled House of Stuart and its campaign to be restored to the three kingdoms of the British Isles. Yet without the two remaining factors the Stuart cause would have been as futile as that of the Bourbons after 1830 or the Romanovs after 1917. One was the financial and military backing of an external power with an interest in limiting or reversing British expansion. The other was a social group internal to Britain whose dissatisfaction with the existing state was great enough to make them take up arms against it. In one sense the failure of Jacobitism was caused by the inability of these two factors ever to interlock at critical moments. Where the internal opposition was unprepared to rise in significant numbers, then external powers were insufficient to force the issue, as can be seen from the relative seriousness of the different risings. The '08 was a fiasco brought about because both the French regime and the exiled House of Stuart mistook popular opposition to the Union as support for a restoration. The '19 was merely a tactical feint on the part of the Spanish state that did not even attain the dignity of a fiasco. Only two—the '15 and the '45—had the indispensable element of relatively widespread backing within Scotland to bring them within striking distance of their goal, but these nevertheless still failed because foreign support could not be provided in time to influence events. What were these internal and external forces?

The external force was absolutist Europe. The years from 1716 to 1741 saw an Anglo-French Alliance (although it might be more appropriate to describe the period as one of Anglo-French Cold War), and until the latter year opposition to British expansion was partially taken over from France by the Spanish Empire and other lesser powers such as Sweden and Prussia. The resumption of hostilities between Britain and France took place as part of the War of the Austrian Succession from 1740, with both states gradually becoming ever more directly involved on the sides of their respective allies.

What social force within Scotland gave France its internal leverage? In a few celebrated cases the bourgeois revolution took the form of a direct onslaught on the feudal regime, leading to the reconstruction of state and society on a new class basis. More commonly it took the form of a gradual internal reconstruction driven by the need to compete with, and hence emulate, those nations which were already reconstructed on capitalist lines. But what if there was no longer a state to be either overthrown or transformed? In Scotland, the defunct state apparatus had embodied a transitional society, in which feudal economic and military relations, although modified, still prevailed. This had been carried directly over into the Union. We might have expected these relationships to disintegrate from within in the manner outlined by the Hungarian Marxist Georg Lukács, where 'those parts of the feudal and absolutist superstructure that were not eliminated by "revolution from above" would collapse of their own accord when capitalism was already fully developed'.[25] But what if parts of the feudal superstructure were artificially preserved with outside support, so that they retained a social and political power far greater than their shrinking economic base would otherwise have justified? The Scottish nobility escaped the consequences of successful revolution in England through a combination of their own geographical inaccessibility and the political expediency of all the English regimes from the Restoration onwards. Jacobitism represented the aims of a declining section of this class. The Union had preserved the feudal powers of the lords, but could not protect them from the encroachments of capitalism, or 'commercial society' as it was called by the Scottish Enlightenment. In these circumstances the lords had three alternatives. First, they could throw in their lot with the new society and undergo a voluntary self transformation into capitalist landlords, introducing commercial tenures and production for the market. Second, they could maintain existing relations on their estates but simply attempt to extract a greater surplus from the peasants. Third, they could participate in a political attempt to turn the clock back—or at least make it stop—by restoring the dynasty whose commitment to feudal reaction was undoubted. This did not necessarily involve any great affection for the Stuarts as a dynasty. As the Duke of Kilmarnock admitted to Argyll while awaiting execution after the '45, 'My Lord, for the two kings and their rights, I cared not a farthing; but I was starving, and by God, if Mohammed had set up his standard in the Highlands I had been a good Mussulman [Muslim] for bread and stuck close to the party; for I must eat'.[26]

All three courses of action presented their own difficulties. The first was only guaranteed to succeed for the very greatest of the feudal lords, like the dukes of Argyll, who had the financial reserves to sustain them through the period of transition to capitalist agriculture. The second ran up against the fact that the level of exploitation could only be increased by a limited degree without physically destroying the peasants on which the lords depended to produce their wealth. The third involved the certainty of civil war, and the risk of meeting death in battle or the grim fate of execution as a traitor; nevertheless, it had one very great advantage to commend it.

Unlike any other feudal class west of Poland, the Scottish landowning nobility could still raise an army from their tenants, either as a result of tenurial arrangements that specifically involved military service, or simply because of the pressure that they could bring to bear through the heritable jurisdictions. And it is crucial to understand that these powers were not restricted only to the Highlands. The '15 demonstrates this most clearly, since the heartland of that rising was in the north eastern Lowlands, where the Episcopalian lords of Banff-shire and Aberdeenshire raised the majority of the Jacobite force from among their tenants. What the preservation of military feudalism effectively meant was that Scotland experienced a form of dual power between 1707 and 1745. In the English and the French (although not the Russian) revolutions the centres of dual power opposed to the absolutist state were in territories seized through military onslaught or urban insurrection by forces opposed to the regime. In Scotland the situation was reversed, as feudal enclaves continued to function after the fall of absolutism within the overall territory of a state otherwise dedicated to the accumulation of capital. Why then did the British state allow the Heritable Jurisdictions to continue after 1707, especially when a number of other articles of the treaty were broken? If they had originally been preserved as a contingent measure to sell the Union to the Scottish ruling class as a whole, then their continuation was the result of two different and contradictory considerations.

One consideration was an awareness that some of the most committed supporters of the revolution settlement and the Union were themselves beneficiaries of these institutions and in a social crisis would employ them in support of the regime. To alienate these men was to risk depriving the state of their local military apparatus and even of pushing them into support for the Stuarts.

The other consideration was also related to the question of state power. Neither the juridical nor military aspects of the English state had been reproduced in Scotland; partly because it would in any event take time to overcome the uneven level of development between the states, and partly because of the suspicion with which the English ruling class continued to regard their new partners. This weak nation-within-a-state was weakest precisely across the area north of the Tay, and successive administrations were prepared— indeed, were forced— to tolerate the continued functioning of local jurisdictions as a form of substitute. The situation was far from ideal, to the extent that attempts to counterbalance the weight of the jurisdictions was made directly after the Union with the establishment of justices of the peace, who were intended to hold judicial and administrative responsibility for particular geographical areas. As a judiciary, they were concerned with upholding law and order and the collection of the new tax revenues introduced by the Treaty of Union. As an administration, they were responsible for maintaining the means of transportation and incarceration, fixing wage rates, enforcing contracts and supervising weights and measures. Yet in spite of the state controls which theoretically existed over appointments to the Commission of the Peace, many justices of the peace were Jacobite in politics. Consequently, in the aftermath of the '08, members of the commission responsible for testing the loyalty of suspected Jacobites were themselves supporters of the Stuarts. Even a purge following the '15 left in place many Jacobites who would later rise for Charles Stuart, like John Gordon of Glenbucket and James Moir of Stoneywood, and they would shortly be joined by more of their comrades. The problem for the central state was that, since the justices were unpaid, there was a shortage of suitable candidates, the shortfall often being made up by the lesser landowners who sought the position to further their political ends. In short, the social influence of the class upon which Jacobitism was most reliant could not be avoided, at least in the northern half of Scotland.

1745

By the beginning of 1744 France was drawing up plans for an invasion of Britain with the 24 year old Charles Edward Louis John Casimir Silvester Xavier Maria Stuart, grandson of James VII, as figurehead. What did France hope to gain from raising the stakes in this way? Fundamentally, Louis wanted to reverse the British rise to world power status which had begun with the Wars of the Spanish Succession and which had been consolidated at the Treaty of Utrecht in 1713. If the Stuarts were restored then land titles acquired since their expulsion would be in question. But the real threat would be to the Whig financial and mercantile interest through the cancellation of the National Debt and concessions which the French state would require by way of restoring lost colonies and trading privileges.

In the end, bad weather conditions at the end of February 1745 scattered the fleet and made the Channel impassable, but the idea of an invasion supported by internal rebellion had now been seriously raised as a strategic option. Early in March France formally declared war on Britain. For Charles, who had largely taken over from his father as the active leader of the exiled court, it was imperative that he take action while the war continued and France had the most pressing need to intervene directly in Britain. The very successes of the French army made it appear that peace might be secured through military victory before another attempt could be made. On 11 May France was victorious at Fontenoy over British troops led by George II's youngest son,

William, Duke of Cumberland. Their forces then began a march across the Austrian Netherlands (present day Belgium) taking one town after another before the climatic seizure of Ostend on 12 August. The significance of this for Britain was immense. The Austrian Netherlands had been partially subdued but, more importantly, the United Netherlands, the only state in Europe to which Britain was allied through a comparable socio-economic structure rather than military convenience, was now threatened with conquest. As a result of this crisis the vast majority of the British army—over 34,000 men—was on the European mainland. In Britain there were less than 4,000 men scattered across Scotland and less than 6,000 in England, most of them concentrated in London. On 5 July, while the French were making their triumphal progress across the Low Countries, Charles Edward Stuart set sail for Scotland with around a dozen companions, the majority of them Irish Jacobites. The extent to which the French court was aware of his intentions is unknown—his father was certainly ignorant of them—but Charles expected support in Scotland. A Jacobite group known as the Association had been in existence since 1739 and had been in contact with both the French and Stuart courts between then and the '45. Yet the backing that they sought from France always included at least 6,000 regular troops together with sufficient money and weapons to guarantee support once a landing had been made. Charles had some money, but no weapons and not even the promise of manpower from His Most Christian Majesty. Prospects for a rising therefore depended on whether the second element needed for a serious attempt—internal support—was forthcoming.

The first news to greet Charles after landing on Eriskay in the Outer Hebrides was not encouraging. A number of chiefs whose adherence he might have expected sent word that they refused to join him, not because they had abandoned the cause but because, without the type of support previously asked for by the Associators, they considered that any rising was doomed to failure. Charles sailed for Arisaig on the mainland where he waited for ten days, meeting the local chiefs and trying to persuade them that success was possible. What seems to have swayed a sufficient number of what (in an English context) could be called the 'declining gentry' to join the rising was the adherence of Donald Cameron Younger of Locheil who perfectly embodied both the crisis of the lesser nobility and the social power that they still possessed.

On the one hand, he had been technically bankrupt for at least 15 years before 1745. A tenant on his estate, who had also been employed by the family, gave evidence some years after the '45 as to the financial condition of Locheil at this time:

> Donald Cameron of Locheil was understood to be in straited circumstances, borrowing money wherever he could find it, and particularly that the Deponent lent him 6,000 merks upon a Wadset; and the Deponent believes, that this was occasioned by his Experience about his House, by building Parks, a Summer-House, and making a fine Garden, and by his great Expense, when he went from home.[27]

On the other hand, he could still mobilise both his tenants and clansmen for war. In 1776 Adam Smith reflected on the fact that such power had been exercised in Scotland so recently: 'It is not 30 years ago since Mr Cameron of Locheil, a gentleman of Lochaber in Scotland, without any legal warrant whatever, not being what was then called a lord of regality, nor even a tenant in chief, but a vassal of the Duke of Argyll, and without being so much as a justice of the peace, used, notwithstanding, to exercise the highest criminal jurisdictions over his own people.' And in the case of Locheil, these feudal jurisdictions were also linked to his role as chief of the local branch of Clan Cameron. 'That gentleman', Smith notes, 'whose rent never exceeded £500 a year, carried, in 1745, 800 of his own people into rebellion with him'.[28]

On 19 August Charles raised the Jacobite standard at Glenfinnan and waited. By the end of the day the Jacobite chiefs had arrived with between 1,000 and 1,500 men, enabling the rising to begin with a march across country to Edinburgh recruiting and raising 'contributions' from the burghs. He was joined by a number of Lowland lords en route. For Locheil and his ilk the choices may have been limited, but their tenants and clansmen, who comprised over half the army, had no choice at all. Two points need to be made regarding their participation. First, by this stage the supposed difference between 'clan' and 'feudal' levies is less significant than it appears, since many of the clan territories in fact corresponded to the areas where the members held their tenure. Second, the distinction between those who went willingly and those who were forced out is irrelevant—those who 'chose' to go would have been forced even if they had not so chosen. Smith's use of the term 'carried' is certainly correct, as many of Locheil's 'people' were less than enthusiastic about participating in the rising. A deposition made after it was crushed gives some examples of how the 'gentle Locheil' managed to raise his force. According to this account, on 15

August 24 men, led by the tacksmen, arrived in Rannoch where they 'went from house to house on both sides of the Loch Rannoch...and intimated to all the Camerons, which are pretty numerous on both sides of the loch, that if they did not forthwith go with them, they would that instant proceed to burn all their houses and hough [ie hamstring] all their cattle; whereupon they carried off all the Rannoch men, about 100, mostly of the name of Cameron'.[29] Even among those who did go willingly, the need for economic survival took precedence over cultural deference. It is instructive in this context to contrast the response of clansmen in the western Highlands who experienced this final push into willing rebellion and the Atholl clansmen in Perthshire—on the very border of the Lowlands—who did not, and consequently had in the majority of cases to be forced out. Many chiefs had responded to their need for revenue by increasing the rents due from their tacksmen, who in turn passed these on to their sub-tenants. This pressure was compounded in the western Highlands by severe climatic conditions that produced a run of bad harvests from 1741 onwards, particularly in 1743 and 1744, and to starvation among the cattle herds. The consequent absence of stock to sell at the markets induced a precipitous decline in income among the tenants and sub-tenants for whom cattle grazing was the main non-subsistence economic activity. Inevitably these peasants had difficulty paying their rent.

'Forcing out' was not confined to the Highlands and also occurred on the Hanoverian side in, for example, the regiment raised by Lord Loudon, but this merely emphasises the extent to which these feudal levies were still generally operative throughout Scotland, regardless of political affiliation. Of course, the majority of British troops were not forced out in the technical sense, but were usually compelled to join the forces by economic compulsion and sometimes even by the press gang. While the alternatives may have been almost equally grim for those concerned—although there is no record of even the press gang burning down the family homes of their victims—the difference between 'unfree' compulsion and the 'freedom' to starve is almost a textbook example of the difference between a feudal and a capitalist labour market.

The Jacobite army faced no opposition as they marched south east to the capital along the roads so carefully constructed by General Wade 20 years before. By 4 September they had taken Perth, where they were joined by, among others, Lord George Murray, the greatest military leader to support the cause since Claverhouse. By 16 September the rebels had arrived at the suburbs of Edinburgh and, in the early hours of the next morning, a contingent of Highlanders successfully rushed the main gate. At daybreak on 21 September the Hanoverian army was attacked at Prestonpans by the Jacobite army using the Highland charge for the first time since Killiecrankie, and to similar effect. Although the opposing armies were roughly the same size, there was no way that the exhausted Hanoverians, most of whom were invalids who had never expected to see serious combat, could face an onslaught of this nature. Most broke and ran after ten minutes, leaving behind the broadsword-mangled corpses of their comrades, although, contrary to what was later claimed, there is no evidence that the Jacobites killed prisoners or mutilated bodies after the fighting had ceased. Charles found himself with Scotland at his feet, and with only one serious confrontation with the enemy.

How was this possible? It was not because of support from the Lowlands population, who were unremittingly hostile. Lord Kames, who may be taken as representative of contemporary Enlightenment thought, saw the opposition between the Jacobite movement and the Hanoverian state in the starkest terms: 'Are we to follow the Rules of England or France? Are we to be guided by the Law as at present established, or as it was three Centuries ago?' This sense of crisis allowed him to reassert the case against Divine Right in terms unheard since the eclipse of the Radical Whigs and Fletcher after 1688, writing that 'hereditary Right may be laid aside altogether without any Crime; since the Good of the Society is an Object of much greater Importance than the Right of any particular Family can be'.[30]

More important were the views of the Presbyterian ministers, because they were guaranteed an audience among the poorer and middling sort. A Jacobite victory would not only cost them their individual posts—in the same way that the Williamite victory of 1689 had cost those of the Episcopalians—but would in all likelihood spell the end for the Kirk By Law Established as an institution. Adam Ferguson, an even greater Enlightenment figure than Kames, was at this time a minister by profession and, in a speech to Hanoverian Highland troops, he gave reasons both political and religious for opposing the rising. One was that a Jacobite victory would inevitably mean domination by France:

> But even let us suppose the French only meant to seat this Pretender on the Throne of Britain, and leave him afterwards the free Management

114

of the Kingdom. What can we expect in our civil and religious Concerns from a Popish King, but the Subversion of our Liberty, and the entire Corruption of our Religion?

Under the present regime, he argued:

Your Persons and Liberty is [sic] secured, your Religion is established pure and undefiled, according to the Word of God. What Change for the better this Rebellion would bring, is not easily conceived.[31]

The last point was the most convincing, since it did not require listeners to believe that the Hanoverian world was the best possible, simply that a Jacobite one would be worse. Similar arguments, no doubt less eloquently expressed, were being put in parishes across the Lowlands. In many places they continued to be put even under Jacobite occupation.

Hostility was not solely the preserve of those with most to lose—Enlightenment intellectuals, Presbyterian ministers and Whig dignitaries. All in all, seven Lowland towns between Stirling and Berwick, including those which were occupied by the Jacobites, proclaimed Loyal Addresses when to do so still involved an element of risk. There were a number of occasions in which the citizens of the conquered towns mounted some form of resistance against the Jacobites. In some cases this took a mainly passive form, but in Dundee, Perth and Stirling it ascended to the level of armed resistance. While Charles was occupying Perth, 200 to 300 Highlanders had captured Dundee on 8 September. The town was defenceless, and the magistrates declined to offer resistance. The Highlanders arrived on Saturday, and during church service the following day Presbyterian ministers continued to argue support for the Hanoverian regime. The council swore allegiance to George on 26 September, and on 30 October his birthday was celebrated with the usual fireworks and bonfires, after which the crowd chased the Jacobite imposed governor out of town. A similar pattern is visible, in even more extreme form, in Perth. After the bulk of the rebel army had marched on to Edinburgh, the crowd similarly turned on the notorious Jacobite zealot Oliphant of Gask who was acting as treasurer and deputy governor of the town. Gask and his supporters were only saved by the arrival of 300 members of Clan MacIntosh. The rising against the Jacobites seems to have brought a response, since the town council minutes are silent from 11 November to 8 February, suggesting that the magistrates were prevented from meeting. What is certain is that, in response to opposition by the kirk, services were halted from mid-December. But events in Perth were not alone in showing a level of opposition to Charles extending to physical resistance.

The Jacobites laid siege to Stirling from 4 January 1746, to be met by opposition from the inhabitants as well as a lesser number of militia. The magistrates, on the other hand, wanted to surrender the town. Accordingly, on the morning of 8 January 1746 the militia were ordered to hand in their weapons at the castle. Some of the civilian defenders, however, refused to concede defeat, took up arms themselves, elected their own officers and resumed the defence. In the end the burgh surrendered several days later, after receiving assurances that it would neither be sacked nor taxes be raised from the inhabitants. It is frequently argued that the Scottish population below elite level were neutral with regard to 'the two kings and their rights', and as far as the Highlands were concerned this may well have been the case. The evidence from the Lowlands, however, suggests that at least a large minority in some of the bigger burghs were prepared to physically oppose the Jacobites when they had the chance. It was not a matter of indifference to them who won.

In reality Jacobite success was down to three factors. The first was the lack of any central state authority in Scotland capable of mobilising opposition to Charles. During the '15, opposition to the Jacobites had been generated from within civil society itself by Argyll and a host of lesser Hanoverian lords who had mobilised their tenants against the rising. This did not happen during the '45. The government, in a typical act of mean spiritedness, had refused to reimburse its supporters for their expenditure 30 years earlier, which made most of these increasingly cost conscious gentlemen unwilling to incur the same costs twice. Even those prepared to do so would have found it difficult. The government had passed a Disarming Act after the defeat of the '15, but the only clans to do so were government supporters: opponents held onto their guns. The fruits of failing to replicate the British-state-in-England north of the border, while discouraging or demobilising the loyal local powers that had acted as a substitute, were now being harvested.

The second factor was that, conversely, the Jacobites were armed and had a tactical advantage in a small mobile army of irregulars whose officers were at least ideologically committed to their cause. The very archaic militarism of the Jacobites gave them an initial advantage in a society now geared to making money rather than making war, at least at home. In these circumstances the Jacobites did not have to be a tremendously efficient fighting force—merely the fact that they *were* a fighting force in an otherwise demilitarised society was enough, as the good burghers of Edinburgh had realised.

The third factor was that the men who staffed the state apparatus suffered from overwhelming complacency. Having cynically exaggerated the extent of the Jacobite danger for electoral purposes at the time of the Hanoverian succession and the '15, the majority of the dominant Whig party—especially in England—appear to have convinced themselves not only that the threat was extinguished, but that it had always largely been of their own invention. It was for this reason, and not only because of the necessity of supplying troops to fight the French in Flanders, that Britain was virtually unprotected when Charles landed.

Charles understood that it was necessary to invade England. London was the heart, and only by aiming for it could he persuade the French to invade in his support. Most of the Jacobite lords opposed the invasion, and it was only carried by one vote in the Council of War on 30 October 1745. Crucial to winning even this slim majority was a promise by Charles that his counter-revolution would be joined by both a supportive rising in England and an invasion from France.

Would the London government have washed their hands of the entire business and allowed Charles to retain an independent Scottish kingdom had the Jacobites remained in Scotland? It should be clear that in the context of the inter-systemic rivalry between Britain and France this outcome was absolutely excluded. In fact, as Charles correctly saw, the Jacobites had no choice but to invade England. Every day they remained in Edinburgh saw their funds diminish and any attempt to raise money through the systematic collection of the Malt Tax could have turned the passive resentment of the population into active hostility. The threat of desertions would increase and the chances of a Hanoverian counter-attack become more likely. But there was also a deeper logic at work. A strike at England was required because only with French aid could Charles hope to retain power, and the only way to persuade the French that it was worth their while committing troops was to aim for London, to offer them the prize of removing the greatest rival of the French state from the international arena.

Some 5,000 foot soldiers and 500 cavalry left Edinburgh on 31 October for the march south. Almost as soon as they had gone the Whigs retook the town with troops from the castle with a minimum of difficulty. Their territorial base in Scotland now gone, much now depended on the level of support which would be forthcoming in England. Contrary to what Charles had claimed, this was minimal. During the preparations for an abortive French invasion in 1744 a Jacobite emissary called James Butler—actually the Pretender's equerry—was sent to England to assess the situation. Sir James Hynde Cotton, a man thought correctly by the French to be one of the most important English Jacobites, and who had promised his full cooperation in the event of an invasion, first declined to meet Butler, and then protested about January as the proposed date on the grounds that it would be too cold to conduct a campaign. No doubt Cotton was concerned lest such conditions prevented him from consuming his customary six bottles of claret a day. It is sometimes said that had Charles reached London he would have been greeted enthusiastically by a population only too glad to be rid of the unpopular Hanoverian regime and its corrupt parliament. Given the apparently unstoppable Jacobite advance, there was little to stop them doing so, yet less than 400 responded, mostly Catholics. As Ian Gilmour puts it, in his best Tory-Marxist mode, 'Whatever their words, the actions of the English Jacobites were in favour of the [Hanoverian] regime'.[32]

The Jacobites reached as far as Derby, 130 miles from London, avoiding engagement with the enemy except for a successful, if largely irrelevant, siege of Carlisle. Now they were faced with the prospect of being caught between three separate forces, many of whose soldiers were veterans recalled from Flanders as an earnest of how seriously the government now took the situation. His own Council of War forced the retreat from Derby on Charles. While Charles sulked in his tent, Murray staged a brilliant tactical retreat back to the Highlands, winning a minor encounter at Clifton in the north of England and achieving a decisive victory over the Hanoverians at Falkirk on the way. None of this mattered, for the real balance of forces now began to reveal itself. Conflicts within the French court over the prospects for the rising had delayed the launch of a supportive invasion until December, at which point it had to be postponed as the result of bad weather. The French never regained the initiative, and thereafter British naval superiority ensured that neither military nor financial aid crossed the Channel. Meanwhile, the Hanoverian army, commanded by George's youngest son, William, Duke of Cumberland, moved deep into Scotland, deeper than any army had done since the days of Cromwell, burning as it went.

The Jacobites were exhausted, hungry and below full strength when Charles chose to confront the Hanoverians on Culloden Moor near Inverness on 16 April 1746. The decision to make a stand at this point was not simply because of the incompetence of his mainly Irish advisers; the blockade of France had prevented money reaching the rebels and this meant that the situation was unlikely to improve. The Hanoverian troops were supported by artillery and equipped with flintlock muskets and bayonets. And, even though they outnumbered the Jacobites by something like 9,000 to 5,000, the majority of the government troops were not even required to fight, for to compound the military imbalance still further, the site was flat boggy terrain (the Gaelic name for the moor translates into English as 'Yellow Bog') which deprived the Highland contingent of any element of surprise and provided their opponents with unprotected targets for their mortars and cannon. No previous Jacobite rising had been faced by a British army shaped by the 'Military Revolution'; it was only now that the full military might of the British state was brought to bear on internal rebellion for the first time. 'As exposure to the atmosphere reduces all mummies to instant dissolution', wrote Marx, 'so war passes extreme judgement on social systems that have outlived their vitality'.[33]

Charles waited for Cumberland to attack, but the Hanoverian cannon instead subjected his army to bombardment at close range—latterly with grapeshot—for at least a quarter of an hour, firing at men who were given orders neither to retreat nor advance but were simply left presenting themselves as targets until Charles and his advisers decided what strategy to follow. When the order to charge finally came the Jacobite forces ran straight into the rifles and bayonets of the Hanoverian troops. Few even made it as far as the enemy lines, and those that did fared little better. As the Jacobites understandably turned to flee they were pursued by dragoons and horse, 'and then followed a general carnage', by the end of which, 'The moor was covered with blood; and our men, what with killing the enemy, dabbling their feet in the blood, and splashing it about one another, looked like so many butchers'.[21] In such circumstances it is no surprise that the outcome was decided in less than half an hour. A comparison of the respective casualty lists tells its own story: 60 Hanoverian dead; over 2,000 Jacobite. Yet many of the latter were killed, not on the battlefield, but on the road from Culloden to Inverness.

With the Jacobites in full flight, the Hanoverians began a systematic sweep of the moor, clubbing, stabbing, bayoneting and shooting the wounded as they lay on the ground. And the slaughter did not stop on the day of battle itself. Of all the troops who fought at Culloden, the only ones who were allowed to surrender were the French, who were, in the eyes of the Hanoverian state, fellow civilised Europeans and not dirty savages like the Highlanders who were little better than Native Americans (who were of course shortly to be treated in much the same way). The fate of those who were not summarily executed varied. Of the 3,463 listed, 88 died of wounds or illness in prison, 120 were executed (including 40 deserters from the Hanoverian army), 936 transported, 348 banished (including 126 who were allowed to go to America), 1,287 set free (including 387 French and Spanish) and 684 whose fate is unknown, although a large percentage of these must also have died of neglect in the prison hulks to which the prisoners were taken. Beyond these recorded casualties, however, hundreds, perhaps thousands, of civilians suffered for a cause which was never theirs.

What was the cause of this savagery? The Hanoverian army did not 'lose control'—the favourite excuse for British atrocities from Culloden down to Bloody Sunday in Derry and on to the Basra road. Nor will it do to blame the remnants of the Jacobite leadership for refusing to submit immediately after the battle, as if the atrocities would somehow have remained uncommitted had they not briefly reassembled at Ruthven in Baddenoch in the days immediately after the battle. In fact, the ferocity of the Hanoverians was both licensed and encouraged from the top. The brutal behaviour of systematically brutalised men—schooled both in the lash and the rigours of continental service—was deliberately fostered by black propaganda concerning Jacobite ill treatment of prisoners after Prestonpans, and orders to give 'no quarter' before Culloden. These allegations had little substance, and nor did the Jacobite rank and file commit atrocities unsanctioned by their officers. Even the bitterest critics of the Jacobite army conceded their discipline. In fact, the Hanoverian High Command decided on these tactics for two reasons. The first was to avenge, but also retrospectively to justify, their previous defeats by portraying the Jacobites as superhuman savages against whom any actions were permissible. The second was the grim logic which said that the only way to prevent any regrouping of the enemy or any future rising was to unleash such a tidal wave of violence that no one who survived it would ever again consider rising against the new order.

The worst examples of this ferocity were displayed by Lowland Hanoverians towards Highland Jacobites, both on the battlefield and in the subsequent harrying of the Highlands. This has been a major factor in fixing the war as a cultural—or, as we would say nowadays—

'ethnic' clash. There is no need, however, to employ such useless metaphysical notions. There is always a danger when using terms like 'ethnic cleansing' from a position of support for, or at least of sympathy with those being 'cleansed', that the historian comes to accept that there are indeed real 'ethnic' differences between the groups involved. There were in fact no 'ethnic' differences between the Lowlanders and the Highlanders, only social differences that had steadily been increased during the preceding century, as the pace of feudal and then capitalist development in the Lowlands outstripped that of the Highlands. From the 1640s the Highlanders had increasingly come to be described in terms of 'Celtic' as opposed to 'Saxon' racial characteristics. This racism reached its climax in the aftermath of Culloden. The issues involved were, as is usually the case, political.

The rising in England had produced a ferocious xenophobia towards the 'Rebellious Scots' whom the national anthem, written at this time, enjoins George II to crush. It is important to note, however, that this was a relatively new development. Lowlanders had generally been taken as typical Scots, but the rising temporarily reversed this identification; the Highlanders were now taken to stand for the Scots as a whole, and the Highlanders, as several outraged English subjects now came forward to testify, were barbarians or worse. The double identification of the Highland Clans with Jacobitism as a political movement on the one hand, and the Scots as a nation on the other, made it easier for those at the top of the Hanoverian state apparatus to adopt the attitude they did towards the Scots as a people. For the Scottish ruling class and their ideologues it was therefore of paramount importance that those areas that had remained loyal turned the distinctions between themselves and the rebels from matters of degree into those of absolute difference.

The great Enlightenment thinkers, for whom the Highlands represented everything from which they wished to escape, later theoretically enshrined the ideological manoeuvre whereby the Highlands were to be regarded as completely distinct from the Lowlands. It should be added, however, that this was a retreat from their earlier clarity regarding the feudal nature of the Highlands, a retreat which was compounded by the later romanticisation of the (largely mythical) Highlanders which became fashionable from the 1760s onwards. The theory of social development bequeathed by the Scottish Enlightenment is one of the great intellectual achievements of the modern epoch, but the fact that they identified the inhabitants of the Scottish Highlands as examples of the first and most primitive stage of that development helped contribute towards an obscurantism—the supposedly absolute social difference between the Highlands and the Lowlands—whose dismal effects are with us still.

The measures to ensure that the '45 could never be repeated took the form of a barrage of new laws. The Tenures Abolition Act itself abolished wardholding—whereby personal and, more importantly, military services were performed in exchange for grants of land—and replaced it with nominal cash payments. The Disarming Act re-asserted earlier legislation forbidding the possession of arms, and this of course complemented the abolition of military service. Equally significant were two other clauses. The first banned the bagpipes and all outward expression of clan identity, old (the plaid) and new (the kilt), as weapons of war. The only groups exempt from these prohibitions—and they were very important indeed—were the Highland regiments, some of whom had already seen service against the clans at Culloden. The second struck at the heart of the Episcopalian ideology that had sustained Jacobitism since 1688. It insisted that all tutors, masters and chaplains in private schools or households publicly take an oath of allegiance to George II and 'his heirs and successors' in order to qualify to teach at all. The penalties for unqualified preaching or teaching, or for employing someone unqualified to do so, extended to transportation. The most significant legislation of all was the Heritable Jurisdictions Act of 1747. The way in which the jurisdictions had been used to mobilise support for the rising meant that their relative usefulness to the British state was well and truly at an end. Now they were all to be swept away, with the exception of the Baron Courts, which were retained for the purposes of enforcing payment of arrears and adjudicating on small claims. Abolition covered the entire country, and no exceptions were granted even for those, like Argyll, who were the most loyal supporters of the regime.

International comparisons

The most helpful comparisons with the revolution in Scotland, and the events which followed it, can be found over 100 years later, in nations which did not exist during the period between the Glorious Revolution and the '45. During the 1860s the unifications of Italy, Germany and the US marked the climax of their respective bourgeois revolutions. In each case these were mainly imposed from above by the state power of the most advanced geographical area—Piedmont, Prussia and the North respectively—expanding its control over the backward adjacent regions and incorporating them into a new nation state. Despite the resulting internal unevenness, each was then set irreversibly on the road to capitalist industrialisation. In fact, of the three examples, the US experience, although on a much greater scale than that of Britain, provides the closest parallel. For whereas the Piedmontese and Prussian forces came to dominance by defeating, intimidating, bribing or even persuading smaller states to join them in new political formations, the North initially entered the American Civil War to prevent the secession of a major part of the existing nation state. Of course the Jacobites were not merely involved in an attempt at secession for Scotland, but in overthrowing the existing state throughout the territory of the British Isles. Ultimately, however, this was also the goal of the Confederacy in relation to the United States. Once battle was joined, the aims of the Confederacy were to expand slave production northwards to areas where it had never previously existed, retarding the advance of industrial capitalism and free wage labour and, as a result, placing the US as a whole under the informal control of the British Empire for whom most of Southern cotton exports were destined. The analogy cannot be pursued too far—Scotland was itself divided by civil war in a way that the Confederate states never were—but it nevertheless indicates the pattern of 'revolution from above' into which the Scottish Revolution falls, or rather, foreshadows. By some point in the second half of the 18th century, even before the French Revolution, the capitalist system had taken on a purely economic momentum which made bourgeois domination unstoppable and irreversible, regardless of the temporary political setbacks suffered by individual revolutions in, for example, 1848. Gettysburg did not, therefore, have the same significance as Culloden. For, even if the Confederacy had won that battle and gone on to win the Civil War, the ultimate victory of industrial capitalism across the entire territory of what is now the US would sooner or later have followed, either through a renewed attempt by the North or adaption by the Confederate ruling class to the new capitalist order, in the manner of the Prussian Junkers or Japanese Samurai. This was not the situation in Scotland during 1745-46.

Had the Jacobites, and through them, absolutist France, been victorious, Britain, the most dynamic economy in the new system and the only significant state geared to capitalist accumulation, would have been severely weakened and its greatest opponent given a further lease of life. The Jacobites would have been incapable of reimposing feudalism over the whole of Britain—the relative economic weight of Scotland was too slight, and the development of capitalist agriculture elsewhere too great for that to be possible—but they could have established a regime more subservient to French absolutism than even that of Charles II the previous century. In practical terms this would have removed the main obstacle to French hegemony in Europe, opened up British colonial possessions to its embrace and, at the very least, reversed the land settlement—particularly in Ireland—that resulted from the English Revolution. Britain would have been, of necessity, reduced to a satellite of France. For, even assuming that the seizure of London had miraculously restored the Jacobite convictions of wavering supporters, their very lack of a firm social base in England would have forced the new regime to rely on the force of French arms for its existence.

The '45 was therefore far from being the historical anomaly inevitably doomed to failure that is so often portrayed. This violent irruption of the old world into the new finally bestirred the British bourgeoisie into performing its final act as a revolutionary class. For this was a war fought by them, not only to defend the achievements of the revolutions that brought them to power, but also to preserve the independent existence of their state. In that context, Culloden was not a minor event, significant, if at all, only to the Scots, but one of the most decisive battles in British and world history.

The revolution after the revolution

The very fact that Culloden had been necessary indicated how backward the indigenous forces of Scottish capitalism remained compared with those of England. What were in England the economic and social preconditions for revolution would in Scotland have to be the consequences of it. The Union would always be 'incomplete' so long as this unevenness prevailed. Before the '45, the process of combined and uneven development in Scotland involved borrowing enough from the more advanced English society to keep the backward Scottish society in place. After the '45, Scotland was still underdeveloped in relation to England, but the removal of institutional impediments to capitalism now allowed a quite unprecedented transformation of Scottish life. The resulting 'skipping over of intermediate stages' would, in the space of decades, bridge the unevenness that had separated the two societies. In

1814 Walter Scott completed his first novel, *Waverley*, which recounts the adventures of the eponymous hero during the '45. Near the end, the omnipresent narrator looks back from his vantage point in 1805 at the changes which had taken place in Scotland over the preceding 60 years. His summary is a classic description of the process of combined and uneven development as it now impacted on Scotland:

> There is no European nation which, within the course of half a century or little more, has undergone so complete a change as the kingdom of Scotland. The effects of the insurrection of 1745—the destruction of the patriarchal power of the Highland chiefs, the abolition of the heritable jurisdictions of the Lowland nobility and barons, the total eradication of the Jacobite party, which, averse to intermingle with the English, or adopt their customs, long continued to pride themselves upon maintaining ancient Scottish manners and customs—commenced this innovation. The gradual influx of wealth and extension of commerce have since united to render the present people of Scotland a class of beings as different from their grandfathers, as the existing English are from those of Queen Elizabeth's time.[35]

There were two aspects to this process.

The first aspect was the dominance of an unfettered capitalist economy. Some Marxists, in reaction to unfeasably heroic depictions of the rise of the bourgeoisie, have tended to exaggerate the extent to which feudal landowners had voluntarily transformed themslves into agrarian capitalists by the mid-18th century, or even the mid-17th century. The case is overstated even for England and completely misleading for the rest of Europe. In so far as 'self transformation' was a common European experience, it was one which can be dated from after 1815 and, more specifically, after 1848, when the surviving absolutist regimes attempted, with widely differing degrees of enthusiasm and consistency, to reconstruct the state machine so as to compete more effectively against their modernised British and French rivals. Prussia, or rather Imperial Germany, had by 1871 clearly emerged as the most successful of these. Similarly, their predominantly agrarian ruling classes were sufficiently impressed with the productivity of English and Lowland Scottish agriculture to seek to emulate its achievements. Yet no other nation would ever again have the luxury of the prolonged emergence of agrarian capitalist relations which characterised English history between the Black Death and the passing of the Enclosure Acts. The alternatives were either to make minimal adjustments and run the risk of peasant revolts comparable to those which accompanied the French Revolution—which was ultimately the fate the Russian autocracy—or replace the existing methods of exploitation with those which prevailed in Britain. As with the recasting of the state, it was Prussia which was at the forefront of this process, so much so that, looking back from his vantage point at the beginning of the 20th century, Lenin discerned two distinct paths towards capitalist agriculture in Europe and its overseas extensions, which he defined respectively as the 'Prussian' and 'American' paths:

> The survivals of serfdom may fall away either as a result of the transformation of the landlord economy or as a result of the abolition of the landlord latifundia, ie, either by reform or revolution. Bourgeois development may proceed by having big landlord economies at the head which will gradually become more and more bourgeois and gradually substitute bourgeois for feudal methods of exploitation. It may also proceed by having small peasant economies at the head, which in a revolutionary way, will remove the 'excrescence' of the feudal latifundia from the social organism and then freely develop without them along the path a capitalist economy. These two paths of objectively possible bourgeois development we would call the Prussian path and the American path, respectively.[36]

In fact, the American path was exceptional; the Prussian path typical (except in France, where the victory of peasant smallholding during the revolution established an enduring obstacle to further rural capitalist development). It is in this context that the earlier experience of Scotland is important, for the Lowlands were not only a component of the admired British model, but had been the first region to undergo what became known as the 'Prussian' path and which should be more accurately referred to as the 'Scottish' path instead. The introduction of what the theorists of the Scottish Enlightenment called 'commercial society' into the countryside, together with the profits from the tobacco and linen trades, provided the capital which allowed the industrialisation of the Lowlands to take place.

The core of the Scottish economy remained agriculture, and it was in this sector more than any other that feudal obligations still prevailed. The social power of the lords had been systematically destroyed in so far as it represented a potential threat to the British state, but their economic power over tenants remained in place. Local changes to tenurial relationships had of course taken place before 1746. But as long as these were not generalised across Scotland the possibilities of increasing productivity (and proprietorial income), let alone of feeding a growing population or accumulating capital for the purpose of investment, would remain unrealised. The revolutionary epoch was therefore followed by an intense period of socio-economic change, in which agrarian capitalism was finally introduced on a general basis by a self appointed radical elite. The revolution from above that this involved was perhaps the purest bourgeois experience in history. Unconstrained by feudal nobility behind them (since it had been destroyed by the military and juridical apparatus of the British state), unafraid of a working class before them (since it had not yet come into existence in significant numbers and would only do so as a result of their activities), the Scottish bourgeoisie were free, as no other bourgeoisie had been or would ever be, to restructure society as they wished. The greatness of the Scottish Enlightenment is at least partly explained by the need its theoreticians felt to consciously remake their world. As late as the first edition of *The Gentleman Farmer* in 1776 Lord Kames, who perfectly exemplifies the unity of theory and practice attained by the Scottish Enlightenment, thought this was some way off: 'May we not hope that our progress may be rapid; and that agriculture will soon be familiar among us, and as skilfully conducted as in England?'[37] It is instructive, therefore, to compare this very tentative optimism with the following verdict from an anonymous supplement to the sixth edition of the same book in 1815:

> It may suffice to observe in general that there never were greater agricultural improvements carried on in any country than there have been in Scotland during the last 30 years; that the progress of the most correct systems of husbandry has been rapid and extensive beyond what the most sanguine could have anticipated; and that, in short, when we contrast the present state of agriculture in the south eastern counties with what must have been its state about the middle of the last century...the efforts of several centuries would seem to have been concentrated in the intermediate period.[38]

Some unsystematic but suggestive indices of economic growth show what flowed from the transformation of agriculture. In 1755 the Scottish population was calculated as being 1,265,000, virtually the same as in 1688; by 1801 it had risen to over 1,600,000, and by 1831 to well over two million. In 1700 Scotland was only the tenth most urbanised country in Western Europe; by the 1750s it was seventh, by 1800 it was fourth and by 1850 it was second only to England. And the rate of urban growth was the highest anywhere. Let one measure of economic buoyancy—the increase in rent—stand for all those that could be cited. Between 1660 and 1740 the national average of real rent doubled, between 1660 and 1770 it increased threefold, between 1660 and 1793 it increased by 7.6 times and between 1660 and 1811 it increased 15-fold. When the rate of increase finally began to stabilise at the end of the Napoleonic Wars in 1815, the total increase in real terms from 1660 may have been of the order of 15.6 times. In a relatively short time the Scottish economy had risen to equal that of England, and may even have surpassed it: between 1750 and 1800, Scottish overseas commerce grew by 300 percent, compared to a 200 percent increase in England. In short, if the Scottish economy had been separated from that of England, it could truly be said to have 'caught up and overtaken' the latter: change on such a scale would not be seen again until the industrialisation of Russia after 1929.

But Scotland was no longer separate from England, and this was of crucial importance for the second aspect of Scottish development: the formation of a national consciousness in Scotland. The completion of the bourgeois revolution involves more than the elimination of feudalism and its replacement by capitalism. Whatever the form taken by the revolutionary process, the content has typically involved the creation of a capitalist nation state with an attendant national consciousness among the population. In Scotland, of course, far from the nation state being born with the revolution, the embryo was aborted before the revolution was anywhere near completion. Scottish national consciousness did not exist in 1320, nor in 1560, nor even in 1707. The Lowlands were in the process of developing a sense of nationhood by the latter date, but this was a process from which the Highlands were largely excluded and which was in any event cut short by the Treaty of Union. It follows then that the Scottish national consciousness that we know today arose after the Union and could not have been preserved by institutions carried over from the pre-Union period. Consequently, Scottish nationhood was a product of the Union, for only after the Union were the material obstacles to nationhood—lack of capitalist development and the divide between the Highlands and the Lowlands—overcome. The historical events that are supposed to prove the existence of Scottish nationhood before 1707 were in fact presented in this way only after that date, when they were retrospectively assimilated to the national myth. A Scottish national consciousness did arise, but only within the context of the British state and in tandem with the formation of a British national consciousness. Highlanders played an important role in the formation of both. In particular, their role as colonists and soldiers in North America—occupations they had been forced into as a result of the destruction of their society after the '45—brought the admiration of the honest burghers who had once trembled at their approach. There is a bitter irony in the fact that the Highlander again came to stand for the Scottish nation as a whole, not as the enemy within, but as the warrior vanguard of British imperialism.

Although the majority of Scots have a dual national *consciousness*, comprising different combinations of Scottishness and Britishness, the former has, for all practical purposes, always been subordinate to the latter. From some point between 1746 and 1820, all classes in Scotland began, for different reasons, to treat the British aspect of their national identity as *politically* decisive, and to regard the Scottish aspect as an essentially cultural matter. The political identification with 'Britishness' has by no means been an unconditional good—where it has encouraged working class identification with the British state, then it has acted as barrier to socialism—but where it has involved recognition of the collective interests of the British working class, then it has offered the best possibility of achieving it.

Conclusion

I began this essay by outlining some of the theoretical difficulties which Marxist historians have found with the concept of a Scottish bourgeois revolution. I want to end by looking at another reason why the process has been so little recognised by the left, particularly in Scotland itself. This is not a failure to recognise the existence of revolution through a deficient theoretical model, but rather a refusal to recognise it because the revolution does not play the role expected from it as the emotional centrepiece of a national tradition of popular radicalism.

Socialists are often tempted into assessing the significance of bourgeois revolutions in so far as they leave us examples of popular mobilisation that can inform and inspire our own activities. This is the wrong emphasis, and not only because so few bourgeois revolutions can actually play this role. For Scottish socialists the Scottish Revolution cannot occupy the same place that comparable events do for socialists in England and France—or even in Italy and the US. On the one hand, unlike 1642 in England or 1792 in France, at no point in the Scottish Revolution were popular interventions *decisive* in shaping the outcome. The key turning points do not involve the revolutionary crowd storming Edinburgh Castle or a *levée-en-masse* overwhelming royalist armies against all odds, but deals struck in snuff-filled rooms off Edinburgh High Street and royal troops hunting down defeated peasants across Culloden Moor. On the other hand, unlike 1870 in Italy or 1871 in Germany, the end result was not the establishment of a modern nation state, but the dismantling of its foundations and their absorption into a new state dominated by an historic enemy. Whichever way the matter is approached, both 'the people' and 'the nation' are absent.

The Scottish Revolution took a particular form that indeed makes it difficult to celebrate as part of a revolutionary tradition. It seems to me mistaken to argue that it could have been different—since the alternatives did not exist—and pointless to argue that it should have been different—since this presupposes a normative model of revolutionary development wholly at odds with the actual historical record. The completion of the Scottish Revolution was, at the same time, the completion of the British Revolution. The formation of the Scottish working class was, at the same time, part of the formation of the British working class. These facts make it unlikely that there will ever be a second, proletarian Scottish Revolution separate from one in Britain as a whole. We can, however, be certain of one thing. Any revolution that the Scottish working class does help to make will, of necessity, be quite unlike the one which brought it into existence.

Notes

1   This essay summarises, in schematic form, the argument of my two forthcoming books, *Discovering The Scottish Revolution: The Decline of Scottish Feudal Society and the Origins of the British Capitalist State, 1688-1746* and *The Origins of National Consciousness in Scotland*. Evidence to support the various claims made here can be found in their accompanying references.

2   See J Foster, 'Capitalism and the Scottish Nation', in G Brown (ed), *The Red Paper On Scotland* (Edinburgh, 1975), pp143, 144, for an example of the first position, and J D Young, *The Rousing of the Scottish Working Class* (London, 1979), p29, for an example of the second.

3   See for example E J Hobsbawm, 'Scottish Reformers of the Eighteenth Century and Capitalist Agriculture', E J Hobsbawm et al (eds), *Peasants In History* (Calcutta, 1980), p7.

4   See for example 'Notes of the Month: "Scottish Nationalism",' *International Socialism* 68, first series (April 1974), p7.

5   See for example J McGrath, 'Introduction' in J McEwen, *Who Owns Scotland?* (Edinburgh, 1978), pp1-2; T Nairn, 'Scotland and Europe' in T Nairn, *The Break-Up Of Britain* (second, expanded edition, London, 1981), p109.

6   I borrow the concept of an epoch of bourgeois revolution from V I Lenin, 'The "Peasant Reform" and the Proletarian-Peasant Revolution', in V I Lenin, *Collected Works*, vol 17 (Moscow, 1963), pp125-126, although not the three conditions outlined here. See also A Gramsci, 'The Modern Prince', in A Gramsci, *Selections from the Prison Notebooks of Antonio Gramsci*, edited and translated by Q Hoare and G Nowell-Smith (London, 1971), pp179-180.

7   Marxist accounts of Scottish development which argue that the bourgeois revolution opened with the Reformation are therefore wide of the mark, even though these tend to identify the closing date correctly as 1746. See, in particular, the interesting essay by George Kerevan, written before he turned from orthodox Trotskyism to free market Scottish nationalism, 'The Origins of Scottish Nationhood: Arguments Within Scottish Marxism', *The Bulletin Of Scottish Politics*, vol 1, no2 (Spring 1981), p128. See also N Davidson and D Gluckstein, 'Nationalism and the Class Struggle in Scotland', *International Socialism* 48, second series (Autumn 1990), p111. Generally speaking, the sections of this article which deal with pre-capitalist Scotland—for which I was solely responsible—repeat many of the misconceptions about Scottish history which I now criticise here.

8   J Steuart, *An Inquiry Into The Principles Of Political Economy*, edited with an introduction by A S Skinner (2 volumes, Edinburgh and London, 1966), vol 1, p108.

9   T Kirke, 'A Modern Account of Scotland by an English Gentleman', in P Hume Brown (ed), *Early Travelers In Scotland* (Edinburgh, 1978, facsimile of the 1891 edition), p261.

10 D Stewart, *Sketches of the Character, Institutions and Customs of the Highlanders of Scotland: With Details of the Military Service of the Highland Regiments* (new edition, Inverness, 1885), p58.

11 L D Trotsky, *The History of the Russian Revolution* (London, 1977), p27.

12 H R Trevor-Roper, 'Religion, the Reformation and Social Change' in
    H R Trevor-Roper, *Religion, Reformation and Social Change* (London, 1967),
    p33.

13 *The Complaynt Of Scotland... With An Appendix Of Contemporary English Tracts*,
    re-edited from the originals with an introduction and glossary by J A H Murray
    (London, 1822), p106.

14 F Engels, 'The Peasant War in Germany', in K Marx and F Engels, *Collected
    Works*, vol 10 (London, 1975), pp469-470.

15 Cromwell to the General Assembly of the Church of Scotland, 3 August 1650,
    in T Carlyle (ed), *Oliver Cromwell's Letters and Speeches: With Elucidations*, vol 3
    (London, 1872), p18.

16 [T Margetts], '[News-letter from Scotland]', 24 October 1648, *The Clarke Papers:
    Selections From The Papers Of William Clarke, Secretary To The Council Of The
    Army, 1647-1649, And To General Monck And The Commanders Of The Army In
    Scotland, 1651-1660*, edited by C H Firth with a new preface by A Woodrych (2
    volumes, London, 1992), vol 2, p46.

17 T Thomson (ed), *Acts Of The Scottish Parliament*, vol 7, part 2 (Edinburgh,
    1822), p89.

18 Ibid, vol 9, pp38-39.

19 Matthew 6.21.

20 Council of Caledonia to the Governor of Carthegena, 11 March 1699, *The Darien
    Papers: Being A Selection Of Original Letters and Official Documents Relating to the
    Establishment Of A Colony At Darien By The Company Of Scotland Trading To
    Africa And The Indies, 1695-1700*, edited by J Hill Burton (Edinburgh, 1859), p92.

21 T Thomson (ed), op cit, vol 11, pp404-406.

22 A Fletcher, 'Speeches by a Member of the Parliament Which Began at
    Edinburgh the 6th of May, 1703', Speech 13, 9 September 1703, in J Robertson
    (ed), *Political Works* (Cambridge, 1998), pp160-161.

23 *A Short Letter to the Glasgow Men* (1706), p2.

24 [J Hodges], *War Between The Two British Kingdoms Considered...For The Mutual
    Interest Of Both* (London, 1705), p40.

25 G Lukács, 'Critical Observations on Rosa Luxemburg's "Critique of the Russian
    Revolution",' in G Lukács, *History And Class Consciousness* (London, 1971),
    p282.

26 Quoted in C Petrie, *The Jacobite Movement: The Last Phase 1716-1807* (London,
    1950), p126.

27 'Donald Cameron of Clune's Evidence at the Trial of John Cameron of
    Fassifern', 15 February 1754, quoted in J Stewart, *The Camerons* (Stirling,
    1974), pp307-308.

28 A Smith, *An Inquiry into the Nature and Causes of the Wealth of Nations*, edited
    by A S Skinner (Harmondsworth, 1970), p511.

29 *The Prisoners of the '45*, edited from the State Papers by B G Seton and J G
    Arnot, vol 1 (Edinburgh, 1928), pp270-271.

30 Lord Kames, *Essays Upon Several Subjects Concerning British Antiquities*
    (Edinburgh, 1747), pp205, 208. See also p217.

31 A Ferguson, *A Sermon Preached in the Ersh Language to His Majesty's First
    Highland Regiment of Foot, Commanded by Lord John Murray, at their Cantonment
    at Camberwell on the 18th Day of December, 1745* (London, 1746), pp18-19.

32 I Gilmour, *Riots, Risings And Revolutions* (London, 1990), p114.

33 K Marx, 'Another English Revelation', in K Marx and F Engels, *Collected Works*, vol 14, op cit, p516.

34 *The History of the Rebellion in 1745 and 1746 Extracted from 'The Scots Magazine' with an Appendix Containing an Account of the Trials of the Rebels; the Pretender and His Son's Declarations Etc* (Aberdeen, 1755), p198.

35 W Scott, *Waverley; Or, 'Tis Sixty Years Since*, edited by A Hook (Harmondsworth, 1972), p492.

36 V I Lenin, 'The Agrarian Programme of Social Democracy in the First Russian Revolution 1905-1907', in V I Lenin, *Collected Works*, op cit, vol 13, p239.

37 Lord Kames, preface to Lord Kames, *The Gentleman Farmer: Being An Attempt To Improve Agriculture By Subjecting It To The Test Of Rational Principles* (6th Edition, Edinburgh, 1815), pxii.

38 'A Supplement, Containing An Account Of The Present State Of Agriculture, And The Improvements Recently Introduced', ibid, p537.

Chapter 4

Imperialism and Scottish culture

Angus Calder

There are three eminently contentious terms in my title. Definitions of 'imperialism' abound. 'Culture' can be applied narrowly to the folk arts and/or 'high arts' of a particular aggregation of people, or exhaustively to all their lived practices. And the delimitation of 'Scottish'-ness is not easy. I hope that what I say later may helpfully ease us through these problems of definition, but I am going to begin exactly where you might expect me to start—with popular fiction by one of Scotland's best known and best loved authors, who was happy to call himself an 'imperialist' and lived and wrote in the heyday of 'imperialism', whether this is defined as the dominant ideology of the British state, as a phase in Western capitalism, or merely as a phenomenon in popular culture.

John Buchan began to publish thrillers featuring Richard Hannay—later General Sir Richard Hannay—during the First World War. *The Thirty-Nine Steps* came out in 1915, *Greenmantle* in 1916 and *Mr Standfast* in 1919. All three feature conspiracies by diabolically clever master spies against British power. Their plots depend on amazing coincidences and involve nightmarish sequences in which Hannay is pursued over awkward terrains by fiendish adversaries, changing clothes and accents repeatedly to disguise his identity. In his dedication of *The Thirty-Nine Steps* to Thomas Arthur Nelson, in whose publishing business Buchan had been a partner, he confesses to his affection for the works of light fiction known as 'dime novels' in the US and 'shockers' in Britain—'where the incidents defy the probabilities and march just inside the borders of the possible'. His short novel derived from a serious bout of illness in which he felt 'driven' to write a 'shocker'

135

for himself. But now, with the Great War raging, 'the wildest fictions are so much less improbable than the facts.' So he has it both ways. He admits that his fiction is not serious in its intention, yet insinuates that it somehow corresponds, albeit inadequately, to contemporary reality... Buchan, over age for service, and initially unfit, did not enjoy the Great War at all when he finally found his way to France as an Intelligence Corps officer. Numerous dear friends, including Nelson, were killed. But Buchan's faith in the British Empire, its peoples and its beneficent destiny, enabled him to present the war, in his 'shockers', as a contest between victorious Good and thwarted Evil.

Having it both, or all, ways turns out to be typical of Buchan's discourse, matching salient features of his biography. Born in Perth, a son of the Manse, in 1875 and schooled in Glasgow, he nevertheless identified most strongly with the landscape and traditions of the Borders where he spent boyhood summers. From Glasgow University he proceeded to Brasenose College, where he shone academically and socially and acquired an abiding devotion to the landscapes of Oxfordshire. He diverted from his chosen career at the London Bar to serve Lord Milner, the statesman sent out to reconstruct South Africa after the Boer War. He was not the first or the last Scot to fall in love with Africa, where, employed on various administrative tasks over a couple of years, he roamed vast unspoilt tracts of 'Nature'. His first famous novel, *Prester John*, had an African basis. His Hannay is an idealised self projection. Hannay is not a deep intellectual, like Buchan. His posture as a self proclaimed bear (as it were) 'of very little brain' at times recalls his exact fictional coeval, P G Wodehouse's Bertie Wooster (like Hannay created with the US market very much in mind—a Brit for Yank consumption). Hannay shares Buchan's own devotion to field sports. Unlike Buchan, though, he is a serious fighting army officer. He has been formed by years roaming the Southern African *veld*, and has spent relatively little time in the Scotland of his forebears. But he is as much at home as his creator in rugged Scottish landscapes and with Scottish people of all classes.

Indeed the notion of 'Scottishness' which Buchan's shockers communicate virtually assimilates it with the famed capacities of the chameleon. Hannay's friend, Sandy Arbuthnot, another Anglo-Scot with whom he teems up in *Greenmantle*, is an astonishing linguist and master of disguise who is able to lead a cult of Middle Eastern devotees and pass himself off as a Mohammedan Messiah. In Turkey, Hannay refers to 'straths' and 'glens' as features of the local landscape, but everywhere he is haunted by memories of the South African *karoo*, revived for him by his close comradeship in thwarting Kaiser Wilhelm with an ageing Boer big game tracker, Pieter Pienaar. Scotland might be said to represent ancestry and danger, South Africa beauty and freedom. But Hannay, in *Mr Standfast*, falls for a perfect English rose, identified in his imagination with the spot in the Cotswolds where he first meets her, and where they settle when married.

Just before he is introduced to Mary Lamington, to whom Buchan rather impishly gives the name of a Scottish Border village, Hannay has:

> a kind of revelation. I had a vision of what I had been fighting for, what we were all fighting for. It was peace, deep and holy and ancient, peace deeper than the oldest wars, peace which would endure when all our swords were hammered into ploughshares. It was more; for in that hour England first took hold of me. Before, my country had been South Africa, and when I thought of home it had been the wide sun-steeped spaces of the *veld* or some scented glen of the Berg. But now I realised that I had a new home. I understood what a precious thing this little England was, how old and kindly and comforting, how wholly worth striving for. The freedom of an acre of her soil was cheaply bought by the blood of the best of us.[1]

Yet when Hannay later, in a tight corner, is restored by the thought of Mary—'looking again beyond the war, to that peace which she and I would one day inherit...a vision of a green English landscape'—there comes to his mind 'a line of an old song, which had been a favourite of my father's...

> There's an eye that ever weeps and a fair face will be fain
> When I ride through Annan Water wi' my bonny bands again!'[2]

Buchan called his engaging autobiography *Memory Hold the Door*. But his own identity seems to go round and round in a revolving door. Oxford, he claims:

> enabled me to discover Scotland. Before I came [note, not 'went'] up I had explored a great part of the Lowlands with the prosaic purpose of catching trout; but apart from my own Borders, the land, though I was steeped in its history, made no special appeal. Scottish literature, except the ballads and Sir Walter Scott, was scarcely known to me, and I had read very little of Robert Burns. but now as a temporary exile I adopted all the characteristics of a Scot abroad. I became a fervent admirer of

Burns and a lover of Dunbar and the other poets of the Golden Age. I cultivated a sentiment for all things Scottish and brought the Highlands and isles into the orbit of my interest.[3]

The physical self transformations of Hannay—rarely seen in the same clothes for more than a few pages at a time—match the psychological prestidigitation of his creator. 'Empire' gave Buchan an umbrella of identity under which he could identify passionately with South Africa and later with Canada, of which he was appointed Viceroy, while promoting the publication of new verse in the old Scots tongue (some of which he wrote himself) and professing a Scottish patriotism which verged on outright nationalist sentiment—all the time responding wholeheartedly to that vision of Deep England which inspired the English nationalist school of composers—Elgar, Vaughan Williams, Butterworth, Moeran, etc. Buchan can only be called a 'racist' in so far as he traffics freely in the racist stereotypes of his day—the brutal, methodical German, the foppish but vicious Turk, the honest Boer in tune with the natural world and so on. He is avid to find good in all 'races'—Hannay admires the spirit of a 'Portuguese Jew' who conflates in one person two often despised racial types.

Buchan's idealisation of England, as transmitted through Hannay, suggested that it represented past peace, enduring peace, and the future peace of a world civilised by the British Empire. Reminiscing in 1940, he wrote of his South African days when:

a vision of what the empire might be dawned upon certain minds with almost the force of revelation... I dreamed of a worldwide brotherhood with the background of a common race and creed, consecrated in the service of peace; Britain enriching the rest out of her culture and traditions, and the spirit of the Dominions like a strong wind freshening the stuffiness of the old lands. I saw in the Empire a means of giving the congested masses at home open country instead of a blind alley... Our creed was not based on antagonism to any other people. It was humanitarian and international; we believed that we were laying the basis of a federation of the world.[4]

While the idealism of Milner's 'Round Table' group of imperialists, so named after the journal which it published, belonged very specifically to a particular historical conjuncture, marked by the achievement of Dominion status by Australia, New Zealand and South Africa, following Canada, and early steps towards Indian home rule, the terms on which Buchan embraced England and Englishness had been long prefigured in the writings of fellow Scots, and admitted by sometimes envious Englishmen. In the novels of Buchan's boyhood and lifetime hero, Walter Scott, the peace and prosperity which had followed the suppression of the last Jacobite Rebellion represented a necessary accommodation of Scottish violence, clannishness and fanaticism with English stability and commercial prowess. Thomas Carlyle had extolled the dumb strength of John Bull—great doer, not great thinker—with the implication that he needed Scots to intellectualise for him. David Livingstone, passionately Scottish in spiritual and intellectual formation, was usually happy to be regarded as an Englishman. In Thomas Hardy's great fable, *The Mayor of Casterbridge*, a charming Scottish wanderer named Farfrae literally takes over a Wessex, west Saxon, Deep English town, representing the success of many 'Scots on the make' in English, Welsh and Irish trade and industry, in the City of London, and perhaps above all in the Colonies. Buchan flourished and wrote at a moment when the English public boarding schools exercised cultural and political hegemony, when wealthy Scots sent their sons to them, then on to Oxford and Cambridge universities, and when a composite British ruling class moved freely between clubs in London and sporting estates in the Scottish Highlands, both shared and shared alike between Anglo-Scots and their wealthy English friends. English toffs had learned to play golf; Scots played cricket. But the chameleon Scot might be seen as acting a part which the Englishman performed naturally. He could equally well identify with South Sea Islanders like R L Stevenson, with the wilds of North America, like John Muir, or with the International Workers of the World, like R B Cunninghame Graham, 'Don Roberto' to admiring Argentinians who named a city after him.

So far what I have said might seem likely to produce an argument as follows: in the heyday of the British Empire some Scots attached to the British ruling class and its strategies, represented—with charm and idealism—by Buchan, who was both politician and best selling writer, infected Scottish culture with imperialist ideas. Along with Buchan one might range the distinguished Scottish composers Alexander Mackenzie and Hamish McCunn who contributed, with Edward Elgar, compositions performed in the Empire Pageant at the 1924 British Empire Exhibition at Wembley—Mackenzie was represented by his *Britannia Overture* and McCunn by *Livingstone Episode* and *Camp and Kaffir Melodies*.[5] One might mention Harry Lauder, the former coal miner, knighted in 1919, who sang Scottish songs all over the empire to thronged halls, and was delighted in Rangoon to meet Mr Lim, 'known all over India as the Sugar King' and 'reputed to be one of the richest Chinamen in the world', who greeted him in his opulent mansion: 'Man, Harry, it's a braw, bricht moonlicht nicht the nicht, is it no? Hooch aye,' and proceeded: ' Say, Harry, ma cock, hoo wad ye like me to gie ye a blaw on the pipes?'—upon which he performed in fine style, confiding later that he had been pipe major in the Dollar Academy pipe band.[6] One might further allude to the high minded John Reith directing that great institution the BBC as it linked the empire through the airwaves and promoted a homogenised Standard Received Pronunciation, and the equally stern John Grierson, pioneering British documentary cinema at the Empire Marketing Board and moving on via the GPO Film Unit to develop documentary cinema in Canada.

But the idea that Scotland's destiny lay within the English speaking 'Commonwealth of Nations'—the very term had been coined by a Scottish politician, Lord Rosebery, in the 1880s—was not confined to people obviously hitched to the imperial establishment. One might discount as establishment axe grinding a prominent feature of the Scottish National War Memorial unveiled in 1927 in Edinburgh Castle, where above the door of the innermost shrine the branches of the Tree of Empire supported the arms of Scotland along with those of the Dominions and India. However, the memorial, under the overall charge of the architect Sir Robert Lorimer, and realised in detail by distinguished sculptors and craftsmen inspired by the arts and crafts movement, was far from being a crassly jingoistic project. In that decade when Presbyterian clerics inveighed darkly against Catholic immigration, it was not surprising that the arms of Eire, a Free State within the Commonwealth since 1923, were not represented. But that status achieved by Southern Ireland seemed to some a precedent for a self ruling Scotland. In 1928 the Reverend James Barr, an Independent Labour MP, supported by the so called 'Red Clydesiders' (Maxton, Johnston, Kirkwood and all), put forward a bill in the Commons designed to give Scotland self governing status within the empire, and this was hailed as a proposal 'within the true lines of imperial development' by none other than C M Grieve, whose verse in Scots as 'Hugh MacDiarmid' Buchan had encouraged, and who shortly figured as one of the great founders of the National Party of Scotland. For Grieve, Scotland was 'one of the great founder nations of the empire'.[7] So one might say that the ideology of empire as a beneficent force permeated even oppositional elements in Scottish political and artistic culture. Pittendreigh Macgillvary (1856-1938), though nationalistic as artist and poet, had been honoured with the title King's Sculptor in Scotland in 1921. He was naturally asked to join the General Committee organising the British Empire Exhibition at Wembley. He resigned when his suggestion that Scottish sculptors should be exhibited separately from English colleagues was turned down. But it seems just as significant that he had agreed to join the committee in the first place.[8]

It seems to me that all that I have so far suggested might seem embarrassingly self evident. In a period when Glasgow was proud of being the second city of the empire, and would host its own impressive Empire Exhibition as late as 1938, when Clyde built ships were sinews of imperial commerce and the Royal Navy, when a century of large scale emigration had linked Scottish families to far continents, when Scottish missions and the schools attached to them were profoundly influential in India and Africa, when Scots contributed a disproportionate number of regulars, volunteers and casualties to the British military effort on the Western Front of 1914-18—Scottish culture at all levels was affected by imperial sentiment, and even the opposition to the war by John Maclean was garnished by the boast that Glasgow, so important in world trade and industry, could become a second, bigger and better, Petrograd. Only retrospectively could ignorant people suggest that Scotland had been a colonised country, a victim of the English imperial drive in which, in fact, Scots had very willingly participated.

Analytically, Scotland's position in the empire had been utterly different from that of Ireland, a country colonised and subordinated by England from the 16th century, and indeed from that of Wales, a backward region where industrialisation from the 18th century had depended on English—and Scottish—capital. During a period of resurgent nationalism in all three Celtic countries, Michael Hechter's book *Internal Colonialism: The Celtic Fringe in British National Development*, published in 1975, gained a certain amount of credence, and fed into ideas suggested by Immanuel Wallerstein's theses about core and periphery in capitalist expansion. But the differing courses of politics in the three countries since then can only be explained by Scotland's lack of any overall history of colonial oppression and exploitation. While Ireland's heritage of violent resistance had a grisly sequel, and the language issue and English immigration had explosive, and divisive, power in Welsh political life, Scotland proceeded decorously, without any serious violence, towards the recovery of its own parliament in 1999. As a nation, Scotland had never ceased to exist. Under the 1707 Treaty of Union it had retained its own established church, its own system of education and, crucially, its own law and legal system. MacDiarmid's claim that it had been 'one of the great founder nations of the empire' would not have seemed at all absurd to a Canadian, New Zealander or Malawian.

I will now retreat, as I promised, to the problem of definition. I will try to be summary without being clumsy, but I hope you can forgive my simplifications.

Let us run with the broad definition of terms. When we speak of a 'indigenous American culture', we refer to all lived practices of an aboriginal people. 'Scottish culture' would accordingly refer to everything we do in Scotland—how we drink, how we marry, how we sing. Attempts have been made to isolate 'imperialism' as a recurrent phenomenon in human societies which can be studied from ancient pre-capitalist examples as well as modern ones. But it seems wisest to apply the term to the processes which first created the development of modern capitalism in Europe, from the 15th century, then generated industrial revolution, which permitted European powers and the US, in cooperation as well as rivalry, to dominate, in effect, every part of the world and opened up virtually all the earth's material resources, and most of its human populations, to profitable exploitation by metropolitan capital. 'Globalisation' such as we live with today is the latest phase of this process, and I myself would readily describe it as intrinsically 'imperialistic'.

In this context, to differentiate between Scottish 'culture' and those of other industrialised Western countries will be difficult. As both Marxist and 'social scientific' approaches to history and society have insisted, the situation of a factory worker or typist in Scotland is very similar to that of counterparts elsewhere. Differentials such as literacy rates and mortality statistics may suggest local peculiarities. (Russians clearly drink too much vodka.) Deep fried Mars bars and haggis suppers are no doubt rare in Milan, but McDonald's hamburgers are now eaten in every modern city. For several centuries a Western lifestyle has been emerging which is now adopted in Eastern societies and by Southern elites and could be described as 'Americanised', with the qualification that American lifestyle has incorporated or adapted features from many other cultures. Curries and paellas assort with pizzas and fried potatoes in our postmodernist world of instantaneous world-wide communication. Country and Western music, perversely deplored by some in Scotland as an American intrusion, is in fact a development from Scottish, Irish and English musical styles. Harry Lauder's Mr Lim had as much right to his bagpipes as we have to Peking duck.

But geographical and chronological factors have given Scotland a peculiar position in the history of imperialism/globalisation which makes it analytically possible to assign special characteristics to Scottish culture. They also serve to explain peculiarities in the work of great Scottish storytellers—Scott, Stevenson and Buchan.

Geographically, Scotland is a country slashed deeply by the sea with a relatively low ratio of fertile land. These factors have made emigration salient in history and culture. It is estimated that 100,000 people emigrated to Ireland from Britain before 1641. Some 30,000 of these were Scots and, concentrated in Ulster, they had a disproportionate effect on Irish and then, by further emigration, on North American history. But in the first four decades of the 17th century, greater numbers of Scots—40,000—are said to have emigrated to Poland, and a further 30,000 to Scandinavia.[9] Though the population of Scotland at this time was less than a million, this effusion was not of course comparable to the mass exodus from Ireland during and after the mid-19th century famine. But it did mean that the Wandering Scot—soldier, farmer, trader—was well established as prototype by the 17th. Nationalists in Scotland have latterly said a lot about our 'European' outlook as compared to the insular English. One might extrapolate backwards from, and forward to, the fictions of Smollett and Scott, Stevenson and Buchan, and argue that Scots, often short of opportunity in their own land, have long been attuned to accommodating themselves to foreign tastes, prejudices and customs. An interesting example would be Episcopalian clergymen, of a persuasion first unpopular, then, after the Glorious Revolution, outlawed in Scotland itself. Such Scots could find employment abroad, as chaplains in the unsavoury forts of the Royal African Company, or emissaries in America of the Society for the Propagation of the Gospel. The first Episcopalian bishop of the infant US was accordingly consecrated, after the American Revolution, in Aberdeen.

Another geographical factor was proximity to England. This had the effect in the 14th century of exciting Scots to a precocious nationalism and moving them towards the potentially revolutionary doctrine that kings ultimately had authority only through the consent of the people. Emulation of a dangerous and richer southern neighbour helped to inspire notable Scottish achievements around 1500, when William Dunbar consciously developed from and vied with the great master Chaucer, when James IV's navy preceded the Tudors' in solving the problem of how to mount a really heavy gun on a sailing ship, and Scottish seamen were developing a lead over English in the arts of deep sea navigation.[10] While Tudors planted English colonies in Ireland, James VI came up with the notion of colonising the Scottish *Gaeltacht*. His exploitation, after the Union of Crowns, of English conquest of Ireland gave scope for fellow Scots in colonisation, and some proceeded later in the 17th century to make East New Jersey a distinctively Scottish colony on the American seaboard. After such experience, the idea of creating a Scottish colony on the isthmus of Panama was not so daft as historians of the Darien Company of the 1690s have tended to assume. Its failure merely matched those of attempted settlements by English and other European peoples in various parts of the tropical world in the early phases of capitalist imperialism.

The English could not have stopped Scots penetrating their colonies in the 17th century even if they had seriously tried to do so. The exclusive, 'mercantilist' English Navigation Acts from 1651 onwards did not check the probes of Scots interlopers. From the Union of Parliaments in 1707, Scots were entirely within their rights to operate as equals in any British settlement. They developed overweening influence in some of the West Indian sugar colonies, and as every schoolboy *should* now know, Glasgow rose to opulence on the basis of a virtual monopoly position in the trade in Virginian tobacco. No Scottish port specialised in the slave trade, but, through sugar and tobacco, African slavery was as important to Scotland's economic progress as to England's. Burns was drawn to the idea of mending his fortunes as an overseer in a West Indies sugar plantation, and Scott was permanently mortified by the cowardice displayed by his brother when he confronted a slave rebellion in just such a position. As early as the 1720s Robert Walpole saw East India Company patronage as an aid to making the Scots amenable to Whig government and we can descry the first fabulous fortunes accruing to lucky Scots in the East. Overseas fortunes, brought home, energised improving agriculture and modern industry in Scotland.

By the 19th century disproportionate Scottish influence in British trade, soldiering and politics in India was taken for granted, as was the dominant position of Scots in the fur trade of the vast region now included in Canada. Much has been made of the plight of Highland Gaels forced into emigration after Culloden and in the Clearances of the 19th century. But it has to be said that they were normally likely to prosper more overseas not only than impoverished Irish Gaels, but also than their compatriots at home. Scottish regiments and their wailing bagpipes developed fierce and proud traditions within the British army. It has been customary for nationalistic historians to suggest that the Scots were recruited as mercenaries and, as it were, upper servants, of the English in the dirty work of empire. This seems more plausible as a view of the Irish contribution to British expansion overseas. Ireland fed men disproportionately into the British army, though it must be added that Ireland, too, supplied colonial governors, generals and entrepreneurs to the imperial project.

Scots, with traditions of a war of liberation against English rule, conscious of links with a doomed aboriginal Gaelic culture, and with chameleon-like propensities, were perhaps imaginatively predisposed to greater sympathy with Native Americans and Maoris, Sikhs and Bantus than many English readily displayed. John Mackenzie has argued that Scots brought a distinctive vision of civic morality to the government of overseas empire which so many of them found themselves conducting.[11] But only a gross aversion to blatant evidence could sustain the notion either that Scots were less zestful in empire than the English, or that their attitude to the English involved cultural cringe. Scotland's middle classes on balance did very well indeed out of empire and its labouring classes were largely sustained by industries exporting to the empire or importing from it.

If England seemed to a man like Buchan a centre of calm and a reservoir of spiritual values at the heart of empire, this must have been partly because the Scots were dashing about so conspicuously far and wide to energise it. Surely no English city, after Liverpool lost its slave trade, lived in symbiosis with tropical empire matching Dundee's with Bengal. In 1937 Evgenia Fraser, daughter of a Russian father and a mother from Broughty Ferry, reared in Scotland, arrived to join her husband Ronnie on the banks of the Hooghly. He was the *kerani*, the man in charge of the office of a jute mill and all its clerical staff:

> The keranis of the mills, up and down the river, were young men recruited from Dundee and its district. Most of them had a grammar school background and had served their apprenticeship in the offices of

jute mills and brokers. They had also attended the Dundee technical college... Usually after a certain time working as keranis in the mill offices they were promoted as salesmen in the various head offices, situated mostly in that promised land of Clive Street, Calcutta. The other men, the overseers, in different departments of the mill had held similar positions in the mill in Angus and had also attended the technical college.[12]

Besides geography, the other factors differentiating Scottish culture from English imperialism, and European imperialism in general were asynchronicity and ideology, closely related to each other. Seventeenth century Scotland had close links with the Netherlands, at that point leading Europe not only in intercontinental trade and colonisation, but also in advanced agricultural methods. The English, with their greater resources, were temporarily better placed to imitate, and then surpass, the Dutch. But when agricultural improvement and overseas trade rather suddenly began to burgeon together in Scotland towards the middle of the 18th century, Scottish economic and social thinkers were well placed to discuss the resulting Industrial Revolution, its theoretical dimensions, and its moral implications. The achievements of the Scottish Enlightenment resulted from this conjuncture. In the same country Scottish thinkers saw coexisting the traditional economy of the *Gaeltacht* and the cutting edge practices of trade in tobacco, the Carron Iron Works, Lothian husbandry and new textile technology. Watt's steam engine and Adam Smith's political economy coincided with the worldwide impact of Macpherson's versions of Gaelic poetry and, not long after, the Scots verse of Robert Burns and his wonderful reworkings of traditional song. Scotland had the unique and unrepeatable distinction of pioneering simultaneously in the recovery of traditional cultures for modern man and the spelling out of the gospels of economic and technological progress. Walter Scott, bringing all these elements together in a genre of historical realism in fiction which he effectually invented, established parameters for Scottish identity within which his fellow countrymen lived comfortably for a century.

The Scottish past was wondrously lively, an incomparable source of song and story, but self interest dictated that Scots should abandon heroics and lost causes and accommodate themselves with commerce, industry and the British imperial project. Storytelling which in Scott was still at first geared to experience—he had spoken to old Jacobites and living devotees of the true Covenanted faith—led in less factually rooted romances by him to variations on the theme of the wandering Scot, transmuted in Stevenson and Buchan into a wholly freewheeling type of adventure narrative which might be seen as achieving its final sublimation in the ahistorical but in a sense historic creation by an Anglo-Scot, Ian Fleming, of James Bond 007, duly fixed in global culture by our incomparable Edinburgh milk roundsman 'Big Tam'. And aptly so. Sean Connery, never able to escape his Lothian accent entirely, whatever nationality producers have cast him into, has been an ironic obverse of Hannay and Arbuthnot, masters of disguise: the Scot who cannot be other than he is, and now indignantly demands the severance of his own country at last from England—but also the Scot who defined triumphant Englishness for moviegoers worldwide, tacitly usurping the imperial mastery of the Southron at the moment of its terminal decline after the Suez fiasco. This is perhaps a lesser feat than the usurpation of the English literary tradition and the English language itself by Yeats, Joyce and Heaney. But it is one of many examples of 20th century Scottish creativity which make it meaningful to discuss Scottish culture as a distinctive element within the postmodernist global pot pourri.

Notes

1   J Buchan, *The Complete Richard Hannay* (Penguin, 1992), p360.
2   Ibid, p649.
3   J Buchan, *Memory Hold the Door* (Hodder & Stoughton, 1940), pp80-81.
4   Ibid, pp124-125.
5   J Mackenzie, *Propaganda and Empire...1880-1960* (Manchester University Press, 1984), p110.
6   H Lauder, *Roamin' in the Gloamin'* (Hutchinson, no date), pp255-256.
7   Special Correspondent (C M Grieve), *Stewartry Observer*, 12 April and 3 May 1928, in H MacDiarmid, *The Raucle Tongue: Hitherto Uncollected Prose*, vol II (Edited by A Calder, G Murray and A Riach, 3 vols, Carcanet, 1996-98), pp107-111.
8   H MacDiarmid, *The Raucle Tongue...*, vol I, op cit, p290.
9   J H Ohlmeyer, 'Colonisation within Britain and Ireland', in N Canny (ed), *The Origins of Empire: The Oxford History of the British Empire*, vol I (Oxford University Press, 1998), pp139-140.
10 N A M Rodger, 'Guns and Sails in English Colonisation', in N Canny (ed), op cit, pp84, 89.
11 J Mackenzie, 'Scotland and the Empire', *Inaugural Lecture*, Lancaster University, 13 May 1992.
12 E Fraser, *A Home by the Hooghly* (Corgi, 1991), pp22-23.

Chapter 5

Robert Burns, the patriot-bard

Jock Morris

In the month of January 1793 Louis XVI was executed by guillotine, Thomas Muir of Huntershill was arrested and charged with sedition, and Robert Burns was desperately defending himself to his employers against the charge brought by government spies that he was the head of a disaffected party in Dumfries. Recent research by Patrick Scott Hogg, author of *The Lost Poems*, has revealed that there was an organisation of the Friends of the People in Dumfries at this time. It is almost certain that this is the disaffected party that Burns stood accused of being the leading member of.

In his letter to his employer, however, his defence is complete denial and ignorance:

> I know of no party in this place, either Republican or Reform, except an old party of Burgh-reformers, with which I never had anything to do… Individuals both Republican and Reform we have, though not many of either; but if they have associated, it is more than I have the least knowledge of; and if there exists such an association, it must consist of such obscure nameless beings as precludes any possibility of my being known to them, or they to me.[1]

He was also accused of being involved in a near-riot in the theatre in Dumfries. It had started in the pit, the cheapest part of the auditorium, where the tradesmen and others of the lower orders would gather. At the end of the performance, the audience were supposed to sing 'God Save The King'. From the pit, there was a commotion and demands, instead, for the singing of 'Ça ira', the popular anthem of the French Revolution. Again his defence was denial:

I was in the Playhouse one night when 'Ça ira' was called for... I was in the middle of the pit, and from the pit the clamour arose... One or two individuals with whom I occasionally associate were of the party, but I neither knew of the Plot, nor joined in the Plot; nor ever opened my lips to hiss or huzza, that, or any other Political tune whatever.[2]

This is a defence not unknown to some who have been arrested on picket lines.

To the accusation of uttering invectives against the king, the author of 'A Dream', in which he satirises the whole royal family in turn, and numerous Jacobite songs, slyly dissembles:

His private worth it is altogether impossible that such a man as I can appreciate.[3]

Then he simultaneously hides behind his Masonic oath and reminds his investigator of their common membership of the Freemasons:

...and in his public capacity, I always revered, and ever will, with the soundest loyalty, revere the Monarch of Great-britain, as, to speak in Masonic, the sacred KEYSTONE OF OUR ROYAL ARCH CONSTITUTION.[4]

As to the accusation that he supported reform principles, he successfully used the same defence that the Friends of the People resorted to:

I look upon the British Constitution as settled at the revolution (1688), to be the most glorious constitution on earth, or that perhaps the wit of man can frame.

However:

...we have a good deal deviated from from the original principles of that Constitution: particularly, that an alarming System of Corruption has pervaded the connection between the Executive Power and the House of Commons...this is the Truth, the Whole truth, of my reform opinions.[5]

He even resorts to a tactic employed by the Convention of the Friends of the People when under increasing attack for not suspending their reform agitation at a time when the lower orders were excited by the events in France. Strikes, riots and raisings of Trees of Liberty were breaking out all over the country. The Friends of the People were accused of opening the door to anarchic and revolutionary ambitions among the ignorant, illiterate and unpropertied. They adopted the defensive tactic of making public declarations in the newspapers, supported by signatures testifying to their loyalty to the 1688 constitution, to their abhorrence of riots and any violent activities, and their willingness to serve in militias to put down the former. They even declared their intention to help in controlling the populace by buying a Brown Janet, a cannon, a plan which backfired on them at the later trials. Hence Burns:

> I never...had the least connection with any political association, except that when the Magistrates and principal inhabitants of this town met to declare their attachment to the Constitution, and their abhorrence of Riot, which declaration you would see in the Papers. I, as I thought my duty as a subject at large, and and a Citizen in particular, called upon me, subscribed the same declaratory Creed.[6]

He denied having supplied any political poetry to the *Edinburgh Gazeteer*, the journal of the Friends of the People, and offered to cancel his subscription, although only two months earlier he had greeted its editor with ecstatic enthusiasm:

> If you go on in your Paper with the same spirit, it will be the first (best) of its kind in Europe... Go on, Sir! Lay bare, with undaunted heart and steady hand, that mass of corruption called Politics and Statecraft![7]

Of his reputed sympathy for the French Revolution, his only recourse was to recant:

> As to France, I was her enthusiastic votary in the beginning of the business. When she came to shew her old avidity for conquest, in annexing Savoy, etc, to her dominions, and invading the rights of Holland, I altered my sentiments.[8]

Burns was by this time an excise man, a customs officer, a salaried government employee. If found guilty, the least that would have happened would have been the loss of his position, and his family's reduction to destitution, which was a very real fear for him. Or worse, as he wrote later:

> The shrinking bard adown the alley skulks,
> And dreads a meeting worse than Woolwich hulks,
> Though there, his heresies in Church and State
> Might well award him Muir and Palmers fate.[9]

The Woolwich hulks were the prison ships where convicts were held while awaiting transportation, and where Muir and Thomas Palmer did indeed lie for several months.

Burns was lucky. The official terror against reform had not swung into top gear and, unlike Muir, he was not being judged by the dreaded reactionary Lord Braxfield, nor a rigged jury. He was in the hands of relatively well disposed employers who perhaps balked at the prospect of finding guilty their already famous and revered employee. He had been made a Freeman of the town of Dumfries six years before on the strength of his first published volume of poetry. The second edition, which many of them would have subscribed to, was to be published the following month.

Burns promised his employers:

> My Reform opinion…which before I was aware of the completion of these innovating times, I too unguardedly (now I see it) sported with: but henceforth , I seal up my lips.[10]

Yet six months later, in late August, Burns sent George Thomson, a song publisher, a new song he had written.

> Scots, wha hae wi' Wallace bled,
> Scots, wham Bruce has aften led,
> Welcome to your gory bed
> Or to victorie![11]

In a postscript, Burns said he was inspired by Bruce's 'glorious struggle for freedom, associated with the glowing ideas of some other struggles of the same nature, not quite so ancient'. He was referring, of course, to the French Revolution and to the radical movement for parliamentary reform and for republicanism it had inspired in Britain. On 30 August 1793 the date of trial had been fixed for Thomas Muir for, among other things, the dispersal of seditious literature. The seditious literature referred to was Tom Paine's *Rights of Man*. Burns' apparently patriotic speech put in the mouth of Bruce to rouse his troops before battle was in fact a disguised anthem in defence of the reform movement now under ferocious attack, with the trial of Thomas Muir being a crucial part. Burns wrote this song in solidarity with Thomas Muir.

So, Burns had not only dispersed seditious literature, he had written it , appealing to fellow Scots to rediscover the fighting spirit of those who had fought with Bruce and Wallace, not to fight for Scottish independence, but to stand up for the struggle for political liberty, ie the extension of the franchise, as the only way to combat political corruption and the ruination of the country.

The song goes on:

Now's the day, and now's the hour:
See the front of battle lour,
See approach proud Edward's power
Chains and slaverie![12]

For Edward, read William Pitt and Henry Dundas, the Scottish secretary, and for the front of battle which was louring, the Tory government's onslaught on the reform movement and on civil liberties. Chains and slavery were indeed to be the sentence passed on Thomas Muir—14 years transportation to Botany Bay.

The final stanza declares:

Lay the proud usurpers low!
Tyrants fall in every foe!
Liberty's in every blow!
Let us do, or die![13]

Burns cries out for a fight against tyrants or despots or monarchs who are usurpers of power, and for liberty—the clarion calls of the French Revolution, and of the American revolutionaries 20 years before. Liberty was an extremely dangerous word to be using in a poem at this time:

'Let us do, or die!' is an adaption of a French revolutionary oath. More or less the same words were the final triumphant chant of the Convention of the Friends of the People in late 1792.[14]

Burns allowed the song to be published in a radical newspaper, but only anonymously. It was far too dangerous to allow his name to be attached to it. He was only to live for another three years, but he continued, anonymously and under various pseudonyms, to provide radical, republican and even insurrectionary poetry for radical newspapers, like the *Edinburgh Gazeteer*, the *Morning Chronicle* in London and the *Glasgow Advertiser*, forerunner of the *Glasgow Herald*. Among them, in 1793, was 'The Tree of Liberty', celebrating the symbol of the French Revolution and the guillotine. In 1794 he wrote 'The Irregular Ode for General Washington's Birthday'. This poem saluted the man who had become the international icon of the reform movement, while bewailing the loss of fighting spirit and submission to despotism in Wallace's Scotland and King Alfred's England, a return of whose supposed universalist constitution Thomas Muir and other Friends argued for. In 1795 Burns wrote 'A Man's a Man for a' That', a song which, stripped of its class content and depoliticised, has become a pious hymn to equality:

> In 1795, it was undoubtedly a seditious and treasonable song... The historical and cultural context of the song is important. Scotland still had many working people who were bonded to a master, and Scottish 'slaves' still worked in the early mines of Fife.[15]

And if Patrick Scott Hogg is right, and he makes a very convincing case, there are a number of others lying silently hidden in the pages of those radical papers of the 1790s.

So how do we square this Burns, this tortured champion of liberty struggling to keep the flame alive under conditions of dreadful oppression, with the Burns that still dominates popular imagination? This Burns combines a number of misunderstandings, misuses and abuses. There is the heaven taught ploughman, the untutored, inspired son of the soil who intuitively composes timeless lyrical verse. There is the marketing icon Burns of shortbread tins ringed with tartan. (He is unlikely to have seen very much tartan, as it, along with the pre-Jacobite version of kilts and bagpipes, was illegal in his time. The Victorian Romantic revival would not create the mythical Scottish tartan history until decades after his death.)

Most importantly for us is the Hanoverian bard who becomes the one nation Tory Burns. By being taken out of its historical context, or selectively quoted, the language of his poetry is robbed of its political force. In 'Man was Made to Mourn', the speaker is an old peasant:

> See yonder poor, o'erlaboured wight,
> So abject, mean and vile,
> Who begs a brother of the earth
> To give him leave to toil:
> And see his lordly fellow-worm
> The poor petition spurn,
> Unmindfu', tho' a weeping wife
> And helpless offspring mourn.[16]

It is the aristocracy who refuse work to the unemployed poor, careless of the suffering they cause. Further:

If I'm designed yon Lordlings slave
By nature's law designed
Why was an independent wish
E're planted in my mind?
If not, why am I subject to
His cruelty, or scorn?
Or why has man the will and pow'r
To make his fellows mourn?[17]

The fact that man is capable of hoping for freedom proves that a system based on the power of one class over another is not the natural order of things. It finishes pessimistically, but with ironic compensation:

O Death! the poor man's dearest friend—
The kindest and the best!
Welcome the hour my aged limbs
Are laid with thee at rest!
The great, the wealthy, fear thy blow,
From pomp and pleasure torn:
But oh! a blest relief to those
That weary-laden mourn![18]

From this powerful and compassionate poem, full of anger at the injustice of the class system, are lifted and misused the internationally famous lines:

Man's inhumanity to man
Makes countless thousands mourn.[19]

This is not a poetic encapsulation of original sin—that we are all guilty of being nasty to one another. The countless thousands are the poor, labouring masses. Those guilty of inhumanity towards them are the aristocratic and ruling classes.

The depoliticised Burns floats in an ahistorical, pre-industrial, agricultural, even ageographical idyll. The south west of Scotland exists almost independently of the rest of Europe, America and the East. As soon as we place Burns' feet firmly on the ground of his historical times, that myth disappears like a wraith.

He lived in the second half of the 18th century. He was born in 1759, a year before the coronation of George III. He lived for 37 years, so George III was king throughout his life. If you have seen the films *The Madness of King George* , or *Tom Jones*, or *The Scarlet Pimpernel*, you will have a flavour of the period. This was a time when gentlemen wore their hair powdered, when the distinctions of social class—or rank, as Burns called it—were plainly visible in the quality and form of people's appearance and dress.

It was also one of the most important and exciting thirds of a century in human history, during which the most cataclysmic events took place—the American Revolution, the French Revolution, the Industrial Revolution and, in Scotland, the Agrarian Revolution. Burns' life and poetry were interlinked, in one way or another, with all of these.

Neither did he exist in isolation from other important figures of his day. As McIntyre puts it:

> Scotland's national poet was born in the same year as William Pitt, Schiller and Mary Wollestonecraft, the near contemporary of Robespierre and Mozart, of Nelson and of William Blake.[20]

McIntyre goes on to mention Voltaire, John Wesley, Henry Cavendish, Captain Cook, Thomas Jefferson and, among numerous others, Benjamin Franklin:

> The 53 year old Franklin—printer, scientist, moralist and sage—was installed in London as agent for the Pennsylvania Assembly, pleading the cause of the colonists against the Proprietors. He travelled north in that year [1759] to receive an honorary degree from the university of St Andrews (the town had 3,000 inhabitants, 42 ale houses and 20 students).[21]

Scotland was still a very poor country when Burns was born. Only 25 percent of babies survived their first year of life. Only 50 percent of those who made it to the age of one survived to ten. And only 25 percent of the survivors, three in every 100 born, lived beyond the age of 48. So, even though conditions improved rapidly in the second half of the 18th century, Burns' early death was not so very unusual. What killed people? Smallpox, tuberculosis, rheumatism, various fevers and malaria became widespread. Malaria was one of the biggest killers in 18th century Scotland, because the land was so sour and swampy. But it was a form of rheumatism which may have killed Burns.

Agricultural improvement was only beginning. The rural landscape of Ayrshire was nothing like it is now—a patchwork of fields and hedgerows, woods and copses, in turn now disappearing with the growth of agribusiness. There were hardly any trees, and what trees there were were mainly on the river banks. There were no hedges or fences or walls, and particularly no dry stone walls. There had been riots in Galloway where the rioters knocked down the new dry stone walls and in Monymusk where secret night raids were organised to rip up new plantations of trees.

The farms were still ploughed in the rig system, very long thin rigs dispersed between families, very badly drained, yielding very poor crops. The priority of the agricultural improvers in 18th century Scotland was drainage. The landlords would establish an area of land as a farm, let it to a tenant on condition that he improved it by draining it, building walls, planting woods and building a stone farmhouse instead of clay. It took a lot of capital to do that, and many of these early improving tenants were ruined. Burns was one of them. He was set up in Ellisland by a gentleman patron after his first book of poems was published, on condition he improved it, including the building of a stone farmhouse. He was unable to do so, and it is this that drove him to seek a job in the excise.

So Burns was born into a social class which was being squeezed out of existence. The iconoclasts who have attacked the myth of the heaven taught ploughman, the innocent, uneducated peasant visited suddenly and mystically by the spirit of poetry, have concentrated on Burns' education, pointing out how, given the standards of the time, he was relatively well educated and how well read he made himself. There is a danger though of losing sight of the fact that he was a ploughman. He was a peasant. His schooling, in fact, was intermittent—two years as a child with an 18 year old tutor hired by his father along with other local farmers, and a few months of mathematics at the age of 15.

He was born in a cottage built by hand out of clay by his own father. He was raised from birth to hard backbreaking toil. At the age of 15 he was the main labourer on the farm. He and his brother were sent to school on alternate weeks for a period because one of them had to be available to work on the farm.

He was a poor peasant. But he was also a voracious reader and became profoundly interested in the prevailing intellectual debates of the day. He was aware of, and sympathetic to, the lives the poor had to lead, because he lived it himself, and he sought explanation in the ideas of the Enlightenment.

But his early political poems express an idealising of this impoverished life as a kind of defence against the contempt the poor were held in by their 'betters'. In 'The Twa Dogs', he imagines a rich landlord's dog and a ploughman's dog sitting down for a blether together over the affairs of state. The dogs are called Caesar and Luath, Luath from an ancient hound in Macpherson's *Ossian*, which Burns adored and which had not long been published. The poem is a fine satire on the follies of the wealthy, but it is Caesar, the rich man's dog, who struggles to enlighten Luath, the sheepdog, about his poverty. Luath replies:

> They're nae sae wretched 's ane wad think:
> Tho' constantly on poortith's brink,
> They're sae accustomed wi' the sight,
> The view o't gies them little fright.
>
> Then chance and fortune are sae guided,
> They're in less or mair provided;
> An' tho fatigued wi' close employment,
> A blink o' rest's a sweet enjoyment.[22]

And they conclude that the solution to the problems of country life would be provided by landlords staying at home to look after their estates rather than going off to be corrupted in London and abroad.

He is even drawn in admiration towards those members of the gentry and nobility who express enlightened and reformist views and behave fraternally towards their inferiors. In 'Extempore Verses on Dining with Lord Daer', he amuses himself with exaggerating his nervousness, then finishes with:

> Then from his Lordship I shall learn
> Henceforth to meet with unconcern
>   One ranks as well's another;
> Nae honest, worthy man need care
> To meet with noble youthfu' Daer,
>   For he but meets a brother.[23]

This Lord Daer would appear later in the story as a leading figure in the first Convention of the Friends of the People.

His satirical attacks on the Calvinist church are much sharper. The 18th century is the age of the Scottish Enlightenment. The universities were employing professors who were challenging the idiocies of the theory of the salvation of the elect, and promoting deist forms of religious belief, a common sense belief in a benign creator God, based on Newton's physics. Anatomy was beginning to investigate the human body. Burns read David Hume and Adam Smith. Burns became a freemason, whose ideas were rooted in the Enlightenment, as Mozart's were. So he was part of an intellectual milieu which was challenging the old religious order. And yet he was unable to publish 'Holy Willie's

Prayer' in his lifetime. Like much of his dangerous poetry, it was circulated privately.

'The Cotter's Saturday Night' was viewed by the Victorian bourgeoisie as his finest poem. It is no wonder—here are the deserving poor, content with their poverty, leading well ordered, affectionate and pious family lives. And yet it was enormously popular with the common people too. They enjoyed the flattering and by now nostalgic picture of themselves. This poem had a similar effect when published as *Uncle Tom's Cabin* later had, but it ends in an apocalyptic patriotic rage:

> How he, who lone in Patmos banished,
> Saw in the sun a mighty angel stand,
> And heard great Bab'lon' s doom pronounc'd by Heaven's command.[24]

St John of Patmos was author of the biblical Book of Revelations and saw a vision of the destruction of Babylon, a common source of inspiration for lower class thinkers and agitators over a long period.

> Then howe'er crowns and coronets be rent,
> A virtuous populace may rise the while,
> And stand a wall of fire around their much-lov'd isle.[25]

The true spirit of the nation is embodied in the common people who will rise to defend it when the monarchy and aristocracy are incapable. Finally:

> O' thou who poured the patriotic tide,
> That streamed thro' Wallace's undaunted heart,
> Who dared to, nobly, stem tyrannic pride,
> Or nobly die, the second glorious part:
> (the patriot's God, peculiarly Thou art,
> His friend, inspirer, guardian, and reward!)
> O never, never Scotia's realm desert:
> But still the patriot and the patriot-bard
> In bright succession raise, her ornament and guard.[26]

Patriot is a confusing word here. John Wilkes, the patriot, campaigned for parliamentary reform and supported the Americans against his own country in the war. The word patriot meant one who believed it was the right and duty of the common people to control the affairs of their own country. Patriot equalled democrat. It is in that context that Dr Johnson declared that 'patriotism is the last refuge of a scoundrel'.

George Washington was for Burns the modern Wallace. He became a hero of the reform movement internationally. He would be an icon of the French revolutionaries. Later, Burns would write the 'Irregular Ode to Washington's Birthday', again calling on the spirit of Wallace.

'The Cotter's Saturday Night' was written in 1785, two years after the colonists had won the war. Burns saw himself as the patriot-bard, the poetical spokesman for the democratic movement in Scotland.

George Washington was another member of the enlightened freemasons of this time, along with Thomas Jefferson and many others, and it was the great historical events in America that gave an impulse to the political movements in Europe. If Great Britain could be defeated by a bunch of ragamuffin colonists, then there was hope for real historical change.

There is a superb but not well known poem from this period, certainly not one that is taught in schools or recited at Burns Suppers. It combines a hatred of the aristocracy with compassion for the poor and a faith that the ideas of the American Revolution can overcome oppression and liberate and empower the poor. And it shows a different side to what has become the popular idea about emigration—the clearances, poor peasants driven from their ancestral land by rapacious improving landlords. In 18th century Scotland, poor people organised themselves to escape poverty and oppression by emigrating to the colonies. It is a dramatic monologue, a device he was very fond of. The speaker is Beelzebub. It is called the 'Address of Beelzebub', and is addressed from hell. It is introduced with the note:

> To the Right Honorable the Earl of Breadalbane, President of the Highland Society, which met on the 23rd of May last, at the Shakespeare, Covent Garden, to concert ways and means to frustrate the designs of 500 Highlanders who, as the society were informed by Mr McKenzie of Applecross, were so audacious as to attempt an escape from their lawful lords and masters whose property they were, by emigrating from the lands of Mr MacDonald of Glengarry to the wilds of Canada, in search of that fantastic thing—LIBERTY.

Burns always wrote the word 'liberty' in capital letters.

Long life, my lord, an' health be yours,
Unskaith'd by hunger'd Highland boors!
Lord grant nae duddie, desperate beggar,
Wi' dirk, claymore, or rusty trigger,

May twin auld Scotland o' a life
She likes—as lambkins like a knife!
Faith! you and Applecross were right
To keep the Highland hounds in sight!
I doubt na! they wad bid nae better
Than let them ance out owre the water!
Then up amang thae lakes and seas,
They'll mak what rules and laws they please:

Then a litany of American revolutionary heroes:

Some daring Hancock, or a Franklin,
May set their highland bluid a-ranklin:
Some Washington again may head them,
Or some Montgomery, fearless lead them:
Till (God knows what may be effected
When by such heads and hearts directed)
Poor dunghill sons of dirt and mire
May to Patrician rights aspire!

Then the British parliamentarians and soldiers:

Nae sage North now, nor sager Sackville,
To watch and premier o'er the pack vile
An' whare will ye get Howes and Clintons,
To bring them to a right repentance?
To cowe the rebel generation,
An' save the honor o' the nation?
They, an' be damned! what right hae they
To meat or sleep or light o' day?
Far less to riches, pow'r or freedom,
But what your lordship likes to gie them?

Then Burns whips himself into a rage at the treatment of the poor
by the wealthy, and strips bare their class hatred:

But hear, my Lord! Glengarry hear!
Your hands owre light on them I fear:
Your factors, grieves, trustees and bailies,
I canna say but they do gaylies:
They lay aside a' tender mercies,
An tirl the hullions to the birses;
Yet while they're only poind and herriet,

They'll keep their stubborn Highland spirit.
But smash them! crush them a' to spails,
An rot the dyvors i' the jails!
The young dogs, swinge them to the labour:
Let wark an' hunger mak them sober!
The hizzies, if they're aughtlins fawsont,
Let them in Drury-lane be lesson'd!
An' if the wives an' dirty brats
Come thiggin at your doors an' yetts,
Flaffin wi' duds, an' grey wi' beas',
Frightnin awa' your ducks an' geese;
Get out a horsewhip or a jowler,
The langest thong, the fiercest growler,
An' gar the tatter'd gypsies pack
Wi' a' their bastards on their back!

And finally the promise of the most prestigious seat in hell:

Go on, my Lord! I lang to meet you,
An' in my 'house at hame' to greet you;
Wi' common lords ye shanna mingle,
The benmost neuk beside the ingle,
At my right han' assigned your seat

The seat is assigned amidst a catalogue of legendary sadistic tyrants:

'Tween Herod's hip an Polycrate;
Or (if you on your station tarrow),
Between Almagro and Pizzaro,
A seat, I'm sure ye're well deservin't;
An' till ye come—your humble servant,
BEELZEBUB[27]

Again, 'The Address of Beelzebub' was not published in his lifetime, but circulated privately.

But it was the French Revolution that inspired the most radical political uprising from below of the century. Like the American Revolution, it opened up the possibility to large sections of people in Scotland of actually achieving real fundamental change in society. Burns was one of them. The movement was particularly vigorous in Scotland, although it was never as advanced and organised and consciously revolutionary as in Ireland.

Scotland was starting from even further back in the democracy stakes than England. So few people were allowed to elect MPs that most of them could be bribed, and were. The bulk of the 45 MPs were in the pocket of Henry Dundas, the Scottish secretary.

By the late 1780s, the Scottish economy was really feeling the benefits of the union. The Carron Iron Works was the most productive of its kind in Europe, the Forth and Clyde Canal had been completed, cotton was being produced in factories in New Lanark, silk being woven around Paisley, and linen production was booming. The urban population was increasing, Edinburgh and Glasgow almost doubling in 30 years, wages improved, leisure time increased, newspaper production rose from eight in 1782 to 27 in 1790, and the mills became centres for political debate and organisation:

> I travelled, says a writer in 1790, through some places where not many years ago the people were wretchedly poor, want sat upon every brow, hunger was painted on every face: neither tattered clothes nor their miserable cottages were a sufficient shelter from the cold; now the labourers have put off their long clothing, the tardy pace, the lethargic look of their fathers, for the short doublet, the linen trousers, the quick pace of men who are labouring for their own behoof, and work up to the spirit of their cattle, and the rapid revolution of the threshing machine.[28]

The first strike or combination of importance took place in July 1787:

> ...the weavers of Glasgow refused to work at the usual rates of pay. Having assembled on Glasgow Green, they proceeded to appoint committees 'to meet with the masters, receive their ultimatums and report'. Negotiations having proved fruitless, the strikers took the webs out of the looms of those willing to work and carried them in procession through the town. A riot followed; the military were called out; and as a result of the firing that ensued three of the weavers were killed and three mortally wounded. In the following July, Lord Eskgrove sentenced one of the strikers to be whipped and banished for seven years.[29]

A combination of things set off widespread political agitation in Scotland: the Corn Bill of 1791, the rejection of the Burgh Reform Act, attempting to extend the franchise, the defeat of the first Abolition of Slavery Act, the proclamation against seditious writings directed against Tom Paine's *The Rights of Man* (the suppression of which produced a huge increase in demand) and particularly the progress of the French

Revolution. The defeat of the Duke of Brunswick's 'army of despotism' at the Tuileries on 10 August 1792 and the victory of the revolutionary army at the Battle of Valmy went through Europe and the world like an electric shock. Suddenly the forces of the *Ancien Regime* could be defeated by the common people, and radical change seemed attainable.

The *Edinburgh Gazeteer* rejoiced:

> Every patriotic heart must rejoice at the brilliant successes of the French in every quarter. Despotism has now been shook to the centre on the continent and before the conclusion of next summer the Tree of Liberty will occupy the soil that has long been usurped by tyranny.[30]

Brims comments:

> By the end of the year virtually every town south of Aberdeen had its own parliamentary reform society as did many of the villages of central Scotland. The Scottish Association of the Friends of the People had become a force to be reckoned with.[31]

And the lower orders were also on the move:

> Millenarian handbills circulated containing the prophecies of the 13th century Thomas the Rhymer—after 'a violent struggle' Scotland's liberty would be made 'perfect', that after terrible convulsions in church and state, military, civil and religious despots would be forced to flee in shame, and that afterwards, peace would reign, trade would flourish and 'true religion and an universal love to mankind shall be established unto the end of the world'.[32]

Risings of working people rose and spread throughout the country. In the month of November it was at its height. Amongst others:

> ...in Perth 'several hundred of the lower class' burnt Dundas in effigy...and even boys shouted 'liberty, equality and no king!'... The entry of Dumouriez into Brussels was celebrated by the erection of a Tree of Liberty at the Cross. The bells were rung from eight in the morning till six at night, and the inhabitants were compelled to illuminate their windows...in Dundee, a few people assembled in the High Street, where they attempted to plant a Tree of Liberty, but some young gentlemen pulled it down. On the Monday following, a mob threatened to unload a cargo of meal which could not be landed because of the corn laws. Next day...hundreds paraded the streets shouting 'Liberty and Equality', carrying the effigies of the gentlemen who had pulled down their tree. A man with a flaming barrel on his head led the way.

They broke the windows in the town hall, went back to the High Street, erected a Tree of Liberty, bearing the scroll 'Liberty, Equality and no Sinecures', decorated it with apples and lit it up with a lantern and candles. The disturbances were not put down till the following Monday by troops.[33]

The connections being made here between the economic complaint about the famine caused by the Corn Laws and political demands for liberty and equality are hugely important:

In Aberdeen, the sailors, following the example of Leith and other British seaports, went on strike...they unrigged the vessels going to sea.[34]

There was a 'national' seamen's strike going on!

During the 18th century rioting had been almost the only method of popular protest, but such tumults had never been associated as they were now with universal principles of reform and even of revolution.[35]

The year 1792 saw consciously political strikes, demonstrations and riots in towns and villages all over Scotland by the lower orders. Unfortunately, H W Meikle, like other commentators on the period, sees this as being the problem—what he calls 'the adverse influence of the French Revolution on Scottish reforms', rather than evidence of the incredibly exciting possibilities of the moment.

It was at this point, in early December, that Burns wrote to a correspondent about political unrest in Dumfries and the commotion in the theatre. On 12 December, the second day of the first General Convention of the Friends of the People in Edinburgh, he sent to another friend, for private circulation, the newly written 'Why Shouldna Poor Folk Mowe?' 'Mowe' is a metaphor for fornicate. The chorus goes:

And why shouldna poor folk mowe, mowe, mowe,
And why shouldna poor folk mowe:
The great folk hae siller and houses and lands,
Poor bodies hae naething but mowe.

In the context of the times, this was class conscious, politically committed satire. The song goes on to ridicule the Duke of Brunswick for his defeat at Valmy in September:

When Brunswick's great prince cam a cruising to France
Republican billies to cowe,

Bauld Brunswick's great prince wad hae shown better sense,
At hame with his princess to mowe.

He goes on to express passionate solidarity with the oppressed Poles
by taking a vicious swipe at Empress Catherine of Russia, who made
her lover, Stanislaus Poniatowski, puppet ruler in Poland:

Auld Kate laid her claws on poor Stanislaus,
And Poland has bent like a bow:
May the diel in her ass ram a huge prick o brass
And damn her in hell with a mowe!

He finishes with a 'scurrilous' mock sychophantic toast:

Here's George our good king and Charlotte his queen,
And lang may they tak a good mowe.[36]

This was in December 1792, when the lower orders were turning
out for a republic. So much for the 'heaven taught ploughman'.

Thus in the midst of this tumult of popular manifestations inspired
by the French Revolution, the Friends of the People had their first convention, with 160 delegates from 35 towns. That they had styled their
meeting in the French revolutionary manner was not lost on the forces
of reaction. Dundas and Pitt agreed that the situation was so serious
that the only sensible response was a policy of repression at home and
war abroad with France.

In vain did the convention denounce the actions of the lower orders,
offer to join in putting down disturbances, and declare their loyalty to
the constitution and the king. The reformers were held responsible—
at best foolishly, at worst deviously—of having stirred up the ignorant
population to aspirations beyond their natural station.

A series of state trials began with small fry—three printers, sentenced to nine months imprisonment for having drunk a toast to
'George the Third and last and damnation to all crowned heads!'[37]
and having promised the soldiers in Edinburgh Castle a pay increase
if they joined the Friends of the People. For fear of contamination by
the local population, barracks had been set up for the first time ever
instead of billets in the towns for the soldiers.

Thomas Muir was a much more prominent target. As well as circulating *Rights of Man*, he was charged with exciting disaffection by seditious speeches, and reading and defending the Address of the United
Irishmen in the convention. Prominent amongst the evidence against
him was his possession of a seal inscribed with the words 'Ça ira'.

Lord Braxfield's summing up to the jury is breathstopping:

> I leave it to you to judge whether it was perfectly innocent or not in Mr Muir, at such a time, to go about among ignorant country people, and among the lower classes of people, making them leave off their work, and inducing them to believe that a reform was absolutely necessary to preserve their safety and their liberty, which, had it not been for him, they would never have suspected to have been in danger.

And:

> A government in every country should be just like a corporation; and in this country, it is made up of the landed interest, which alone has a right to be represented. As for the rabble, who have nothing but personal property, what hold has the nation on them? What security for the payment of their taxes? They may pack up all their property on their backs, and leave the country in the twinkling of an eye. But landed property may not be removed.[38]

Thomas Muir was sentenced to transportation to Botany Bay for 14 years. Alongside the state trials, local authorities and influential local loyalists blacklisted known and suspected supporters of the Friends of the People:

> Lawyers of allegedly Jacobin sympathies were deprived of briefs, radical journeymen and schoolmasters were dismissed from their employments, and master tradesmen and shopkeepers of democratic political views were boycotted.[39]

The state trials and the local witch hunts were supported by a loyalist propaganda campaign—parliamentary speeches, sermons, pamphlets, newspaper articles, and so on—with all the power of the state at their disposal. Ranged against them were the radical newspapers, pamphlets, handbills, songs and poems of the likes of Alexander Wilson, the Paisley weaver, Robert Burns and many others: 'Soon every village was divided into camps of Government Men and Democrats'.[40]

The intimidation and harassment took its toll. Many of the gentry, who had supported the Friends, ran for cover, fearful both of the rising from below and the terror from above. Local meetings grew smaller. Charles Fox, the leading Whig, supported the argument for a tactical suspension of reform demands until the common populace had calmed down.

The trial of Thomas Palmer, a Unitarian minister, followed a month after Muir's. He was sentenced to seven years transportation for writing an address against the war, issued by the Dundee Friends of Liberty.

A few months later, the third (British) convention was broken up by the constables and Skirving, Margarot and Gerrald arrested. All three were tried and given the same sentence as Muir. This British convention (in Edinburgh), by now much more artisan in character, had shifted to the left. It declared itself for universal suffrage and annual parliaments and against the war.

> In imitation of the French, they had called each other 'citizens', divided themselves into 'sections', some of which were headed 'Vive la Convention!' and ended with 'Ça ira'.[41]

It was at the trial of Joseph Gerrald, one of the English delegates, that Braxfield made one of his most notorious remarks. When Gerrald argued that Jesus Christ himself had been a reformer, Braxfield chuckled to his fellow judges, 'Muckle he made o' that; he was hanget.'

Maurice Margarot, another of the English delegates, became the hero of the people. A demonstration escorted him to the courtroom carrying a Tree of Liberty shaped like the letter 'M', with a scroll inscribed 'Liberty, Virtue, Reason, Justice and Truth': 'No series of trials in Scottish history ever created such worldwide interest'.[42]

Motions of support came from the US and France and from reform societies in England. The US intervened with a ship to rescue Muir. Resistance continued to flare intermittently, but the Friends of the People never recovered from the dispersion of the third convention and the trials.

If the first of the trials was ludicrous, the last was grotesque. It involved Robert Watt, the first of Dundas's spies at the beginning of the political 'excitement'. He had been sacked, but with the zeal of the convert he kept a fragment of the Friends going, ordered pikes and halberts to be made and, absurdly, planned an insurrection. He was charged with high treason.

> He was found guilty and hanged at the Tolbooth of Edinburgh. His body was then cut down and laid on a table. The head was cut off, the executioner exclaiming as he held it up to view, 'This is the head of a traitor'.[43]

We should be careful not to overemphasise the power of the oppression. While hundreds of individuals genuinely suffered, the main intention was to use fear of possible consequences to intimidate the mass of the people out of actively pursuing democratic aims. In spite of the repression, unrest continued. One interesting item of evidence was the appointment in May 1794 of lords-lieutenant and sheriffs-principal for the first time in Scotland.

> One of their duties was to was to make arrangements for the defence of the country against invasion…[but] special emphasis was laid on that part of their instructions which dealt with 'internal tranquillity'… They were to organise…companies of…Volunteers, all were to be men of known loyalty to his majesty's government…deputy lieutenants were 'to inform themselves respecting the dispositions of those living in their districts', and to prepare lists of such as were willing to assist the civil magistrate in quelling tumults or illegal meetings.[44]

In January, 1795, while he was writing 'A Man's a Man for a' That', Burns could write to his patron, Mrs Dunlop, about Louis XVI and Marie Antoinette:

> What is there in the delivering over a perjured blockhead and an un-principled prostitute into the hands of the hangman, that it should arrest, for a moment, attention, in an eventful hour, when, as my friend Roscoe in Liverpool gloriously expresses it—
> When the welfare of Millions is hung in the scale
> And the balance yet trembles with fate![45]

Yet in the same month Burns signed a petition to set up the Dum-fries Volunteers and wrote them an anti-French anthem, published under his name:

> Does haughty Gaul invasion threat?
> Then let the loons beware, Sir!
> There's wooden walls upon our seas
> And volunteers on shore, Sir![46]

Indeed, the Volunteers fired a volley at his funeral. How do we make sense of this contradiction? Part of the answer is supplied by Meikle:

> For those who now prudently renounced their democratic zeal, the Windsor blue was a conspicuous sign of repentance. Burns, like many others threatened with the loss of their post, sought to reinstate him-self in the good graces of his employers. Those who clung stubbornly to their opinions were distinguished, like the Roundheads of old, by having

their hair closely cropped. Attired in trousers and gaiters...these 'Crappies' were as obnoxious to Government Men as the 'Black Nebs' who refused to join the volunteers.[47]

Anti-French war frenzy pervaded all classes. Intimidation and harassment of those suspected of disloyalty were widespread. Strikes were put down ruthlessly. Adherence to democratic principles was equal to Jacobinism, therefore pro-French, deadly dangerous and traitorous.

Furthermore, by now the organisation that democrats like Burns had looked to to lead a campaign for reform, the Friends of the People, had been crushed. Even in France, Robespierre and the Jacobins had been overthrown and guillotined by the Directory, and the revolution itself had changed course.

Reformers and republicans were isolated and organisation was atomised. Burns took a pragmatic course. Privately, he kept the company of like-minded friends, among them Dr William Maxwell, a friend of Muir's, who had been a member of the national guard responsible for escorting Louis XVI to the guillotine. He secretly provided poems and songs for publications which were rapidly being closed down. Publicly, he kept his mouth shut, not always successfully, and played the loyalist. 'Does Haughty Gaul' finishes ambiguously and ironically:

Who will not sing God save the King
Shall hang as high's the steeple;
But while we sing God save the King,
We'll ne'er forget the people.[48]

He was, of course, in a very difficult personal position. He was employed as a government officer and was therefore under double pressure to conform and keep quiet. He was married with children and his family's income depended entirely on his wages. He had no land or capital to fall back on. He was born a peasant, a social class which was being squeezed out of existence. His fame as a poet provided him with influential connections which enabled him to escape upwards to the dizzy heights of a post as a salaried government officer, while most others were crushed down into penury, the new landless labouring classes or emigration. He had no income from his writing and was never allowed to enter the ranks of the gentry:

From his conversation he seems to be frequently among the Great—but no attention is paid by people of any rank to his wife.[49]

He was welcome personally in the homes of Whig gentlemen for his wit, political conversation and entertainment value, but to have invited his wife would have been to provide them both with a social recognition to which they were not 'due'.

He was a very low level professional who was utterly dependent on patronage to keep him in the most hated job in the country. And exhausting and health breaking work it was too—200 miles a week on horseback, all the year round, in all weathers. Even membership of the Volunteers, whose job it was to put down the meal riots in Dumfries in early 1796, did not save him and his family from suffering the 'actual famine' which the wealthier were able to avoid.

Men make their own history but not in circumstances of their own choosing. Burns dealt with his situation with what we would call working class horse sense. He chose survival for himself and his dependents rather than martyrdom, a fair enough option in a period of defeat, and one that rings with everyday familiarity to working class militants. 'A Man's a Man for a' That' finishes with a prayer for a future egalitarian republic, not an imminent one:

And let us pray that come it may
And come it will, for a' that,
That Sense and Worth o'er a' the earth
Shall bear the gree an a' that!
For a' that an' a' that,
It's comin yet for a' that,
That man to man the world o'er
Shall brothers be for a' that.[50]

Nothing has changed. The world is still as unjust and senseless as it was, the forces of reaction have prevailed, but, in spite of all that, they cannot stop the coming of the future, classless society.

We should not look for a consistent lifelong revolutionary in Burns. There never was such a being. His politics grew out of his circumstances, the changing ideas and events of his time. Born dirt poor into hard agricultural labour and a milieu of Enlightenment ideas challenging the old ways of thinking and being, he always knew he was in opposition to the existing order of things—to Calvinist doctrine, and the idiocy and injustice of the class system. He did not transcend his time. He can only be understood as a man in his time.

His opposition took different forms at different times. He supported the Whigs against the Tories, Fox against Pitt, even the Prince of Wales (often as he lampooned him) against the king. He hated the

Hanoverians and often expressed it as support for the return of the Stuarts, stalwarts of Catholic reaction, of all people; he hated the government and occasionally bemoaned the loss of the Scottish Parliament. He had a mixed, contradictory consciousness.

It was real historical events that gave direction to his political ideas: the success of the American Revolution; the success of the French Revolution; and the formation of an organisation—the Friends of the People—that could lead a campaign for really attainable change. He was a fiercely proud Scot, but no Scottish nationalist; that would be an anachronism—the return of the Scottish Parliament was simply not on the agenda. A just, egalitarian society could be achieved through reform of the parliamentary franchise, first of all with the Whigs for enlargement and then with Paine and Muir for universal suffrage. That is how the 'parcel o' rogues' in a nation could be dealt with.

Neither was he a Scottish socialist (another impossible anachronism) nor a Scottish republican, in the sense of believing that republicanism could be achieved in an independent Scotland.

A Scottish patriot, yes, in the 18th century sense. Burns was a Scot who believed it was the right and duty of the common people to control the affairs of their own country. He believed that the true spirit of Scotland was liberty, which he romantically traced back to Bruce and Wallace, and that it was embodied in the common people and corrupted in the gentry, nobility and royalty. But he believed the same of the common people of England and wanted them and his fellow Scots to emulate the common people of America and France. He styled himself the patriot-bard, whose ambition was to be the poetical spokesman in Scotland for the democratic movement for liberty.

We on the left have a job to do in rescuing the real Robert Burns from behind the myth. We need to re-investigate and re-establish the tradition, that has never gone away, of the poet of the common man, the tradition that carried the legend of his buying and sending four carronades to the French Assembly. As well as daring to write in the language of the common people, conserving and transmitting our oral tradition, peopling his poetry with commoners capable of fine feelings and noble thoughts as well as human foibles, he gave us a catalogue of songs, poems, satire and invective that enriched the struggle against dogma, oppression and a society deformed by class.

Nothing I have written here is new. It is well enough known in academic circles, but it needs to be understood from a working class and Marxist perspective. We need to reclaim one of our own. We need to celebrate and enjoy Robert Burns and understand him better, and in the process bring back to the light of day the incredibly exciting times in which he lived, at the very birth struggle of the working class.

Glossary

ance	once	hizzies	girls
aughtlins	anyway	hullions	slovens
bauld	bold	ingle	fire
beas	fleas	lang	long
benmost	innermost	lesson'd	put to prostitution
birses	bristles	neuk	nook
carronades	small cannons (from the Carron Iron Works)	owre	over/too
		poind	plundered
		poortith's	poverty
diel	devil	rig system	farming method using ridges
duddie	ragged		
duds	rags	shanna	shall not
dyvors	debtors	spails	splinters
fawsont	attractive	tarrow	grumble
flaffin	flapping	thiggin	begging
gar	make	tirl	thrill
gie	give	twin	rob
gree	prize	wark	work
hae siller	have silver	yetts	gates

Notes

1   Letter to Robert Graham of Frintry, 5 January 1793, in A Bold, *Rhymer Rab* (London, 1993), p321.
2   Ibid, p322.
3   Ibid, p322.
4   Ibid, p322.
5   Ibid, p322.
6   Ibid, p322.
7   Letter to Captain William Johnston, 13 November 1792, in A Bold, op cit, p321.
8   Letter to Robert Graham of Frintry, 5 January 1793, op cit, p323.
9   R Burns, 'From Esopus to Maria', in *Burns Poems and Selected Letters* (London, 1959), p443.
10 Letter to Robert Graham..., op cit, p322.
11 A Bold, op cit, p229.
12 Ibid, p229.
13 Ibid, p230.
14 P S Hogg, *The Lost Poems* (Glasgow, 1997), p25.
15 Ibid, pp37-38.
16 *Burns Poems...*, op cit, p42.
17 Ibid, pp42-43.
18 Ibid, p43.
19 Ibid, p42.
20 I McIntyre, *Dirt and Diety: A Life of Robert Burns* (London, 1996), p1.
21 Ibid, p2.
22 A Bold, op cit, p179.
23 Ibid, p203.
24 Ibid, p165.
25 Ibid, p166.
26 Ibid, p167.
27 *Burns Poems...*, op cit, pp173-175.
28 Quoted in H W Meikle, *Scotland and the French Revolution* (Edinburgh, 1912, reprinted New York, 1969), p65.
29 Ibid, p64.
30 Quoted in J Brims, 'Conflict and Stability in Scottish Society, 1700-1850', *Proceedings of the Scottish Historical Studies Seminar, University of Strathclyde, 1988/89* (Edinburgh, 1990), p36.
31 Ibid, p36.
32 Ibid, p37.
33 H W Meikle, op cit, pp96-97.
34 Ibid, p97.
35 Ibid, p97.
36 A Bold, op cit, pp227-228.
37 H W Meikle, op cit, p112.
38 Quoted ibid, p134.
39 J Brims, op cit, p43.
40 H W Meikle, op cit, p116.

41 Ibid, p144.
42 Ibid, p146.
43 Ibid, pp152-153.
44 Ibid, pp148-149.
45 Quoted in N R Paton, *Scotland's Bard* (Fareham, 1998), pp119-120.
46 A Bold, op cit, pp234-235.
47 H W Meikle, op cit, p154.
48 A Bold, op cit, p235.
49 Letter of Robert Ainslie to Agnes McLehose, 1790, in I McIntyre, op cit, p274.
50 A Bold, op cit, p234.

Chapter 6

Hugh MacDiarmid

Jimmy Ross

The political and cultural questions that Hugh MacDiarmid grappled with all his life are still central in Scotland today. Certainly the best known Scottish poet since Robert Burns, MacDiarmid was not content to confine his energies to cultural production. For half a century he poured out not only poetry but polemic. 'My function in Scotland', he claimed, 'has been that of the catfish that vitalises the other torpid denizens of the aquarium'.[1] But what are socialists to make of him today 20 years after his death, both as a poet and as a political activist?

He was born Christopher Murray Grieve in 1892 in Langholm, a small town in the Scottish Borders. His parents came from agricultural labourer and mill worker backgrounds. His father was a postman. As a child Grieve lived in the same building as the local library in Langholm—his mother was the caretaker—and it was there that his life-long love of reading started. In his autobiography, *Lucky Poet*, he tells, 'I had constant access to it [the library] and used to fill a big washing basket with books and bring it downstairs as often as I wanted to'.[2] After leaving school he went to Edinburgh to train as a teacher but quit the college under a cloud after a prank threatened to become a minor scandal. He thereafter took up journalism and that became his main source of earning for the rest of his life which was frequently spent in poverty and debt. He took the literary name 'Hugh MacDiarmid' in 1922. His literary output was enormous and continuous throughout his life: not only poetry but also autobiography, short stories, essays and editing of books and periodicals.

But MacDiarmid cannot be assessed only as a literary and cultural figure. He was also one of the best known Scottish political activists of his day. After the First World War he became active in the Independent Labour Party, the Unemployed Union and the 'No More

War' movement. As a Scottish nationalist he was a member of the Scottish Home Rule Association and later a founding member in 1928 of the National Party of Scotland (the forerunner of today's SNP)— he was expelled from it five years later for his communism. He then joined the Communist Party in 1934 only to be expelled from that in 1939 for his 'nationalist deviation'. Almost 20 years later, at a time when members were leaving in droves after the invasion of Hungary by the Soviet Union, he rejoined the Communist Party and remained a member for the rest of his life. A prolific speaker and debater, he stood in elections for local government, parliament and university rectorships. He indulged in public rows and controversies in his articles and letters to newspapers. When he died in 1978 a verse from his most famous poem, 'A Drunk Man Looks at the Thistle', was written on his gravestone:

I'll hae nae hauf-way hoose, but aye be whaur
Extremes meet—it's the only way I ken
To dodge the curst conceit o' bein right
That damns the vast majority o' men.[3]

This was true in all aspects of his life, both in his poetry and in his politics.

The importance of MacDiarmid's poetry

When MacDiarmid was beginning his career as a writer, literature in Scotland, and poetry in particular, had been dominated for nearly a century by the tradition of the Kailyard (cabbage patch). As the name suggests, its concerns were parochial and its works were sentimental, maudlin and banal. The Scots language which it used had degenerated from the previous high point at the end of the 18th century when Ramsay, Fergusson and most notably Burns had produced the 'last gasp of the Scottish tongue'.[4] With the formation of the British state, standard English had quickly become the only acceptable form of writing and then too of speech. What remained was the music hall charicature of the bowly legged, kilted Scotsman with the ridiculous knobbly stick and the songs about misty glens and 'granny's hielan hames' purveyed by the likes of Harry Lauder. This kind of Scottish 'culture' was anathema to MacDiarmid and he reacted strongly against it. Although active in the Scottish nationalist movement after the First World War, MacDiarmid was at first opposed to the idea that modern poetry should be written in the Scots language because of its Kailyard connotations. He was still arguing as late as 1922 in a letter to the *Aberdeen Free Press*:

For the most part the Doric tradition [writing in Scots] serves to condone mental inertia...and bolsters up that instinctive suspicion of cleverness and culture—so strongly in all peasants—which keeps the majority of the Scottish public wallowing in obsolete and really antinational tastes... Scotland stagnates in an apparently permanent literary infancy owing to the operation of certain forces of which the Doric sentiment is the principal.[5]

That same year also saw the publication of *Ulysses* by James Joyce. MacDiarmid managed to get hold of a copy of the first edition. The book had a profound effect on him. The vitality and virtuosity of the language, the mixing of extremes and the combination of high culture with realistic earthiness made MacDiarmid decide to look again at the Scots language to see if he could use it to write in a modern style like Joyce. The other book which also strongly influenced him at this time was Jamieson's *Dictionary of the Older Scottish Language* which had been published in 1808—a seemingly strange combination of the modern and the ancient. He began to experiment with poetry in Scots. The Scots that he used was an artificial creation and not the language that was in everyday use. Fellow poet Norman McCaig explained, 'Scots and English are common languages with a common ancestor, and it is as absurd to call Scots a dialect of English as it would be to call English a dialect of Scots. By our time, however, Scots had become weathered into dialects of itself and its vocabulary had become sadly impoverished. Hugh MacDiarmid set himself the enormous task of establishing 'a full canon of Scots'—by enriching the vocabulary with whatever words suited his purpose, even if they had been obsolete for centuries. A queer marriage this, you might say, of the dying with the dead. The 'odd thing is, it worked, for himself if not for others'.[6]

Although he had written poetry before this it had been under his own name of C M Grieve and it had all been in standard English. It was at this point that he took the name Hugh MacDiarmid. This was the name under which his first poetic experiments in what he called 'synthetic Scots' appeared. Synthetic Scots was a peculiar linguistic medium. It was not transcribed natural language. 'It is consciously chosen and selectively used language in a way that the Scots of the ballads is not. It is grounded in rural Scots but is, above all, a literary language'.[7] One precedent that MacDiarmid quoted in support of his decision to use this form of language was Dante who had chosen to write his epic poem *Inferno* in vernacular Italian and not in Latin which was the accepted literary language in Italy at the time:

> Dante's conclusion was that the corruption common to all the dialects made it impossible to select one rather that another as an adequate literary form, and that he who would write in the vulgar must assemble the purest elements from each dialect and construct a synthetic language that would at least possess more than a circumscribed local interest; which is precisely what he did.[8]

MacDiarmid published two books of early poems in Scots— *Sangschaw* (*Song Festival*) in 1925 and *Penny Wheep* (*Small Ale*) in 1926. The poems are typically short lyrical poems but in them MacDiarmid succeeded in creating an emotional force of considerable strength in just a few lines. Often the poem will start with an image from the natural world and then suggest a whole series of philosophical concerns behind that. Although the poems were short, written in Scots and used images such as rainbows, larks and moonbeams, MacDiarmid also filled them with modern scientific thought such as Einstein's General Theory of Relativity. The results of his wide reading of world literature, philosophy, theology and science are evident throughout the poems. But his work was also informed and inspired by politics. Events such as the 1916 Easter Rising in Dublin, the Russian Revolution, the General Strike of 1926 and the Spanish Civil War were all to have an important influence on his poetry.

In his introduction to *The Socialist Poems of Hugh MacDiarmid*, the poet Thurso Berwick, the pen-name of Morris Blythman, described these early poems as 'startlingly new and different in language, style and content from anything that had preceded them. MacDiarmid had mastered the Scots language and was releasing from it qualities of utterance that no one had suspected the existence of: rich and fantastic in texture and imagery, they were at the same time clean, clear and stark in their highly imaginative expression'.[9] The *Glasgow Herald* was also impressed: 'The accomplishment of Hugh MacDiarmid is...quite unheralded. The matter is, of course, still Scottish, but it is stripped of all the trite sentimentalities and sanctimoniousness that hung over Northern verse like a drizzling mist'.[10]

In one poem, 'The Watergaw', MacDiarmid harks back to his father's death.

Ae weet forenicht i' the yow-trummle
I saw yon antrin thing,
A watergaw wi' its chitterin licht
Ayont the on-ding;
An' I thocht o' the last wild look ye gied
Afore ye deed!

There was nae reek i' the laverock's hoose
That nicht—an' nane i' mine;
But I hae thocht o' that foolish licht
Ever sin' syne;
An' I think that mebbe at last I ken
What your look meant then.[11]

Although he was an atheist, he had had a thorough education in Scottish Presbyterianism as a youth and his interest in theological matters stayed with him all his life. This too was reflected in his work.

In 'Crowdieknowe' he explores the possible effects of physical resurrection of the dead from a Scottish graveyard he knew as a child:

Oh to be at Crowdieknowe
When the last trumpet blaws
An' see the deid come loupin' owre
The auld grey wa's.

Muckle men wi' tousled beards
I grat at as a bairn
'll scramble frae the croodit clay
Wi' feck o' swearin'.

An' glower at God an' a' His gang
O' angels i' the lift
—Thae trashy bleezin' French-like folk
Wha gar'd them shift!

Fain the weemun-folk'll seek
To mak' them haud their row
—Fegs, God's no blate gin he stirs up
The men o' Crowdieknowe ![12]

Another poem, 'Empty Vessel', shows how MacDiarmid combined the old and the new in his work. He starts the poem by quoting and paraphrasing an old Scots folk song called 'Jenny Nettles' which is about a young girl and her attempts to deal with the problems caused by her illegitimate child. He changes the story to make the child dead and then compares the intensity of the young woman's grief to the effect that the gravity of planets has on light, 'The licht that bends owre a thing' as described by Einstein:

I met ayont the cairney
A lass wi' tousey hair
Singin' till a bairnie
That was nae langer there

Wunds wi' wurlds to swing
Dinna sing sae sweet,
The licht that bends owre a' thing
Is less ta'en up wi't[13]

Despite the success of his early lyrical poems MacDiarmid was restless, looking to move on and develop the scope of his poetry. As Alex Scott put it in his introduction to *The Hugh MacDiarmid Anthology*, 'No Scottish poet had ever had a finer command of the lyric cry and none has been less content with it'.[14]

MacDiarmid's next publication in November of 1926 was far removed from the short lyrical poems of his first two books: 80 pages—2,685 lines—long, 'A Drunk Man Looks at the Thistle'[15] is generally acknowledged as MacDiarmid's masterpiece. It is a long dramatic poem or poem sequence in which a drunk man (the poet) passes out on a hillside on his way home from a drinking session. He awakes on the hillside to be confronted by a giant thistle which represents Scotland. What follows is a meditation on Scotland, the universe and the human condition. In it MacDiarmid explores love and death, the past and the future. It ranges over time and space. The mood of the poem is subject to abrupt changes and shifts of subject as different ideas occur to the drunk. It encompasses elements of comedy, satire, farce, tragedy, lyricism and documentary. There are sections which are based on translations of Russian, French, German and Italian poems. It is written in Scots but is quite clearly a modernist work. It is inspired both by Joyce's *Ulysses* and by Burns's poem 'Tam O'Shanter'—both poems have a drunk as the central character and MacDiarmid also gives the man a wife called Jean.

The poem is split into sections like chapters in a novel. One section near the centre of the poem is called 'The Ballad of the General Strike'. MacDiarmid had been active in the General Strike earlier in the same year. This was how he described his involvement years later in an interview: 'We had the whole area of Angus, Forfarshire; we had it sewn up. I was speaking when the news came through of J H Thomas's [the leader of the rail union] betrayal of the strike. I was speaking to an audience of mainly railwaymen and they all broke down weeping. It was one of the most moving experiences I ever had—middle aged men most of them, weeping like children, you know. It was such a disappointment, because we knew, we knew we had it'.[16]

In this section the thistle, which up until now has been the symbol for Scotland, instead becomes the symbol for the working class engaged in its struggle against capitalism. All the contrary shapes and 'ugsome guises' that the thistle has gone through in the poem are changed utterly as its 'pin-heid flooers' and 'scrunts o' bloom' are transformed and burst out from the thistle:

A rose loupt oot and grew, until
It was ten times the size
O' ony rose the thistle afore
Hed heistit to the skies...

And still it grew until it seemed
The haill braid earth had turned
A reid, reid rose that in the lift
Like a ball o fire burned

The rose has become the workers' struggle in the form of the 1926 General Strike. But then swiftly comes defeat:

Syne the rose shrivelled suddenly
As a balloon is burst
The thistle was a ghaistly stick
As gin it had been curst

But the drunk man/MacDiarmid knows that the betrayal had come from within the working class movement:

The vices that defeat the dream
Are in the plant itsel'
And till they're purged its virtues maun
In pain and misery dwell

The poem moves on, eventually becoming, as the drunk sobers up, more spiritual and finally ending in silence as the drunk man contemplates his return home to his wife, Jean. It finishes with another conscious echo of 'Tam O'Shanter':

O I ha'e Silence left,
—'And weel ye micht'
Sae Jean'll say, 'efter sic a nicht!'

In the 1930s MacDiarmid turned to much more explicitly left wing verse. Although he was one of the first to do this in the 1930s and although most of this poetry was in standard English, the work of others in the field like Auden, Spender and MacNeice became more famous. This is an area of his writing which is often ignored or dismissed by critics as crude Marxist propaganda. This is a pity because, although maybe not his finest work, many of these poems explore interestingly and often provocatively the relationship between art and politics. During this time MacDiarmid wrote three poems entitled 'Hymns to Lenin 1, 2 and 3'.[17] These are not as awful as their Stalinist cult of Lenin titles might suggest. The best bits of them are the conversations between the poet and Lenin where MacDiarmid tells Lenin that he had the easy bit to do, the politics, whereas MacDiarmid was left with the hard bit, the poetry. Yes, he did tend towards the hyper-egocentric.

It was at this time he wrote poems such as 'John Maclean':

Stand close, stand close, and block out the light
As long as you can, you ministers and lawyers,
Hulking brutes of police, fat bourgeoisie,
Sleek derma for congested guts—its fires
Will leap through yet; already it is clear
Of all Maclean's foes not one was his peer.[18]

and 'Krassivy':

...as it was of Lenin in Russia
When you might talk to a woman who had been
A young girl in 1917 and find
That the name of Stalin lit no fires,
But when you asked her if she had seen Lenin
Her eyes lighted up and her reply
Was the Russian word which means
Both beautiful and red
Lenin, she said was 'krassivy, krassivy'
John Maclean too was 'krassivy, krassivy'
A description no other Scot has ever deserved.[19]

'In the Children's Hospital', with its attack on the cult of the royal family, could have been written yesterday:

Now let the legless boy show the great lady
How well he can manage his crutches.
It doesn't matter though the Sister objects,
'He's not used to them yet,' when such is
The will of the Princess. Come Tommy,
Try a few desperate steps through the ward.
Then the hand of royalty will pat your head
And life will suddenly cease to be hard.
For a couple of legs are surely no miss
When the loss leads to such an honour as this!
One knows, when one sees how jealous the rest
Of the children are, it's been for the best!
But would the sound of your sticks on the floor
Thundered in her skull for evermore![20]

He could also be self deprecating, as in 'Lourd On My Hert'. Here
he paints a scene, familiar to socialists today, where he is awaiting an
upturn in class struggle:

Lourd on my hert as winter lies
The state that Scotland's in the day,
Spring to the North has aye come slow
But noo dour winter's like to stay
For guid,
And no' for guid!

O wae's me on the weary days
When it is scarce grey licht at noon;
It maun be a' the stupid folk
Diffusin' their dullness roon and roon
Like soot
That keeps the sunlicht oot

Nae wonder if I think I see
A lichter shadow than the neist
I'm fain to cry: 'The dawn, the dawn!
I see it brakin' in the East'
But ah
—It's juist mair snaw![21]

The final major stage of MacDiarmid's work was his epic poetry.
These poems were huge, often never completed and published only as
fragments—but even these fragments were massive. These were what

he called 'a poetry of facts'. They were written not in Scots but in English. The English, however, was often as strange and difficult as his 'synthetic Scots'. In this poetry MacDiarmid was reacting against couthienesss and the ideas of the Proletkult and socialist realism—against idolising and making a virtue out of poverty and backwardness. He was, he said, opposed to the '"hothouse proletarian" philistinism of the boy meets tractor variety, but a poetry of today, not of the past'.[22]

MacDiarmid had very clear ambitions for his poetry. 'In The Kind of Poetry I Want' he says it should be:

> ...poems like the breadknife
> Which cuts three slices at once[23]

and 'a language like the magnetic needle'.[24]

In 'In Memoriam James Joyce' he writes, addressing the writer:

> So this is what our lives have been given to find
> A language that can serve our purposes,
> A marvellous lucidity, a quality of fiery, aery light,
> Flowing like clear water, flying like a bird,
> Burning like a sunlit landscape.[25]

Elsewhere he advocates:

> Nae simple rhymes for silly folk
> But the hail art, as Lenin gied
> Nae Marx-without-tears to workin' men
> But the fu' course instead[26]

As an artist, as well as a political activist, he is impatient. He wants the new socialist society where new questions, beyond simple survival and the fight against degradation and exploitation take their proper place as the true concern of human beings:

> Oh it's nonsense, nonsense, nonsense,
> Nonsense, at this time o' day
> That breid and butter problems
> S'ud be in ony man's way
>
> Sport, love and parentage
> Trade, politics and law
> S'ud be nae mair to us than braith
> We hardly ken we draw

Freein' oor poo'ers for greater things
And fegs there's plenty o' them
Tho' wha's still trammelt in alow
Canna be tenty o' them[27]

He cannot wait for the time when, as Trotsky described it in *Literature and Revolution*, 'the liberated passions will be channelised into technique, into construction which also includes art. Art will become more general, will mature, will become the most perfect method of the progressive building of life in every field. It will not merely be "pretty" without relation to anything else'.[28] (One of MacDiarmid's later epic poems was in fact called 'Mature Art'.[29])

This tension was described well by Bertolt Brecht:

The practical methods of the revolution are not revolutionary. They are dictated by the class struggle. It is for that reason that great writers find themselves ill at ease in the class struggle, they behave as though the struggle was already finished, and they deal with the new situation, conceived as collectivist, which is the aim of the revolution. The revolution of the great writers is permanent.[30]

In one of his poems called 'Glasgow 1960', which he wrote some time in the 1940s, MacDiarmid speculates on the nature of post-revolutionary society:

Returning to Glasgow after long exile
Nothing seemed to me to have changed its style.
Buses and trams all labelled 'To Ibrox'
Swung past packed tight as they'd hold with folks.
Football match, I concluded, but just to make sure
I asked; and the man looked at me fell dour,
Then said, 'Where in God's name are you frae, sir?
It'll be a record gate, but the cause o' the stir
Is a debate on 'la loi de l'effort converti'
Between Professor MacFadyen and a Spainish pairty.'
I gasped. The newsboys came running along,
'Special! Turkish Poet's Abstruse New Song.
Scottish Authors' Opinions'—and, holy snakes,
I saw the edition sell like hot cakes.[31]

This humorous, almost throwaway little poem is strikingly similar to what Trotsky, writing in *Literature and Revolution*, said about the nature of post revolutionary society, 'People will divide into 'parties' over...a new theatre, over chemical hypotheses, over two competing tendencies in music'.[32] It also envisages a much better use of Glasgow Rangers stadium and reminds us that it was football stadiums that were used by the workers to hold their meetings during the Portuguese Revolution in 1974-75.

But what should the role of art in society be before the liberation that socialist revolution will bring? In 'And Above All My Poetry Is Marxist' MacDiarmid says:

> Fools regret my poetic change—from my 'enchanting early lyrics'—
> But I have found in Marxism all that I need—
> (I on my mother's side of long-lived Scottish peasant stock
> And on my father's of hardy keen-brained Border mill-workers).
> It only remains to perfect myself in this new mode.
> This is the poetry I want—all
> I can regard now as poetry at all,
> As poetry of today, not of the past
> A Communist poetry that bases itself,
> On the Resolution of the CC of the RCP
> In Spring 1925: 'The Party must vigorously oppose
> Thoughtless and contemptuous treatment
> Of the old cultural heritage
> As well as of the literary specialists...
> It must likewise combat the tendency
> Towards a purely hothouse proletarian literature.[33]

It is interesting to compare that with what Diego Rivera and André Breton write in their 1938 manifesto, *Towards a Free Revolutionary Art*:

> No authority, no dictation, not the least trace of orders from above! Only on a base of friendly cooperation, without constraint from outside, will it be possible for scholars and artists to carry out their tasks, which will be more far reaching than ever before in history... We believe that the supreme task of art in our epoch is to take part actively and consciously in the preparation of the revolution. But the artist cannot serve the struggle for freedom unless he subjectively assimilates its social content, unless he feels in his very nerves its meaning and drama and freely seeks to give his own inner world incarnation in his art.[34]

MacDiarmid's politics

MacDiarmid's poetic legacy is a rich and rewarding one, particularly for socialists. His political legacy is less appealing. 'Labour And The SNP Battle To Claim The Literary Heirs Of Authors Such As Hugh MacDiarmid As Their Own' was the headline in the *Observer* on 28 February 1999.[35] Who can rightly claim MacDiarmid as one of their own? Certainly not New Labour. How could they even start to accommodate the man who said that it was his duty 'to keep up a sort of berserker rage…in the way of old heroes',[36] or, 'My job, as I see it, has never been to lay a tit's egg, but to erupt like a volcano, emitting not only flame but a lot of rubbish'.[37] MacDiarmid was motivated all his life by a hatred of capitalism and the ruling class. But that class hatred was also intertwined with an idea that identified Scottishness as being almost the same thing as being working class. For him the ruling class and British imperialism was an English thing. When confronted with Scots who were quite obviously part of the ruling class, MacDiarmid would explain this away by categorising them as Anglified Scots who had sold out to the English imperialist ascendancy. His was a view that saw Scotland most definitely as an oppressed nation that had eventually been defeated first by the 'Parcel o' Rogues'—the members of the Scottish Parliament who had voted for the Union of the Scottish and English parliaments—and then by the crushing of the Jacobite Rebellion at Culloden in 1746. Hatred of the English was a constant refrain in MacDiarmid's life. He even listed 'Anglophobia' as one of his hobbies in his entry in *Who's Who*.[38]

What was the basis for this anti-English attitude in MacDiarmid? Like his hero Joyce, MacDiarmid was a provincial intellectual. Both he and Joyce were concerned about the status of the provincial intellectual and they saw it as a cultural and a national question. Both were treated badly by the English literary establishment. It was not until 1985 with the publication of his complete poems by Penguin that MacDiarmid's poetry was available internationally.[39] Up until then his work had been published only by Scottish publishers and some obscure English ones. Both writers suffered from political and sexual censorship and they in turn rejected the English literary establishment. But Joyce turned his back on Irish nationalism, going to live in continental Europe. MacDiarmid, however, took nationalism as his starting point culturally and politically. Although a founding member of the National Party of Scotland in 1928, MacDiarmid was dismissive of his fellow nationalists whom he described as a 'troupe of gibbering lunatics'.[40] His nationalism was not of the constitutional, parliamentary type. The Easter Rising of 1916 had influenced him greatly. He recalled in a radio interview in 1977, 'I was in barracks [he had joined the army during the First World War], in Sheffield of all places in 1915, and I was there when the Easter Rising took place in 1916. If it had been possible at all I would have deserted at that time from the British army and joined the Irish'.[41]

MacDiarmid's early nationalism was militaristic and conspiratorial in nature. In fact in the 1920s he called for the setting up of 'a Scottish fascism which shall be, where such laws are concerned, a lawless believer in law—a rebel believer in authority'.[42] In 1929 he wrote to the novelist Compton MacKenzie, another co-founder of the National Party of Scotland, 'The party is steadily eliminating the moderatist, compromising, democratic element, and all the young people are coming round to the realisation for the need of—and the readiness to institute—a species of Scottish fascism'.[43] He also claimed to have founded with MacKenzie a secret, militaristic organisation called Clann Albain which he described in the *Scottish Daily Record* as a 'Sinn Fein Movement for Scotland'.[44] He wrote, in May 1930, that the organisation had been building up for two years and is 'on a militaristic basis, and in this resembles the fascist movement'.[45] What basis there was in reality for this organisation is open to much dispute. The history of the nationalist movement in Scotland is littered with such 'secret' organisations, usually modelled on Irish Republicanism, typically with a membership of less than a dozen people—and probably about half of them police spies. Later in his life MacDiarmid, talking about Ezra Pound, the US poet who was indicted for treason for his broadcasts on Rome Radio for Mussolini, argued:

> Most of my friends were fascists in that sense. They were impressed in the early days by the actual practical achievements of Mussolini in draining the Po marshes and so on, and in, partially at any rate, solving the unemployment problem in Italy. Now that was a temporary thing. Mussolini's real objectives became clearer later on with the invasion of Abyssinia and so on.[46]

The naiveté of that justification has got an 'At least he got the trains running on time' ring to it. It illustrates the fatal flaw in all of MacDiarmid's politics. In spite of his hatred of capitalism and the ruling class and his anger at the exploitation and degradation that he saw all around him, for MacDiarmid the agency of change in all of this was never clearly and solely the working class. MacDiarmid was always attracted to the Nietzschean idea of the superman, both as politician and as artist. This helps to account for his elitism, his fascination with and reverence for 'great men'—his heroes were Mussolini, Lenin, John Maclean, Robert Burns, James Joyce and Stalin. It was in Nietzsche that MacDiarmid found the inspiration and justification for his inconsistencies and his contradictions. Another of his heroes was the Russian irrationalist Shestov who argued, 'It is not a vice to be unstable in one's opinion'.[47]

This combination of ideas and his spectacular ability to embarrass the 'respectable' leadership with his extravagant statements and activity made his expulsion from the National Party of Scotland almost inevitable. One of them, John MacCormick, said, 'I am certain that C M Grieve has been politically one of the greatest handicaps with which any national movement could have been burdened'.[48]

In 1934 he joined the Communist Party which was at this point, after the defeat in Germany and the coming to power of Hitler, in the process of adopting the 'Popular Front' policy with its emphasis on cross-class unity. In his autobiography, No Mean Fighter, Harry McShane, who had worked along with John Maclean in the struggle against the First World War and other campaigns and had then gone on to join the newly founded Communist Party, described the period in which MacDiarmid joined:

> Once it was accepted that Communists should work for the unity of all classes, the next step was to start arguing for self government for the Scottish people. Further support for this came from the fact that the personnel of the party was changing—during the Popular Front period many more intellectuals and middle class elements came to the fore.[49]

In this context MacDiarmid argued his nationalist position with some success although he mostly gained support from party members outside of Scotland and specifically from the national executive in London who were closely following the new line from Moscow. The Scottish district committee tried on several occasions to have him expelled only to be overruled. But his expulsion finally came in 1939 after he had attacked English members of the International Brigade fighting in Spain. MacDiarmid had written:

> The Celtic members—Scottish, Irish and Welsh—of the International Brigade found it impossible to work hand in hand with their English

comrades and had to break away from them and join up in a body with the Americans instead... It is obvious at all events that a similar breaking away from the English must take place in other connections.[50]

McShane commented:

We [the Scottish delegation to the Party Congress] were (all except two) of the opinion that MacDiarmid had never done anything for the party, and that he was as much a Scottish nationalist as he was a Communist.[51]

MacDiarmid was to remain a member of no party for nearly 20 years. But for all his stormy relationship with the Communist Party, he never broke from its Stalinism. Ten years after his expulsion from the party he wrote a poem entitled 'Lamh Dearg Aboo (to Stalin)'. 'Lamh dearg aboo' is Gaelic for 'The red hand to victory'—a war cry of the clan MacDonald:

Stalin, when we Scottish Gaels salute you
It is, like all else, by no mere chance
That an old battle-cry of our people at last
Wins on our lips to its full significance
—Lamh dearg aboo!

...Ah, Stalin, we Scots who had our first home
In Caucasian Georgia like yourself see how
The processes of history in their working out
Bring East and West together in general human triumph now.
—Lamh dearg aboo![52]

MacDiarmid was so convinced of the socialist nature of the Soviet bloc of East European countries that were created after the Second World War that when, in 1956, thousands of disillusioned Communist Party members resigned under the double hammer blow of Kruschev's admissions of Stalin's crimes and the Russian invasion of Hungary and the brutal suppression of the workers' rising, he applied to be readmitted to the party. Writing in the Daily Worker in 1957 in an article called 'Why I Rejoined' he said:

While many members have left the Communist Party, allegedly on account of the 'de-Stalinising revelations', or Hungary, I have felt, on the contrary, that this was the time to rally to the party again and throw all my energies into the fight... Mistakes and distortions there have been, of course. But even if the enemies of Communism were accurate, the killings, starvings, frame ups, unjust judgements and all the rest of it are a mere bagatelle to the utterly mercenary and unjustified wars, the ruthless exploitation, the preventable deaths due to slums, and other damnable consequences of the profit motive, which must be laid to the account of the so-called 'free nations of the West'... In the light of the [counter-revolutionary danger in Hungary] the Russian intervention was not only justified but imperative, if unfortunately necessary.[53]

The counter-revolutionary danger in Hungary that MacDiarmid detected was described rather differently by the *Daily Worker's* own eye-witness correspondent in Hungary, Peter Fryer, as 'ordinary men, women and youths... The revolution thrust them forward, aroused their civic pride and latent genius for organisation, set them to work to build democracy out of the ruins of bureaucracy'.[54] The 'mere bagatelle' was the shelling and bombardment by Russian tanks and planes of workers' districts in Budapest resulting in the deaths of more than 20,000 people, the execution of Imre Nagy and his co-ministers and the crushing by 200,000 Russian troops, 3,000 tanks and the Russian airforce of the first genuine workers' soviet in Europe for nearly 40 years.

One of MacDiarmid's other heroes was John Maclean. He admired Maclean for his courageous stand against the First World War, his involvement in workers' struggles and his support for the Bolshevik Revolution which resulted in him being appointed official Soviet Consul in Glasgow. MacDiarmid also seized upon Maclean's attempt, in the last few years of his life, frustrated by the downturn in workers' struggle, to call for a Scottish Workers' Republic. Although a contemporary of Maclean (MacDiarmid was 31 when Maclean died) his espousal of the 'John Maclean line', as he was later to call it, did not come until well after the great revolutionary's death. There is no record of MacDiarmid having worked with or supported Maclean while he was alive. With Maclean's refusal to join the Communist Party of Great Britain at its inception in 1920-21 and his subsequent early death a few years later, he was more or less ignored by the leadership of the CPGB and, if referred to, was dismissed as having been made mad by his imprisonment for anti-war activities. As Ripley and McHugh have noted in their book on John Maclean:

Maclean's memory, however, was kept alive more enthusiastically by a diminishing band of admirers in Scotland. MacDiarmid more than any other was able to keep Maclean's name before a mainly Scottish audience, but it was Maclean as socialist and nationalist. In doing so MacDiarmid ensured that when the Scottish 'new left' emerged in the later 1960s Maclean would be available as an example and inspiration.[55]

Maclean's daughter, Nan Milton, wrote in her biography of her father:

In 1948, the 25th anniversary of his death, a huge mass meeting organised by the Scottish-USSR Society was held in St Andrew's Hall. A unique feature of this event was the presence on the platform of some of Scotland's foremost poets and literary figures, including Hugh MacDiarmid and Sydney Goodsir Smith, who gave readings of poems which they themselves had composed in honour of John Maclean. Thus as a result of the Scottish literary renaissance, which he himself had helped to inspire, the legend took on a new, immortal form.[56]

But the 'new form' of the 'legend' of John Maclean was one that promoted him as a nationalist as much as a revolutionary socialist. MacDiarmid was a key influence here. In 1973 he wrote:

By 1936 I had thoroughly realised that we must revert to the John Maclean line…ie the beginnings of the self education of the Scottish proletariat in their revolutionary tasks *with the aid of their own intelligentsia* [MacDiarmid's emphasis].

But this also involved MacDiarmid presenting a romantic, nationalist Maclean who was important because—his argument ran—Maclean 'united the diverse elements of Scottish life in a unique way—he was of Highland stock, his work lay in the great industrial belt in the Lowlands, and he married a Border woman. The unification of Scotland, Highland and Lowland, rural and urban, was complete in himself'.[57]

This picture of Maclean with its emphasis on nationalism is the contradictory legacy that MacDiarmid has left. One the one hand his unremitting pushing of the 'John Maclean line' has meant that Maclean was not lost to the new generation of non-Stalinist socialists—'the new left' which emerged in the 1960s. On the other hand, the tartan clothes in which MacDiarmid consistently presented Maclean have allowed him to be regarded as one of the pantheon of Scottish heroes along with Wallace and Burns. This has meant a Maclean that the SNP and sections of the Labour left try to claim as theirs and, by playing up the nationalism, remove the real revolutionary, internationalist nature of his ideas and work.

In trying to sum up MacDiarmid, 'contradictory' is the word which comes most readily to mind. He was a socialist but his elitism made him despair of the workers. Neal Ascherson recently described him as 'a rebel who hated all successful movements…he poured scorn on the SNP as its vote soared in the 1970s. He believed passionately in the Scottish people: yet he was an elitist who loathed the mediocrity of the mass'.[58] His biographer Alan Bold wrote that while he was 'in love with the eternal idea of Scotland, he detests the reality of contemporary Scotland'.[59] As MacDiarmid himself put it, 'Modern Scotland is a disease in which everything has turned to mud'.[60] He consistently called himself a Marxist but was attracted to the idea of fascist/militarist organisation, describing Mussolini's ideology as 'an experiment in patriotic socialism…a war of the idealist against the materialist'.[61] His Marxism could accommodate Nietzschean idealism, in particular the attraction of the idea of the 'superman' and especially the artist as the ultimate 'superman'. Although a self declared historical materialist, he also often saw himself as a mystic. He railed against the idolatry of the Burns cult yet would rarely turn down an invitation to speak at a Burns Supper. His attitude to Burns was ambivalent. Sometimes he would be full of praise for Burns and call him one of Scotland's heroes. Then on other occasions he would attack Burns almost as if he were jealous of him:

> Europe is beginning to repudiate democracy, romantic love and other basic elements in Burns' creed, that suggests that Burns' work will speedily become more and more old fashioned and intolerable to modern consciousness. That is as it should be… In conclusion, let me say that I do not object to Burns dinners on temperance grounds… The drinking at Burns Suppers is one of the few elements in the programme which have my invariable and hearty approval. I prefer Burnsians 'speechless'.[62]

For MacDiarmid as a poet, many of these contradictions could be a strength, adding layers of ambiguity and tension to his work. Personally, MacDiarmid took delight in his contradictions, using them to infuriate and often wrongfoot his critics. But as a political activist, despite his anger against the horrors and miseries produced by capitalism and his commitment and determination to fight against the system, MacDiarmid rarely looked to the working class as the force that would bring down capitalism. His elitism led him to look for supermen, for heroes, who would bring about socialism by their bravery and cleverness—socialism from above rather than from below. His lifelong attachment to the cause of Scottish nationalism, his hatred of the English and his Stalinism, which he never recanted, makes it impossible for socialists to claim him as one of our own. His combination of nationalism and top-down socialism was one that has come to dominate much of the left in Scotland today. For these reasons it is as a poet, not as a political activist, that MacDiarmid deserves to be remembered.

Glossary

antrin	occasional, fleeting	loupin'	leaping
a'thing	the universe	lourd	heavy
ayont	beyond	maun	must
blate	shy	muckle	big
chitterin'	shivering	on-ding	storm
feck	plenty	reek	smoke
fegs	faith	sin' syne	since then
forenicht	evening	ta'en up	concerned
gar'd	made	tenty	concerned
gin	if	till	to
laverock	lark	watergaw	rainbow
lift	sky, heavens	yowe trummie	cold wind

Notes

1   H MacDiarmid, *Lucky Poet* (London, 1943), pxxv.
2   Ibid, p8.
3   M Grieve and A Scott (eds), *The Hugh MacDiarmid Anthology* (London, 1972), p27.
4   A Bold, *MacDiarmid, A Critical Biography* (London, 1990), p151.
5   Quoted ibid, p151.
6   Quoted in A Riach, *Hugh MacDiarmid's Epic Poetry* (Edinburgh, 1991), pp166-167.
7   A Riach, op cit.
8   Quoted in A Bold, op cit.
9   T S Law and T Berwick (eds), *The Socialist Poems of Hugh MacDiarmid* (London, 1990), p191.
10 Quoted in A Bold, op cit, p191.
11 M Grieve and A Scott (eds), op cit, p3.
12 Ibid, pp6-7.
13 Ibid, p15.
14 Ibid, pxviii.
15 Ibid, pp23-102.
16 Quoted in A Bold, op cit, p215.
17 T S Law and T Berwick (eds), op cit, pp36-52.
18 Ibid, p54.
19 Ibid, pp54-55.
20 Ibid, p15.
21 T S Law and T Berwick, op cit, p20.
22 Quoted in A Riach, op cit, p15.
23 Quoted in A Bold, op cit, p410.
24 Ibid, p410.
25 T S Law and T Berwick (eds), op cit, p72.
26 Ibid, p40.
27 Ibid, p40.
28 *Leon Trotsky on Literature and Art* (New York, 1970), p61.
29 H MacDiarmid, *Cornish Heroic Song for Valda Trevlyn* (Glasgow, 1943).
30 Quoted in A Riach, op cit, p144.
31 T S Law and T Berwick (eds), op cit, p30.
32 *Leon Trotsky...*, op cit, p61.
33 T S Law and T Berwick (eds), op cit, p30.
34 D Rivera and A Breton, *Manifesto: Towards a Free Revolutionary Art*, in *Leon Trotsky...*, op cit, p120.
35 *The Observer*, 28 February 1999.
36 H MacDiarmid, *Lucky Poet*, op cit, p79.
37 Quoted in A Bold, op cit, p478.
38 Ibid, p469.
39 M Grieve and W R Aitken (eds), *The Complete Poems of Hugh MacDiarmid: 1920-76* (London, 1985).
40 Quoted in A Bold, op cit, p332.
41 A Bold (ed), *The Thistle Rises* (London, 1984), p289.

42   Quoted in A Bold, *MacDiarmid...*, op cit, p170.
43   Quoted in A Riach, op cit, pp3-4.
44   Ibid, p4.
45   Ibid, p5.
46   Quoted in A Bold, *MacDiarmid...*, op cit, p157.
47   Ibid, p157.
48   Ibid, p271.
49   H MacShane and J Smith, *Harry MacShane, No Mean Fighter* (London, 1978), pp224-225.
50   Quoted in A Bold, *MacDiarmid...*, op cit, p428.
51   H MacShane and J Smith, op cit, p225.
52   T S Law and T Berwick (eds), op cit, p97.
53   H MacDiarmid, 'Why I Rejoined', *Daily Worker*, 28 March 1957, quoted in A Bold, *MacDiarmid...*, op cit, pp467-468.
54   Quoted in C Harman, *Class Struggles in Eastern Europe 1945-1983* (London, 1984), p135.
55   B J Ripley and J McHugh, *John Maclean* (Manchester, 1989), p4.
56   N Milton, *John Maclean* (London, 1973), p11.
57   Quoted in J Broom, *John Maclean* (Loanhead, Midlothian, 1973), p174.
58   Quoted in *The Observer*, 28 February 1999.
59   A Bold, *MacDiarmid...*, op cit, p440.
60   H MacDiarmid, *Lucky Poet*, op cit, p236.
61   Quoted in A Bold, *MacDiarmid...*, op cit, p169.
62   Ibid, p265.

Index